The Dobermann

POPULAR DOGS BREED SERIES

THE
DOBERMANN

FRED CURNOW
AND
JEAN FAULKS

POPULAR DOGS
London Sydney Auckland Johannesburg

Popular Dogs Publishing Co. Ltd

An imprint of the Random Century Group
Random Century House,
20 Vauxhall Bridge Road, London SW1V 2SA

Random Century Australia (Pty) Ltd
20 Alfred Street, Milsons Point, Sydney, NSW 2061

Random Century New Zealand Limited
191 Archers Road, PO Box 40–086, Glenfield, Auckland 10

Century Hutchinson South Africa (Pty) Ltd
PO Box 337, Bergvlei 2012, South Africa

First published 1972
Revised editions 1975, 1976, 1979, 1980, 1983, 1984, 1990

Copyright © Fred Curnow and Jean Faulks 1972, 1975, 1976, 1979,
1980, 1983, 1984
New material copyright © Jean Faulks 1990

Set in Baskerville by 𝍫 Tek Art Ltd, Croydon, Surrey

Printed and bound in Great Britain by
Mackays of Chatham plc, Chatham, Kent

British Library Cataloguing in Publication Data
Curnow, Fred
    The dobermann.—8th ed.—(Popular Dogs' breed series).
    1. Dobermann pinschers
    I. Title   II. Faulks, Jean
    636.7′3   SF429.P5
        ISBN 0 09 164750 9

To Julia Curnow
without whose devotion to the Dobermann
this book would never have been written

CONTENTS

ILLUSTRATIONS

Ch. Tavey's Stormy Medallion and Ch. Hensel Midnight Max

Stormy Medallion bred by Mr C. Starns. Midnight Max bred by Mr and Mrs G. Hansen
Both owned by Mrs D. P. and Miss C. Parker

Ch. Tumlow Whinlands Flurry and Ch. Tumlow Impeccable

Whinlands Flurry bred by Mrs M. Hewan. Impeccable bred by Mrs J. Curnow and Miss E. Hoxey
Both owned by Miss E. Hoxey

Ch. Acclamation of Tavey

Bred and owned by Mrs J. Curnow

Vanessa's Little Dictator of Tavey

Bred by Mr E. Edgar and Mrs B. Garner
Imported and owned by Mrs J. Curnow

W.T.Ch. Chaanrose Night Queen T.D.ex, W.D.ex, U.D.ex, C.D.ex

Bred by Miss Rosie Lane
Owned, trained and handled by Mr John Fleet

Ch. Ashdobe's Brown Berry

Bred, owned, trained and handled by Mrs S. Mitchell

Koriston Pewter Strike of Doberean, T.D.ex, W.D.ex, U.D.ex, C.D.ex

Bred by Mrs A. E. Anderson
Owned, trained and handled by Mrs J. Faulks

Training for manwork: (Bob Ling with Gin v. Forell)

Ch. Tavey's Stormy Acacia

Bred by Mrs J. Curnow
Owned by Mrs E. Gladstone

Training with the dumb-bell: (Ch. Tavey's Stormy Willow, Achenburg Heida, Katina of Trevellis, Ch. Tavey's Stormy Master)

Ch. Borains Raging Calm

Bred and owned by Mrs P. Gledhill

Ch. Findjans Poseidon

Bred and owned by Mr M. and Mrs A. Page

AUTHORS' INTRODUCTIONS

It goes without saying that unless you have a love and admiration for dogs it is pointless to own one or, worse still, more than one. A thoroughbred dog is no longer a status symbol; it is demanding on your time and patience and needs a great deal of care. If you have a natural affection for the canine species and require a companion who will return fidelity for love there is no reason at all why a Dobermann should not be considered.

Should you be devoid of kindness and patience it is better to give up all idea of owning or being owned by a dog, because these feelings between dog and man are reciprocal. A natural love of dogs will make the ownership considerably more pleasurable than if you buy one simply as a talking point in the local pub, especially when it comes to lead and house training, etc., which is an essential part of the partnership.

It is for these reasons that Jean Faulks and I have spent a couple of years thinking about and eventually writing this book, and I hope that the chapters contained herein will help newcomers and experts alike more fully to appreciate dogs in general, and Dobermanns in particular.

It is imperative that you have a good knowledge of feeding, exercising and rearing, an idea of how the Dobermann was evolved, and if you have a knowledge of how it has fared in different countries the information should make the possession of this lovely breed all the more enjoyable. The original Dobermann was quite a different animal from the powerful, elegant dog we see these days, and it is up to you, should breeding be contemplated, to make sure that you help the breed to progress and reach an even higher standard instead of allowing it to deteriorate.

When writing this book Jean Faulks and I have tried to cover all aspects of the breed, she handling the working side and I the development of Dobermanns from early days. In addition, chapters have been included that could be of assistance to both newcomers and exhibitors. It is hoped that readers will learn about conformation, choosing and rearing a puppy, training and general care of this wonderful breed.

Incidentally, the Dobermann, with its clean, noble and elegant line, is today one of the most beautiful animals in the world, and while I have concentrated on what is termed the beauty aspect it should not be forgotten that the Dobermann was first evolved as a guard and working dog. Jean has dealt most fully with this characteristic and but for her help in this direction, *The Dobermann* would have been incomplete.

Obviously, a dog that is a show specimen, and with a temperament that makes it an excellent guard, is the ideal companion. There are many Dobermanns in Britain, Europe and the USA that compete successfully in the breed and in obedience and working events, and it must indeed be a pleasure to own such a specimen. In other words, although the Dobermann was originally evolved as a dog with the utmost intelligence, capable of working all day long, he must also be an aristocratic, elegant, noble and beautifully proportioned animal.

In my own opinion the Americans have reached nearer the ideal than any other nation in this respect and it is pleasing to see that while several years ago they were producing rather large specimens, by far the majority these days are of the correct height according to both American and British standards.

In Germany, the original home of the breed, Dobermanns are approximately of the same size as those in Britain, and having seen some of the top exhibits at the Berlin, Düsseldorf, Dortmund and Wiesbaden shows I am convinced that we in Britain have exhibits in both quality and quantity superior to those in Germany. This condition did not exist until a few years ago, prior to which we were some way behind the Germans in overall quality. Having in mind that the breed was practically unknown in Britain until 1947, we can be very proud of the fact that specimens now produced in these isles can compete with those bred in Scandinavia, Holland, Portugal, Belgium, France, Switzerland and Germany.

I am indebted to George Tunnicliff who drew the several sketches which are essential to illustrate certain points and I do most sincerely express my gratitude for this invaluable assistance. Further, I would like to thank Len Charles, my partner, for his help in compiling the chapter on feeding, his knowledge on this subject being superior to most others. Len Carey of the USA, once proud owner and exhibitor of the late Am. Ch. Rancho Dobe's Storm, probably the most successful Dobermann ever to be exhibited, is also to be thanked for his encouragement and suggestions which have enabled me to explain more fully the various parts in the standard of the breed.

Joanna Walker of the USA and Inge Dallman of Germany have also greatly helped with research on Dobermanns in the United States and in Europe and many others have quite unwittingly helped in various ways, especially those with whom I have discussed the breed and from whom much has been learned, and with whom many sincere friendships have been cemented and enjoyed.

As I have already said, this book would have been incomplete without the four chapters (8 to 11) dealing with obedience, working trials, working tests and police service – and I must express my indebtedness to Jean Faulks for having contributed these interesting and educational sections. Jean, in my opinion, is one of the most dedicated and certainly one of the most able amateur trainers of Dobermanns in Great Britain and her chapters have brought out the high qualities of our breed in a manner no other writer could have done.

I am confident that you will, as I did, enjoy reading about the inherent intelligence and ability that every good Dobermann should, if correctly trained, be able to demonstrate. I personally have no penchant for training dogs in obedience competition or working tests, but I have learned from my experiences in the show-ring and by having Dobermanns around me in my own home that one can never bring a dog's intelligence up to the level of that enjoyed by human beings. It is essential that this be fully recognised and an attempt made to meet the dog halfway by raising his understanding to some degree, using his natural bent as a mimic and his ability to absorb everything repetitive, while at the same time employing a little doggy psychology. Hard, brutal methods will get you nowhere because the love and affection a dog is prepared to give an owner he respects will be destroyed unless there is mutual trust and companionship. A dog is not a machine and is capable of giving devotion that no other animal can emulate, so it is up to you to treat him as you would a friendly pupil until such time as you both consider yourselves equals.

The chapter Jean has written on the Dobermann in working trials and the appendices she has compiled are the result of intense research over a long time and as they cover a period of more than twenty years they will, I am sure, from now on be of great value as reference material on what has transpired in working trials, particularly in relation to Dobermanns, over that period.

1972   F.C.

Ten years have elapsed since the original text was written; some revision has therefore been made for the sixth edition and all appendices brought up to date. Preparation has been my responsibility, sadly because of the death of Fred Curnow in November 1981. His widow, the incomparable Julia to whom this book is dedicated, still attends shows, marking results and noting trends in the breed which she and Fred did so much to develop in this country. Other individual breeders have selected and brought in Dobermanns from abroad which widened the choice of bloodlines, and their successes too are recorded within these pages. But it was Fred and Julia's vision and dedication in introducing and establishing the breed which was the continuing factor in its development in the

UK. For thirty years each successive import into their Tavey kennels carried the top winning bloodlines of the day, from the first stud dog from Germany to the last in-whelp bitch from the USA. Appendix E shows that of 205 breed champions to date 38 are directly Tavey-bred and a further 63 have a Tavey sire or dam. Appendix A records the growth of breed registrations at the Kennel Club from 94 in 1951 to 4824 in 1981. In his lifetime Fred saw the Dobermann emerge from 'Any Other Variety' into the Top Ten.

A man of enthusiasm and dedicated purpose, Fred was often outspoken in his views and passionate in defence of what he held to be right. As an exhibitor his presentation and handling were masterly, as a judge he was held in great esteem at home and abroad. Fred was always ready to advise the novice handler or breeder, he encouraged those of us who enjoy training and working our Dobes; he was a generous host and a trusted loyal friend. With these qualities it was appropriate that his favourite breed should be the Dobermann.

1983   J.F.

Julia Curnow lived for five years after Fred's death but died in December 1986, soon after her ninetieth birthday. This was the end of an era unmatched in the world of pedigree dogs. The breed they both loved, and did so much to develop in Great Britain, remains in the top ten of registrations at the Kennel Club and even today, few Dobermanns are without a touch of Tavey in their breeding.

When agreeing to revise this book I knew what changes would be needed in the four chapters which were originally my responsibility. Chapter 6 had already been presented in a different format in two previous editions, and I assumed that only minor revisions of Fred Curnow's main section would be required. This proved a fond illusion! The breed's rise in popularity, the increased number of entries and of opportunities for showing, research into canine diet and the development of new types of dog food, better knowledge of puppies' physical needs and their character development plus the steady addition of new bloodlines through imports from overseas involved more than a simple revision. Better suited to holding a dog's lead than a pen, the task of bringing this book up-to-date has taken me three years to complete.

It has been made possible only through the patience and encouragement of Marion Paull of Popular Dogs; the information on diets personally given by Dr Anna Rainbird of Pedigree Petfoods, Dr John Curgenven of Omega, Messrs Alister Lockhart of Wafcol, Steve Dixon of Febo Professional and Peter Stratford of Beta Petfoods; the help over details of kennel management and construction from Agnes and Fred Anderson (Koriston); the professional interest in the breed of David S. Wilson, B.V.M.S., M.R.C.V.S.; the detailed advice on breeding and puppy-rearing freely offered by many friends and experienced breeders throughout the UK in response to my questions, and the availability and instant help of Peggy Dawson, the breed archivist who, with her usual enthusiasm, has confirmed pedigree details, and checked dates, names and awards. To all of them, I offer my most grateful thanks.

Tracing the development of the breed in this country and recounting its successes in the show-ring and in working trials, obedience and working tests, has been made easier through my having been a competitor. Taking part from time to time in all these activities I have had in turn Pincher, Popsie, Patsy, Prima, Pippin and Polly as my partner. Together we trained, travelled and competed together, sharing fatigue and excitement and meeting with failure and success. They all qualified for inclusion under their registered names in one or more of the appendices to this book. Through them I met most of the top handlers and breeders of the time, and admired the famous dogs that are mentioned in these chapters. For the many friendships and memories now set down in print, I can thank the Dobermanns who have shared our home since 1950.

From the start my husband Deryck encouraged me and has patiently supported my interest in training and qualifying, and periodically in showing, each one of our dogs. His approval has been warm and enduring and has made possible anything I may have achieved in pursuit of a hobby that has now led to a share in *The Dobermann*.

1990   J.F.

1

Origin and Development
of the Breed

The history of the Dobermann, although veiled in mystery, is nevertheless intriguing and fascinating: intriguing because delving into any historical subject, and in particular when dealing with a specific breed of dog, arouses curiosity; fascinating because in tracing the ancestry of a dog the results can be educational and enable correct breeding programmes to be planned.

Many writers have tried to trace the origin of the Dobermann, but as no definite records were kept by the man who evolved this attractive and alert dog, most of what has been written is based on assumption; intelligent assumption, certainly, because due to the colour and conformation of the present-day Dobermann it is reasonable to assume that several breeds, each quite different from the others, were used in its evolution. I suppose that almost all breeds of dogs as we know them today were evolved by accident from a mixture of several types, but what I find fascinating is that although the Dobermann is a relatively new breed no detailed records of how it evolved are easily available.

What we do know, however, is that Louis Dobermann did not produce the breed by accident but used planned methods to arrive at the end result. Louis Dobermann of Apolda in the state of Thuringia, Germany, was a tax or rent collector during the 1880s and, being a dog lover, albeit one who liked aggressive animals, he decided to breed a dog that would be of help and protection to him when making his rounds. He had the added advantage of being the keeper of the dog pound in which all strays within his area were kept.

One can imagine the many cross-breeds, mongrels and pure-bred dogs that eventually found their way into Herr Dobermann's dog pound and the serious thought he must have given before selecting the several breeds necessary towards producing his ideal guard dog. Doubtless he had in mind a dog of average build so that it would scare off intruders and act as a positive guard. He also probably preferred a dog with a smooth, short coat to reduce unnecessary grooming, and, above all, he must have wanted stamina, intelligence and alertness so that his companion could travel with him during the many hours demanded by his work.

At that time there existed the German Pinscher, which was, according to photographs, a rather nondescript dog. However, this Pinscher had the reputation of being aggressive and alert and it was around that breed that Louis Dobermann built his strain.

Even in those far-off days the Germans had developed the habit of cropping the ears of certain breeds and the Pinscher was among those who suffered this operation, the main purpose of which was to give a more alert and fearsome expression. Another reason for cropping was to reduce the size of pendulous ears, thus making it more difficult for other dogs to maintain a firm hold when fighting with those whose ears were almost non-existent. From the date of evolution of the breed and up to the early 1920s it was fashionable to crop ears to quite a small size, but more recently, in an attempt to add elegance and line to Dobermanns, Boxers and Great Danes, both the Germans and the Americans have adopted what is known as 'the long crop'.

The Rottweiler, which readers will know is a massive, solid dog noted particularly for stamina and tracking power, was also introduced into the bloodline and even today we occasionally see in some Dobermanns the slightly wavy coat inherited from the Rottweiler.

It is fact that the Rottweiler did much to bring the Dobermann Pinscher into being and those enthusiasts who work their dogs should deeply appreciate Louis Dober-

mann's forethought when deciding to introduce the blood
of such an intelligent dog into his bloodlines. It is well
perhaps at this stage to remind readers that while our
breed is now known simply as the Dobermann, it was, up
to 1957, known and registered in Britain as the Dobermann Pinscher. Kennel Club permission was given to drop
the word Pinscher when it was pointed out that such
nomenclature literally translated from the German meant
Terrier, which type of dog the present-day Dobermann
does not resemble in any way at all. Germany also
eliminated the word Pinscher even before we in Britain
took this step, but in America and several other countries
the breed is still known by the double name.

It is generally accepted that the Manchester Terrier,
which in those days was probably a larger dog than one
sees in Britain these days, was also used in the evolution
of the Dobermann, thus giving the short, shiny coat and
the distinctive black-and-tan markings.

Undoubtedly the use of Manchester Terrier blood,
besides adding colour and coat type to the present-day
Dobermann, gave something towards the refinement,
elegance and line, and even today we often see the
distinctive black thumb markings which are typical of the
Manchester breed on the toes of newly born Dobermanns.
These dark markings on the toes as well as the white spots
on the chest of young Dobermanns sometimes disappear
by the time the puppy is three to four months of age.

Some French enthusiasts of today consider that
Beauceron blood was also introduced, thus accounting for
size and colour. This is quite feasible because the
Beauceron is also a solid, upstanding, bright and alert
guard dog and the breed, or something very similar, was
known to be in the district of Thuringia during the time
Herr Dobermann was producing his own particular breed.
Another reason for considering that the Beauceron was
used in the evolution of the Dobermann is that this breed
often carries a white patch on the chest, a trait which was
very apparent in the original Dobermanns and still crops
up occasionally today.

From my own studies of the Dobermann I am convinced

that the Pointer, whether English or German type does not really matter, was also used when Louis Dobermann was slowly producing his ideal. Many a time when exercising my own dogs in adjacent woodland where birds and game can be found I have seen my dogs suddenly stop and point with the correct foreleg and tailset of a first-class Pointer.

If we look back at some old photographs of the breed, a few of which can be found in Philipp Gruenig's book on Dobermanns, we find a most extraordinary dog with a harsh coat standing about 22 inches at the shoulder. No doubt Louis Dobermann, although satisfied with the temperament he had bred into his dogs, was not exactly pleased with their lack of physical style. It is reasonable to think (as indeed has been suggested by Philipp Gruenig) that some refinement was introduced by Louis Dobermann or Otto Goeller, or by another later breeder. This probably came from a mating with a Greyhound, most likely black, because of the additional height, stamina and speed inherent in the breed.

What is really surprising is that Dobermanns of today breed so true to type and we must thank both Louis Dobermann and Otto Goeller, who continued his work, for being such highly selective and successful breeders. With no shadow of doubt it can be claimed, after studying photographs of Dobermanns from the 1900s up to the present day, that improvement in type has been tremendously progressive and I am confident that as time goes on, and if breeders will follow the example set by the two German originators who must have devoted much time to the subject, we can by selective breeding produce more and more dogs that tend towards the ideal. Of course, at the present time there are excellent dogs in almost every country in the world, but there are also many more that do not fit correctly into the standard of the breed. It must surely be the wish of serious breeders to see more and more first-class Dobermanns being bred and exhibited and not just a large quantity of mediocre dogs walking our streets. Obviously it is preferable to own something of beauty that actually costs no more to buy and to keep than does something that does not evoke admiration when viewed by friends and the owner.

I have already mentioned Herr Otto Goeller, also of Apolda. The talented successor of Louis Dobermann, he continued breeding successfully for many years after the death of the latter in 1894, and is generally accepted as the chief architect of the breed. It was in 1899 that he organised the National Dobermann Pinscher Club, and a year later he and other enthusiasts drew up their breed standard. Official recognition by the German Kennel Club was immediately obtained. While there is no doubt that Otto Goeller and his associates gradually improved the overall quality of Dobermanns, when the breed was exhibited in 1899 one of the earliest critiques read:

'The Dobermann was still coarse throughout, his head showed heavy cheeks and the dogs had too wide and French fronts; in coats the dogs were too long and wavy, especially long on the neck and shanks. A lot of dogs were built too heavy, appearing more like a Rottweiler. This was the first show where Dobermanns entered in every class. The first Dobermanns were very sharp fellows with straw yellow markings, white spots on chest, sometimes appearing more grey in colour than black on account of their heavy undercoat. They did not make the impression of a uniform and well bred breed. However, exterior body deficiencies were made up by splendid qualities.'

Contrast the dogs described in that quotation with the uniform elegance of the Dobermann one sees all over the world today. The fact that this dog has come so far and so quickly is a credit not only to the founders of the breed and those who succeeded them, but also to the type of dog that has the inherent qualities of watchfulness and alertness, loyalty and fidelity to his family, aloofness to outsiders, as well as a high intelligence and a strong guarding instinct.

It is not possible to go through the evolution of the Dobermann year by year. At each stage in the development of the breed there were dogs of excellent, average and mediocre physical type; some were aggressive, others were cowardly. Nevertheless, the careful breeding programme adopted by the more responsible breeders in Germany helped to standardise type, and further improve the overall refinement as distinct from the cloddy animal of the early years.

During the last year or two of the nineteenth century, there was a noticeable improvement in quality. Although by that time the Dobermann cult had spread into many parts of Germany, it was in the area of Apolda, where the breed originated, that this evolution really took place, due to the breeding programme of Otto Goeller and Goswin Tischler, of the Thueringen and Groenland kennels respectively. Exhibits with the names of Lux, Schnupp and Rambo drew much attention to themselves, and the first-named, mated to Tilly v. Groenland, produced a five-star litter. Otto Goeller mated Schnupp to a bitch registered as Helmtrude, and it was a grandson of these two, registered as Lord v. Ried, that has gone down in German history as a pillar of the breed.

William Schmidt, who was a great authority on the breed way back in the 1940s, did much research over a long period and tells us that each year produced one or two outstanding exhibits. Only a few years after Louis Dobermann had started to produce his type of dog, his colleague and successor Otto Goeller owned Graf Belling v. Thueringen, which sired quite a number of Sieger winners. Apparently Otto Goeller was dominant as a breeder of what in those days were considered first-class Dobermanns. He exhibited and won well with the bitch Ulrich's Glocke v. Thueringen. In 1904, in the same litter as Graf Belling, she produced the brown Sieger, Hellegraf v. Thueringen, one of the mightiest stud dogs of the breed. Philipp Gruenig in 1939 described Hellegraf v. Thueringen as a paragon of beauty, perfection and power, and added that through him the breed took on a new face and stature. Being considered outstanding specimens, both Graf Belling and Hellegraf were used extensively at stud, and both transmitted good bodies and temperament to their offspring. Lord v. Ried, mentioned earlier as a pillar of the breed, and born in 1907, was a son of Hellegraf. Hellegraf in particular added nobility and elegance to the breed, and stabilised the type then being produced. I learn that this dog's strength as a sire was because of his ability to produce Dobermanns of outstanding gait, which in my opinion has been lost to a great degree in many present-day German-bred dogs.

Another brown dog that scored extremely well at the time Hellegraf was being exhibited was the upstanding and elegant Junker Hans v. der Ronneburg. It is as well to mention at this stage that both black and brown exhibits competed on equal terms, whereas today, because of the difference in quality and even in build, the two colours do not compete against each other for the Sieger title.

By 1904 Sieger Leporello v. Main had made an appearance, and here again was a taller and more refined type of Dobermann than had previously been seen in Germany. He excelled in head type, with a full muzzle and decided stop. It was claimed that although Leporello deviated from the standard, nobody could resist his elegant appearance, and the Sieger title could not be withheld from him. Undoubtedly it was because of the emergence of dogs such as Junker Hans and Leporello that the Germans had to alter their ideas of what constituted the ideal Dobermann, and I seem to think that about this time the standard was amended so that these upstanding, yet noble, exhibits became recognised as the type actually required. However, most dogs of this period had long backs, steep hindquarters, French fronts, heads that were too heavy or too short, and stood low on the leg.

In 1906 Otto Goeller was exhibiting Benno v. Thueringen, a dog of excellent build which brought credit to Goeller and added lustre to the breed. In 1906 too, Sturmfried v. Ilm-Athen was born. A double grandson of Greif v. Groenland (one of the five-star litter by Lux from Tilly v. Groenland mentioned earlier), Sturmfried had great presence and refinement, carried rich markings and had great hereditary power. He also had the reflected glory of having produced a grandson, Modern v. Ilm-Athen, whose blood is carried in almost every Doberman in the world today. Including basic Thueringen and Groenland stock, the Ilm-Athen kennel is believed to have benefited also from addition of the blood of the Manchester Terrier, for Dobermanns from this successful kennel were notable for their short, hard hair, dark eyes and rich markings. Born in 1910, and a grandson on his father's side of the great Hellegraf v. Thueringen, Modern v. Ilm-Athen was a tall dog, and proved dominant in producing dogs with a good sweep of stifle, tremendous depth of brisket, excellent forehands and long clean necks. This dog has been criticised because his head deviated from the ideal but this fault was subsequently corrected in his progeny by the judicious use of bitches carrying good head type. Because of Modern's qualities, he should go down in history as one of the greats, probably equal to Graf Belling and Hellegraf. In any case, from 1910 onwards the overall quality of the breed improved and it was possible to see several outstanding exhibits as distinct from only one or two at the various shows held in Germany.

In the early days Dobermanns were either black or brown, and it was not until 1906 that the first blue dog appeared. It would seem that there was no objection to this new colour, so the standard was amended to make all three colours acceptable.

It was in 1912 that the first Isabella-coloured Dobermann was born in Germany, a dog registered as Assad v. Roederberg; he was a direct descendant of the great brown Hellegraf v. Thueringen. I am sure that the oft-repeated assertion that this fawn shade is the result of continued mixture of brown bloodlines is correct. In the USA I have seen a couple of fawn-coloured Dobermanns which quite candidly do not appeal to my sense of good colour, and, at the time of writing this, Isabellas or fawns are not acceptable in the majority of countries throughout the world.

[J.F. notes: Fred Curnow was writing in 1970, when the mode of inheritance of coat colour in the Dobermann was still not fully understood. It is now known that coat colour is controlled by two pairs of genes (see pages 116–117).

The first in its dominant form produces blacks and, in recessive form, brown Dobermanns. The second is concerned with the density of the colour. In its dominant form this pair of genes 'confirms' the black or brown colour, while in its recessive form the 'blacks' appear as 'blue', and the 'browns' as 'fawns'. On this evidence it is therefore illogical that blue Dobermans are acceptable and fawn-coloured Dobermanns, still sometimes referred to as Isabellas, are not.]

Concerning the colour termed Isabella, I have found out that there are several different stories about how this shade obtained its name. Some folk say that Isabella is the colour of old linen, basing their assumption on the tale of Queen Isabella of Spain, who, when her capital city was surrounded by enemies, swore that she would not change her linen until the siege was lifted. A period of three years elapsed before the enemy was dispersed and one can easily imagine that the Queen's linen was by that time the colour of parchment.

Another story regarding this colour is that Queen Isabella, who apparently was a most dominant personality, ordered that all Spain's royal horses should be of her favourite colour, which was a shade of yellow. As a result, all horses of that colour in Europe, much of which was under the influence of Spain in those far-off days, became known as Isabella horses, and apparently this term has persisted right up to the present day. Spanish adventurers sailing to America took many such specimens with them, some of which escaped into the plains and bred in the wild state. From these descended the Palamino, a colour now popular in many countries, so it is fair to assume that the term originally applied to horses may well apply to dogs. However, Isabella is not a precise term of colour and could range equally between parchment and fawn.

Because of conditions in the war years, many Dobermanns were put to sleep. Breeding programmes were severely curtailed, and much of the best breeding stock sold to neutral countries at comparatively high prices. These conditions did of course assist breeders in Switzerland, Holland and Czechoslovakia, and undoubtedly out

of the sorrow and pain experienced by German Dobermann enthusiasts came some good to the breeders from
these countries who purchased their stock.

Philipp Gruenig tells us that on the day he was ordered
to the front line, eighteen of the half-grown puppies in his
kennels had to be put to sleep or died of slow starvation,
and although he kept his two favourites both succumbed
to malnutrition in 1916. It was because of the lack of food
in Germany that many breeders, in order to stay alive
themselves and also because of the love they had for their
dogs, sold them as pets.

If it had not been for the need of the German Army for
Dobermanns as guard dogs and messenger dogs, it is
probable that all breeding would have ceased there during
the war. This would have been an irreparable blow. After
the cessation of hostilities many of the best dogs that
remained in Germany were sold at high prices to American soldiers in the Army of Occupation, and to buyers
from neutral countries. The breeding stock having
become sadly depleted, a few years passed before recovery
was apparent, after which there was a steady improvement
in general quality. Due to the growing popularity of the
breed in the USA in the 1920s, Americans descended
regularly upon the German breeders and, using the
mighty dollar, acquired many of the top dogs in that
country. The Germans did however retain a few of the
best Dobermanns and, with their usual thoroughness and
skill as selective breeders, continued to produce several
outstanding dogs and bitches.

An influential son of Modern v. Ilm-Athen was Edelblut
v. Jaegerhof, an excellent show dog and outstanding sire,
born in 1913. He remained in Germany throughout the
war, and his blood is found in every Dobermann today,
for he was at stud up to 1924, many of his progeny being
reared in Holland. He lived until 1926.

Burschel v. Simmenau, born in 1915, also survived the
war years and was greatly instrumental in resuscitating the
breed when hostilities ceased. Because of several transfers
of ownership, Burschel sired litters all over Germany, and
I imagine almost every exhibit in that country today can

be traced back to him. The bitch Asta Voss, also born in 1915, was a daughter of Edelblut v. Jaegerhof, and a line of fine dogs descended from her. Among the best of these was Lux v.d. Blankenburg, the result of a mating to Burschel v. Simmenau. Born in 1918, Lux v.d. Blankenburg was a late developer, and his potency as a sire was not recognised until he was four years old. He was full of Ilm-Athen blood, which helped to make him one of the greatest Dobermanns of his period. He was extensively used at stud before being sent to America, where he died in 1931.

Leddy v.d. Blankenburg, litter-sister to Lux, proved successful as a breeding force, chiefly through her son Alex v.d. Finohoehe, who before being sold to Czechoslovakia sired Stolz and Lotte v. Roeneckenstein. Lotte proved a bitch of immense hereditary value. In the following year, mated to Lux v.d. Blankenburg (her grand-dam's brother), she produced Ari and Alto v. Sigalsburg, both dogs of great spirit, that excelled in body structure, compactness and gait. Alto remained in Germany; Ari went to America but unfortunately died soon afterwards. A repeat mating of Lotte v. Roeneckenstein to Lux v.d. Blankenburg produced in 1926 Lux II and Lotte II v. Simmenau, both of whom excelled in substance, shoulders and front. Lotte II proved her hereditary worth in Germany before being sent to America. Mars and Modern v. Simmenau, bred from Lotte v. Roeneckenstein in 1927, also went to America. Apparently Mars was well named, being somewhat belligerent; Modern had a more refined appearance and a quieter disposition, and was considered to be one of the best dogs ever brought from Europe.

1926 proved to be a vintage year insofar as several dogs and bitches were born in that year whose progeny in Germany and America produced the foundation stock later imported into Great Britain after the Second World War. Lux II and Lotte II v. Simmenau have already been mentioned. A son of their older brother, Alto v. Sigalsburg, was Hamlet v. Herthasee, the 1928 Sieger, who became the sire of other great dogs, almost all of which were graded 'excellent'. Hamlet's best-known daughters in Germany were Bessie and Bajadere v. Brandenburg. Bessie was bought as a seven-week-old puppy by a novice owner, Mrs Bauer of Berlin, who chose her simply because she was the most extrovert in the litter. By the time she was three years old, Bessie v. Brandenburg had become a German Siegerin, after which she was sold to the USA, where following her show success in Germany she went Best of Winners at Madison Square, New York. Bajadere v. Brandenburg, Bessie's sister, remained in Germany, and was the dam of Desir and Daisy v. Glueckswinkel, who in 1933 took the dog and bitch Sieger titles in Leipzig. Truly an outstanding bloodline. Before he too was sold to America, Hamlet v. Herthasee left behind another daughter, Kora (sometimes given as Cora) v.d. Ruppertsburg, whose name has become famous through the successes of her progeny in the USA.

From the same line going back to Edelblut v. Jaegerhof and Burschel v. Simmenau via Lux v.d. Blankenburg and Asta Voss, came Helios v. Siegestor, a black son of Stolz v. Roeneckenstein (litter-brother to the great Lotte). Said by Philipp Gruenig to be anatomically correct, and with the best possible points, Helios was the subject of great controversy in Germany because he had several cream-coloured toes on one of his hind feet. Nevertheless his hereditary qualities proved outstanding. Mated to a daughter of the great Lotte v. Roeneckenstein, Helios produced Cherloc v. Rauhfelsen, and from a mating with Ilissa of Westphalia (a brown bitch who was the only American-bred Dobermann to win a German Sieger title) came Astor v. Westphalia, who was born in 1929. Astor's early death robbed American breeders of a potentially valuable stud dog. Fortunately he left behind a son, Kurt v.d. Rheinperle, one of the dogs that formed the backbone of American breeding up to and during the Second World War, and whose descendants made such an impact when brought to Great Britain some ten years later.

Cherloc v. Rauhfelsen, the other important son of Helios v. Siegestor, is best known as the sire of two great bitches, Gretl v. Kienlesberg and Jessy v.d. Sonnenhoehe, both born in 1934. On her dam's side, Gretl was a grand-daughter of the great Lotte v. Roeneckenstein; she is described as being a great show bitch, very feminine and of the utmost quality. She became an American champion and was herself the dam of a famous litter when mated to Kurt v.d. Rheinperle.

Jessy v.d. Sonnenhoehe is considered to be the greatest bitch of all. Philipp Gruenig notes that her dam was Alice generally Bella v.d. Sonnenhoehe, so presumably either name may be found on old pedigrees. He describes Jessy as a large, beautifully balanced animal, with a splendid body, beautiful head, great substance and outstanding gait. According to reports she also had a fiery tempera-ment and took quite a lot of handling. The only bitch to have won Best of Breed at the Sieger show in two consecutive years, Jessy became only the second bitch to be top winner at the Dobermann Pinscher Club of America Specialty Show, a success she achieved in 1939. While still in Germany, Jessy v.d. Sonnenhoehe was mated to the great Troll v.d. Engelsburg. In the litter that resulted were three puppies whose names appear in the pedigree of the earliest Dobermanns brought to the UK. They were Ferry, Freya and Frido v. Rauhfelsen. Ferry and Freya both gained their titles of Reichssieger and Reichssiegerin in Germany in 1938. Once again the top-winning dog was sold to America; Ferry v. Rauhfelsen arrived there in 1939 and went Best in Show at the Westminster Show shortly afterwards. He sired eight champions in that country, as well as many other top-class dogs. Freya and Frido remained in Germany, and their names will recur in a later chapter. Meanwhile, their dam, the great Jessy v.d. Sonnenhoehe, had gone to America. As well as show success it was as a brood bitch that she is best remembered. Having already whelped, in Germany, a litter with a Sieger and Siegerin, in the Westphalia kennel in New Jersey she produced seven champions in one litter by Kurt v.d. Rheinperle in 1938, and six champions in one litter by his son in 1939.

The other great Dobermann of the time was Troll v.d. Engelsburg, mentioned above, whose show career was phenomenal. The first male dog to be top Sieger in two successive years (1934 and 1935), Troll also won the title of World Sieger before leaving Germany in 1937, and later became both a Canadian and an American champion. He was the outstanding stud in Germany from 1935 to 1937, where besides the black Sieger and Siegerin mentioned earlier (Ferry and Freya v. Rauhfelsen), Troll sired many other top winners. Among them were World Siegerin Alfa v. Hollingen, and the 1937 Reichssiegerin, a brown bitch Ossi v. Stahlhelm, whose dam was a daughter of Helios v. Siegestor. Troll's sire, Muck v. Brunia, was a grandson of Alto v. Sigalsburg, and his dam was a line-bred descendant of the great bitch Asta Voss, proving yet again the importance of this bloodline.

It is not only for Troll v.d. Engelsburg that his sire Muck v. Brunia is remembered. A mating to Kora v.d. Ruppertsburg (mentioned earlier as a daughter of Hamlet v. Herthasee) produced Asta v.d. Domstadt, the 1934 black Siegerin. From a repeat mating came Blitz and Blank v.d. Domstadt. Blitz was Reichssieger in 1934 and 1936, and being the only well-known dog left in Germany it was his descendants that contributed to the revival of the breed after 1945. Blank v.d. Domstadt was sent to America where he proved of immense value as a sire, as is shown in a later chapter. Both Muck v. Brunia and Kora v.d. Ruppertsburg went to America, and when bred together again they produced seven champions in two litters.

The policy adopted by American breeders in the 1920s and 1930s, of buying the top winners in Germany and using them to strengthen and improve their stock, meant that when hostilities broke out in Europe in 1939, the best German bloodlines were preserved across the Atlantic. During the war years breeding in Germany was cut to a minimum and many dogs were put to sleep. Only a few enthusiasts were able to continue breeding. When hostilities had ceased serious breeding was gradually resumed, but conditions remained very difficult in Germany for several years. German kennels prominent since 1945 that are now familiar names through the dogs and bitches imported into the UK from 1948/9 on, are (in alphabetical and not necessarily chronological order): Brunoberg, Eversburg, Forell, Furstenfeld, Germania, Hagenstolz, Kleinwaldheim, Rauhfelsen, Stahlhelm, Wellborn. Dobermanns bred in these kennels, or bearing their affix, will appear in a later chapter.

One of the first new German champions was Hasso v.d. Neckarstrasse, Sch.H.II, bred from the Bismarcksaule and Rauhfelsen lines. He was breed champion in the Russian Zone in 1947 and 1948, and was in great demand as a stud dog. His working qualifications included a Schutzhund grade; he also qualified as a Messenger Dog. The Russian Zone champion in 1949 was Boris v. Rehwalde, Sch.H.III, a dog largely of Simbach breeding. He became the main stud dog at Herr Felsing's kennel, where many first-class dogs were bred. Boris v. Felsingpass became a champion in 1953, Carmen v. Felsingpass won the bitch championship in 1957, and a litter-brother and sister, Hede and Heide v. Felsingpass, had similar success a year or two later. On a visit to Austria Francis Fleitmann (of the Westphalia kennels in the USA) was greatly impressed by the quality of Carmen v. Felsingpass, and urged his friend Herman Palmer to buy her.

Herr Klein was one of the most knowledgeable breeders. He bred champion Alex v. Kleinwaldheim, who proved himself one of the leading stud dogs post-war, and the brown Casso v. Kleinwaldheim, winner of the Sieger title in 1949.

A top kennel that carried over from before the war was Germania, owned by Herr August Schneider, who up to his death in 1964 had for many years been recognised as a successful breeder. Dobermanns from this kennel had real quality; they were elegant and noble, with long well-balanced heads. The bitch champion title in 1949 went to his Hella Germania, followed in 1951 and 1952 by Ester Germania with many similar top honours right through to 1964, during which time the blue bitch Adda v. Germania, the black dog Titus v. Germania and the brown bitch Cita Germania all became champions.

Herr Herman Palmer of the Furstenfeld kennel bred Dobermanns of similar type to those of Germania. They were elegant and powerful, and had good heads and rich tan markings. Herman Palmer used World Champion Lump v. Hagenstolz, a double grandson of the great Alex v. Kleinwaldheim, as his main sire and as we said before, he bought Carmen v. Felsingpass as principal brood bitch on the recommendation of Francis Fleitmann. Herman Palmer bred champions Citta and Citto v. Furstenfeld; the latter was the sire of champion Ina v. Furstenfeld.

Herr Ernst Wilking's von Forell Dobermanns have won international acclaim, sound temperament and working potential being considered as important as good conformation. A litter containing three champions, Chico, Cherry and Cindy v. Forell, was bred from the brown bitch Cita Germania by Int. Ch. Odin v. Forell (a descendant of World Ch. Lump v. Hagenstolz and of Int. Ch. Dirk v. Goldberg Sch.H.III).

Other leading stud dogs of the early post-war period, some of whose progeny were brought into the UK, were Benno v.d. Schwedenhecke, Ajax v. Simbach (the sire of Alex v. Kleinwaldheim) and Frido v. Rauhfelsen. Benno and Ajax were direct descendants of Blitz v.d. Domstadt; Frido was a son of Troll v.d. Engelsburg; both Blitz and Troll were sons of Muck v. Brunia.

The 1950 black Sieger was Troll v.d. Eversburg, whose brother Tasso v.d. Eversburg came over to the Tavey kennels in England. Their sire was the great Alex v. Kleinwaldheim, line-bred as shown above to Muck v. Brunia, and also a grandson of Gretl v. Kienlesberg and Jessy v.d. Sonnenhoehe, the famous daughters of Cherloc v. Rauhfelsen. Frau Reiners, a well-known breeder of brown Dobermanns, bred champion Etzel v. Romberg, and the 1959 champion Tittau v. Romberg. A brown bitch from this kennel, Frigga v. Romberg, was brought to the UK.

The Dobermann being of German origin, this section has endeavoured to show how the breed evolved in that country, with particular emphasis on the principal lines of breeding that resulted in the dogs and bitches selected for importation into Great Britain from 1948 onwards.

The Dobermann in Holland

Of the Dobermanns imported from Europe to Great Britain a high proportion have been Dutch-bred. It is therefore appropriate to take a look at how the breed was developed in Holland.

Herr H. Kloeppel of the Grammont kennel, in a (very) brief chapter included in Philipp Gruenig's book, emphasises the importance placed by the Dutch on size and substance as well as on good body structure. Although he was writing before 1934, judging by the quality of the Dobermanns imported from Holland the same desired objective is evidently still held by Dutch breeders. Herr Kloeppel also states that although early imports from Germany were extremely sharp, the more phlegmatic Dutch environment (his words) exerted an influence through the years, so that Dobermanns in that country have steadily become more agreeable.

The earliest Dobermanns in Holland were of Thueringen breeding. Little real enthusiasm for the breed was maintained, however, until the arrival from Germany of Sieger Troll v. Albtal. Born in 1912 and largely of Hellegraf blood, this compact dog had great quality and was an influential sire; his name stands behind most of the dogs that proved important in later years.

Dutch breeders of that period used principally dogs and bitches of the German von Jaegerhof line. In the previous section Edelblut v. Jaegerhof was mentioned as being at stud in Germany, with many of his progeny being reared in Holland during the First World War. The kennel names of the most skilful Dutch breeders of the time became known through the quality of their stock, and in the 1920s they attracted buyers from America. Thus it was that names bearing the affixes of Grammont, Rivals, Roemerhof and Koningstad appear in earlier generations on the pedigree of many famous Dobermanns bred in the USA.

Rivals Adonis, Dutch-bred from a Jaegerhof bitch, was considered to be the best dog in Holland in the early years of the First World War. From a daughter of Troll v. Albtal he sired the bitch Bubine v.d. Koningstad. A brown bitch of Hellegraf and Ilm-Athen bloodlines was bought in Germany by the Grammont kennel, where, mated to Edelblut v. Jaegerhof, she whelped in 1915 a brown dog and bitch, Urian and Undine v. Grammont. It appears that Urian was very short-legged, but otherwise was well-made, with a powerful body and good head and expression. A mating of Urian v. Grammont to the black Bubine v.d. Koningstad mentioned above produced Benno v.d. Roemerhof, reported to be the best black dog of the year (1920). He was a big, powerful dog of good character, alert and brave, and was the first foreign-bred Dobermann to win the title of German Sieger. Afterwards he went to America.

Undine v. Grammont proved as good as her brother. In a litter sired by Rivals Adonis she whelped Ajax and Angola v. Grammont, both browns. Ajax, mated to a daughter of Troll v. Albtal, produced Carlo v.d. Koningstad, a dog of most pleasing appearance and correct proportion, according to Philipp Gruenig. Angola v. Grammont was described as the most beautiful bitch of her time; she was also a brood bitch of the highest order. In three successive years, each time mated to Carlo v.d. Koningstad (the black son of her litter-brother Ajax), she produced Elfrieda, Favorit and Ilisa v.d. Koningstad, all of which achieved fame. Elfrieda, born in 1920, was a great show bitch and became a champion in Holland before being bought by the White Gate Kennels in Philadelphia. There, mated to a son of Burschel v. Simmenau, she produced three champions in her first litter and, a year later, the well-known Big Boy of White Gate. Favorit v.d. Koningstad, born in 1921, was a brown dog, well up to size, with a good front and a long, finely chiselled head of the desired type. Bought by the West-phalia kennels in New Jersey, he was said to be the best sire ever brought to America, and was used extensively at stud. He lived until 1934. Ilisa v.d. Koningstad, also brown, was quickly bought and sent to America, where her most famous daughter was Ilissa of Westphalia, the brown bitch that when brought over to Germany became the only American-bred Dobermann to win a German Sieger title.

As far as Western Europe was concerned, there appear to have been no international successes for Dutch-bred Dobermanns in the 1930s, although it is understood that a great many had gone with their owners to the Dutch East Indies and became popular in that part of the world.

Breeding in Holland was resumed after 1945; some new kennel names appeared, a few older names reappeared. Within a few years there were Dutch champions again, and a sufficient stock of top-quality dogs to attract buyers again. Dobberhof, Heerhof and Sudhoek Dobermanns soon provided foundation stock for enthusiasts in England. In Holland the Dutch champion Waldo v.d. Wachtparade, a son of the great Troll v.d. Engelsburg, was in demand as a stud, as indeed was his son, International Champion Graaf Dagobert v. Neerlands Stam, a dog that won twenty-seven international championship awards in seven countries – a record still unmatched. His breeder, Mrs Knijff-Dermout, had started breeding before the war, and resumed at once after it was over. Skilful use of the most suitable German dogs and bitches has maintained the success of this Dutch kennel and built up a most impressive strain. Neerlands Stam Dobermanns have won championships and universal acclaim all over the world, and are still doing so. Mrs Knijff-Dermout's experience is quite unique. Her dogs are of the highest quality, in temperament and character as well as in physique. It is therefore no wonder that dogs of Neerlands Stam breeding were among the first to be brought to Great Britain.

Dobermanns in the USA

It is thought that Dobermanns first came to America in 1908. Certainly in that year a Mr Theodore Jaeger of Rochester, New York, who was of German origin, was granted the kennel name 'Doberman'. There was little interest in the breed, however, until the end of the First World War, when dogs were brought from Germany by American soldiers returning home, and the breed began to attract attention. The Doberman Pinscher Club of America was founded in 1921, and the Standard as recognised in Germany adopted a year later. In 1923 the first of several top German judges were invited to the USA to give their opinion on progress and quality. Among them was the late Peter Umlauff, recognised as one of the leading authorities, and whose daughter continued to take a great interest in the breed. Philipp Gruenig, author of the comprehensive and authoritative account of the development of the breed, also came to judge in America, as did Willi Hirscher, and also Julius Selikowitz from Norway. The popularity of the breed increased rapidly, and breeding stock was steadily expanded with the purchase by American breeders of winning dogs and bitches from Germany and Holland. Not unnaturally it was these European imports that took the prizes at shows. By 1927 the level of importation dropped, American breeders having the experience and knowledge of the breed to build upon the stock available, although, as has been shown, the policy of buying and bringing over to America the top winners in Germany was continued right up to the Second World War.

Glenn Staines was an early enthusiast, who brought winners from Germany to his Pontchartrain kennels, among them the famous Lux v.d. Blankenburg. He continued breeding for many years, was keenly interested in temperament as well as show potential, and began training 'Pathfinder' dogs for the blind in 1936. Glenn Staines assisted in drawing up the first American Breed Standard adopted in 1922. Except for a few minor amendments this remained virtually unchanged until 1969, when fawn (Isabella) was added as an acceptable coat colour. The American Breed Standard currently in operation is given in Appendix C.

Another early breeder was Howard Mohr of the White Gate kennel, who brought from Holland the great Angola v. Grammont, her daugher Elfrieda v.d. Koningstad, and others. It was Elfrieda's son, Big Boy of White Gate, that became the first American-bred winner of a Best in Show award, and later in Germany he was rated 'excellent' at the Sieger show.

Best known of all the early American breeders was the

celebrated Francis F.H. Fleitmann, of the Westphalia kennels in New Jersey. A scholarly man and widely travelled, he studied the breed on both sides of the Atlantic, and had an eye for quality. In 1922 he was invited by the German breeders to judge their Sieger show, and he remained the only American to hold a judging licence in that country (and also in Switzerland, where he retired and died in 1976). 'Hermy' Fleitmann's enthusiasm in importing, breeding and campaigning Dobermanns did much to popularise the breed in the USA, and the Westphalia kennel became famous both for the excellence of its importations and for the quality of its home-bred stock. Carlo v.d. Koningstad was an early import in 1923, also his son and daughter, Favorit and Ilisa v.d. Koningstad, and many others followed from Holland and Germany, of which probably the best known was Jessy v.d. Sonnenhoehe. Of the illustrious 'Seven Sires' born between 1938 and 1941, two were Westphalias and three had one Westphalia parent. 'Hermy' Fleitmann's contribution to the breed spanned more than thirty years. Between 1922 and 1948 he bred and owned forty-three American champions, and Westphalia dogs were still meeting with success in the show-ring during the 1950s.

A kennel in Maryland which had a tremendous influence on the breed's development in the USA was Marienland, the affix of Richard Webster. He kept a large number of dogs and was a loyal supporter of shows in the 1940s. Looking back, several Dobermanns from this kennel, or carrying the Marienland affix, stand out for their achievement. In 1938 the record 'R' litter containing seven future champions was bred in the Westphalia kennel, by Kurt v.d. Rheinperle from Jessy v.d. Sonnenhoehe. Two of the puppies joined the Marienlands, and both became champions. They were Westphalia Rameses and Westphalia Rembha. In a litter bred from Blank v.d. Domstadt (who was sired by Muck v. Brunia) and the brown Siegerin Ossi v. Stahlhelm (sired by Troll v.d. Engelsburg, Muck's son), a brown dog was registered as Domossi of Marienland. He sired twenty champions, one of which, Emperor of Marienland, was in a litter from

Westphalia Rembha. Emperor of Marienland later became the sire of twenty champions. He and his father Domossi and Westphalia Rameses were three of the illustrious 'Seven Sires'.

Another three were Westphalia Uranus (from Jessy v.d. Sonnenhoehe by a son of Kurt v.d. Rheinperle) and two of his sons: Favoriet v. Franzhof, a brown dog, and Alcor v. Millsdod, a black. The remaining one of the 'Seven Sires' was the brown Dictator v. Glenhugel, who in the ownership of Peggy Adamson sired more than fifty champions. Dictator was a full brother of Domossi of Marienland, being sired by Blank v.d. Domstadt from Ossi v. Stahlhelm, but was two years younger.

The 'Seven Sires' were so called by Peggy Adamson (and probably others) who wrote about them and recorded their breeding achievements. Each one produced more than ten American champions. One American-bred bitch attained comparable status at that time, being the dam of a dozen champions from three sires. She was Dow's Illena of Marienland, by Westphalia Rameses from a daughter of Kurt v.d. Rheinperle. Her twelve champion offspring resulted from matings to Domossi of Marienland and two of his sons, Emperor of Marienland and Dow's Dusty v. Kienlesberg. All of these incomparable producers were descendants of the best German imports, and their hereditary power was carried on through succeeding generations by intermarriage with daughters of each other, and through the descendants of their own brothers and sisters. Even though the 'Seven Sires' are by now off the pedigree forms of present-day Dobermanns, their names should be learned and remembered. It was they who so often supplied the foundation dog or bitch from which new breeders in every part of America were able to build up a successful strain, and from these post-war kennels came the dogs and bitches chosen for importation to Great Britain.

The breeding programme of Bert Dow of Iowa produced some outstanding bitches who became the foundation of other successful kennels. Dow's Illena of Marienland has already been mentioned; Dow's Dame of Kilburn,

and Dow's Cora, Dow's Cassie and Dow's Dodie of
Kienlesberg were others that became famous both in the
show-ring and as valuable broods. Bert Dow served in
1943 as President of the Doberman Pinscher Club of
America.

Margaret Kilburn was breeding Dobermanns for barely
five years in the 1940s, but with such skill and success that
'Kilburn' stock became the foundation for later breeders.
Her own foundation bitch was the great Dow's Illena of
Marienland mentioned above. By the selective use of those
of the 'Seven Sires' based on Westphalia breeding, the
Kilburn Dobermanns were of superb quality, and besides
show success proved dominant sires and dams. Their
contribution to the breed was invaluable.

The Doberman Pinscher Club of America (usually
referred to as the DPCA) is a member of the American
Kennel Club and the only national Dobermann breed club
recognised by them. DPCA members are found all over
the States. Besides encouraging breeding and showing,
and holding shows and an Annual Convention, the DPCA
supports obedience training. Obedience trials take place at
indoor or outdoor shows, where the titles CD, CDX and
UD may be gained. These qualifications are awarded to
dogs trained to a high standard of obedience, but their
purpose and scope are different from British working
trials, with which they should not be confused (see page
231).

Peggy Adamson served for many years on the Gov-
erning Board of the DPCA and has been its President. She
is dedicated to the Dobermann. As lecturer, writer,
columnist and judge she has served the breed in a variety
of ways, and is also its historian. Her Damasyn kennels on
Long Island have become internationally famous. The
great brown Champion Dictator v. Glenhugel, bought as
a puppy in 1941, was Peggy's companion and friend for
ten years, as well as one of the most outstanding stud dogs.
In all he sired fifty-two champions, approximately half of
which were brown. He was a superb showman and
extrovert character, and passed on these qualities to his
progeny in addition to excellent conformation and type.

The slight cowlick along the nape of the neck that can still occasionally occur (and which caused controversy when it appeared in litters born in the UK) became known as 'the mark of Dictator', for he was the original source of this coat defect. Dogs and bitches from Peggy Adamson's Damasyn kennels were sent all over the world, but many remained in the USA and became notable champions. Some of them gained an obedience title too, proving that beauty and brains can and do indeed go together. One such was the brown Ch. Damasyn the Solitaire CDX (by Dictator from one of his grand-daughters), who was born in 1951, the year that Dictator died, and took over as top stud.

Other dominant and well-known kennels on the East Coast are those owned by Ed and Judy Weiss, Monroe and Natalie Stebbins, and Ellen Hoffman. The Weiss prefix is Ebonaire, and their breeding programme was based on Damasyn bitches. Since 1948 many champions have come from the Ebonaire line, sometimes three or four in one litter, demonstrating that selective breeding can bring excellent results. Ch. Stebs Top Skipper sired both the 'Football' and the 'Fencing' litters from which came Champions Ebonaire Touchdown, Flying Tackle, Touché, Gridiron and Balestra. All the dogs kept at Ebonaire live in the house, so most of their champions have been owned and exhibited by other enthusiasts.

The Stebbinses used an abbreviation of their own name as a prefix. I well remember judging a huge entry of Dobermanns in Chicago in 1957 where Ch. Stebs Top Skipper became best of breed. He was descended from Alcor v. Millsdod through the illustrious Rancho Dobe's Storm. I learned afterwards that at only his second show, and while still a youngster, 'Hermy' Fleitmann made Top Skipper best of breed. He was an elegant, powerful showman, alert and full of character. In the Dobermann world Monroe is affectionately known as 'Steb'; as a professional handler he delighted in showing puppies that were bred from his own stud dogs and had been sold to other exhibitors. He retired in the early 1970s. Stebs Top Skipper remains an important name in the breed's history;

he was top sire in the USA for three years. Of special interest to British Dobermann owners is that in his first litter was Ch. Alemaps Checkmate, grandsire of Vanessa's Little Dictator of Tavey.

Ellen Hoffman must be one of the smallest handlers of Dobermanns anywhere, but her short stature is more than compensated for by her great heart. She is a mine of information, always willing to help novice handlers and breeders, and has enjoyed much success in the show-ring, where she handles her own dogs. The foundation stud dog at her Elfred kennel was a post-war German Sieger, the foundation bitch a daughter of Ch. Delegate v.d. Elbe, a line-bred descendant of Domossi of Marienland and the Westphalia 'R' litter. Ch. Elfred's Spark Plug, a son of Ch. Stebs Top Skipper, was one of America's most renowned Dobermanns, winning championships too in Canada and three other countries.

Any record of breeders on the East Coast would be incomplete without mentioning Jane Kay, of the world-famous Kay Hill's kennels. First a professional handler, she is now recognised as one of the best judges of Dobermanns and other working breeds, and has a fund of knowledge about the breed which she is always willing to share. In the second litter she ever bred, Jane Kay had three champions, of which Ch. Kay Hill's Paint The Town Red was kept, and as a brood bitch produced eleven champions. Her most famous 'Witch' litters were sired by Ch. Borong the Warlock CD. This important bloodline was later introduced to Great Britain through two litters born in quarantine.

Moving away from the East Coast towards Pennsylvania we find Tess Henseler's kennels carrying the affix vom Ahrtal. Tess Henseler came to the USA in 1928 from Germany. Her first Dobermann, Hasso v. Ahrtal, was bought in 1948 as a companion and farm dog, but trained for obedience he qualified CD and CDX. The kennel's foundation show bitch was Ch. Meadowmist Isis v. Ahrtal, a daughter of Emperor of Marienland from Dow's Ditty of Marienland. Mated each time to Ch. Delegate v.d. Elbe, Isis produced seventeen champions in four litters. More than seventy champions have been bred by Tess, and between 1954 and 1963 she was nominated 'Breeder of the Year' eight times. Obedience training was however not forgotten, and Tess organised a team of sixteen Dobermanns and handlers who regularly gave demonstrations at the larger shows throughout the USA. The two best-known stud dogs from this kennel were Cassio v. Ahrtal, sire of thirty-eight champions, and Felix v. Ahrtal, who sired twenty-eight.

Other well-known kennels are Highbriar, Toledobe and Tedell, all in Ohio. Breeding at the Highbriar kennel was started by Betsy Thomas as a hobby, but between 1953 and 1975 she bred twenty-five champions. The Toledobe kennels of Patrick and Judy Doniere began in 1955; at shows all the dogs are owner-handled. Their first show bitch, Wahlmars Baroness, became a champion, and in two litters by Alemaps Checkmate produced five champions, one of which, Checkmates Chessman, sired Vanessa's Little Dictator of Tavey. Tedell is the affix of Ted (Theodora) Linck, who in 1951 trained her Dobermann to qualify CDX and UD. A serious breeding programme followed, based on the Highbriar and vom Ahrtal lines, and Ted produced eight champions in eight years, and has continued breeding many good winners that carry the Tedell affix. One of the stud dogs used for Tedell bitches was Ch. Singenwald Prince Kuhio, a top-winning dog in the early 1960s. On his pedigree are the names of all the 'Seven Sires'. Prince Kuhio was owned by Dale Rickert and handled by the top professional George Rood.

Going further west, we find in Missouri Jack and Eleanor Brown, whose surname is used as their affix. Their foundation bitch was Ch. Dow's Dame of Kilburn, by Dictator from a daughter of Domossi of Marienland. The success of this kennel came through breeding to the 'Seven Sires', the names of Alcor v. Millsdod, Emperor of Marienland and the bitch Westphalia's Rembha being close behind the top-quality Brown's puppies. Two of their best-known champions were Brown's Eric and Brown's Evangeline, the result of mating Dow's Dame of Kilburn to her father, Dictator v. Glenhugel. Eric is considered to have been the most excellent of all Dictator's sons; a truly dominant stud, he sired twenty-eight champions. One of his daughters, Brown's Bridget, was a small and sickly brown puppy actually at the veterinary surgeon's to be put to sleep when the Browns hastily collected her, and by careful rearing built her up into a top show-winning bitch. Other high-class Dobermanns came from this kennel; the Browns' record has been a proud one.

Much of the information and detail contained in this chapter has come from Joanna Walker, who for many years has kept records of the most important Dobermanns and their breeders. Keith and Joanna Walker's affix of Marks Tey derives from the English village of that name in Essex which was Joanna's birthplace. They purchased the lovely brown bitch Ch. Damasyn the Waltzing Brook CD, and mated her to Brown's Eric. Waltzing Brook was line-bred to Dictator v. Glenhugel, being by his son Damasyn the Solitaire out of a Dictator grand-daughter. From this litter came Ch. Derek and Ch. Dodie of Marks Tey, both of which had great success in the show-ring. Marks-Tey was one of the top kennels in the 1960s and 1970s, Joanna being equal first 'Breeder of the Year' in 1974–5.

A most remarkable dog that attracted considerable publicity was Ch. Borong the Warlock CD. One of a litter of five champions, his sire was of German breeding, a descendant of Casso v. Kleinwaldheim, his dam from the Damasyn line. He became a champion at the age of thirteen months, added Canadian and Cuban championships to his American title, and was also shown in Germany. He gained his obedience title in three straight shows. Borong the Warlock was a house-dog and the constant companion of his owner Henry Frampton, travelling with him by car, plane, train and ship. He won top awards at shows all over America, and when his owner died in 1967 he was put to sleep, and the two were cremated together. As mentioned earlier, Borong the Warlock was the sire of the two famous 'Witch' litters bred from Kay Hill's Paint The Town Red.

On the West Coast Vivienne and Brint Edwards' well-known Rancho Dobe kennels became one of the most esteemed and best known through the quality and success of the Dobermanns they bred. Before 1943 their kennel name was Moorpark, and a bitch from an early litter, Juno of Moorpark CD, is behind every Rancho Dobe Dobermann. She was a daughter of Sieger and American Champion Ferry v. Rauhfelsen. Rancho Dobe's Storm was born in December 1949. His dam, Maedel v. Randahof, was a grand-daughter of Ferry v. Rauhfelsen and of Muck v. Brunia. Storm's sire, Ch. Rancho Dobe's Primo, was by Alcor v. Millsdod from a grand-daughter of Emperor of Marienland. The story of Storm's early days (he was the only male in the litter to survive), his life as a house-dog with his owners Mr and Mrs Len Carey in Connecticut, and his success in the show-ring during 1951 and 1952 are well documented. Handled at all times by Peter Knoop, Storm responded to his slightest signal, showing and moving faultlessly. Never beaten in breed classes, Storm won the supreme award at the 1952 Westminster Kennel Club show in New York, and made breed history by repeating this success at the same show a year later. After that win he was retired from the show-ring, but proved a valuable stud dog. It was a litter sired by Rancho Dobe's Storm that, born in quarantine, made such an impact in Great Britain. Other champions came from the Rancho Dobe kennels, Primo, Presto, Riff, Roulette and Maestro (bred in 1964) among them, but ill-health forced Brint Edwards and his wife to cut back on their activities.

A bitch that came top in show competition in 1965 was the beautiful black Ch. Ru-Mar's Tsushima CD, the first of her sex to win Best in Show at the International Kennel Club in Chicago. Tsushima was owned by Ron and Margaret Carveth, and was by Ch. Rancho Dobe's Cello from a vom Ahrtal bitch. Known to everyone as 'Tish', she was unbeatable in her show career. Tragically, she died whelping a litter in 1968.

Some of the newer kennels in California are those carrying the affixes of Haydenhill, Westwinds and Marienburg. The Marienburg kennels owned by Mary Rodgers is currently one of the most famous in the USA.

A bitch of Rancho Dobe breeding and a Westwinds dog were purchased in 1962 as youngsters, and both became champions. In 1963 two six-week-old puppies from the Stebs line were bought at a bargain price, and they too became champions. The bitch, Sultana of Marienburg, was the top winning Dobermann in 1967, and twice won best of breed at the DPCA Annual Specialty Show. Selective breeding to the older established lines has kept Marienburg in the forefront of success, and a dog from that kennel has recently been brought to England.

Kay and Charles Etner of the Tannenwald kennels in Texas purchased their foundation bitch as a seven-week-old puppy from Jane Kay in 1960. A daughter of Borong the Warlock and Kay Hill's Paint The Town Red, Kay Hill's Soubretta like her father was a house-dog as well as a show champion. She was the dam of eighteen champions, of which one, Dolph v. Tannenwald, was top show dog and top stud in 1971. Dolph's sire was also of Kay Hill's breeding. It is therefore not surprising that two of his grandsons, Phileen's Duty Free of Tavey and Tavey's Satellite, born in quarantine from different bitches, became two of the most influential sires in Great Britain.

There are, of course, important kennels all over the States, and many great dogs and bitches whose names are chronicled in specialist American publications. The purpose of this chapter has been to indicate the principal lines from which individual dogs and bitches were chosen for importation to Great Britain. American breeders think nothing of travelling a couple of thousand miles to use the stud dog they consider best suited for their bitches, or to select a puppy on which to build their own strain. Their dedication and skill, and their love of the breed, have raised the Dobermann to a peak unequalled anywhere in the world.

Dobermanns in Great Britain

J.F. writes: Fred Curnow's account of the origin of the breed and its development in Germany and Holland and in the United States was written before 1972. To bring it up-to-date additional material has been included and some revision made, but his words and opinions have been retained. Turning to the development of the breed in Great Britain, it is easier for someone else to trace its growth and popularity in that country since Fred and Julia Curnow's contribution was of such immense importance and should be shown in true perspective. Over a period of twenty-six years, a total of fifteen dogs and bitches were imported into their Tavey kennels, from Germany and Holland and from the USA, and Fred and Julia continued breeding and exhibiting with success for as long as their health permitted. Sadly they are no longer with us, but their influence and example, and dedication to the breed they loved, will never be equalled.

The choice of foundation stock was carefully made by those breeders who, after the Second World War, wished to introduce the Dobermann into England. The names of two important and dominant pre-war German champions, Troll v.d. Engelsburg and Blitz v.d. Domstadt, have been mentioned earlier. Both of them were sons of Muck v. Brunia, and they are seen over and over again in the breeding of the individuals first chosen for importation.

Lionel Hamilton-Renwick's Birling kennel was founded on a Swiss-bred dog, Bruno v. Ehrgarten, and a Dutch bitch, Britta v.d. Heerhof. Bruno was a grandson of Sieger Astor v. Hollingen (a son of Troll v.d. Engelsburg and litter-brother to World Ch. Alfa v. Hollingen); Britta was from a father/daughter mating, the Dutch Ch. Waldo v.d. Wachtparade, one of Troll's most outstanding sons, having on this occasion been mated to his daughter Alma v.d. Heerhof. From the Birling litter bred in 1949, three dogs and a bitch became regular winners at the early shows and later were all producers of good stock. Birling Rebel was tall and well-made; Wolfox Birling Rogue became the breed's first male champion; Birling Roimond proved a dominant sire, while Birling Rachel is now recognised as a pillar of the breed. She was Best of Breed at Cruft's in 1950 and 1951, when Dobermann classes (without c.c.s) were first scheduled, and she won many other show awards. As a brood bitch she produced puppies of excellent conformation and temperament to whichever of the leading stud dogs she was mated. Importation of a blue Dobermann bitch, Quita of Jerry Run, from America in 1951, was intended to develop further the Birling line of breeding. However, Lionel Hamilton-Renwick's career often took him abroad, and he was not able to continue to build on the foundation so well laid. In later years he served a term as President of the Dobermann Club, of which he had been a founder member, and he is now recognised as an all-round judge of international repute.

Mrs Barbara Butler's Upend kennel had marked success when Birling Roimond was mated to her imported bitch Frieda v. Casa Mia. One bitch, Bridget of Upend, became a champion, and two others, Belle and Bernadette, each bred a champion. From a repeat mating in 1952 came Metpol Fritz, who won the award for the top police dog in London.

Details of Dobermanns used by the police are given in a later chapter. Selected originally by the Surrey Constabulary for their working potential, they were excluded from breeding with civilian stock, except for the dog Mountbrowne Joe which was presented to the Dobermann Club for that purpose. Their most famous dog, the working trials champion Ulf v. Margarethenhof, was in fact brought over from Germany by an American. Ulf's sire was Hasso v.d. Neckarstrasse, mentioned earlier as a post-war German champion of proven working ability. In quarantine Ulf was found to be too sharp to handle, and his owner offered him to the Curnows free of charge. Fred Curnow arranged for the dog's registration at the Kennel Club, but considered he would be best suited to working for the police, and suggested to Harry Darbyshire that he should visit the quarantine kennels and assess the dog for himself. What followed is Dobermann history, and is recorded in a later chapter. The dogs trained or bred by the police at Mountbrowne, Guildford, seemed at the time a separate and distinct type of Dobermann, and were regarded with some awe by civilian handlers. Only later was it realised that, far from being a separate type, the great Ulf v. Margarethenhof, being a grandson of the 1938 Reichssiegerin Freya v. Rauhfelsen, was in reality a cousin of the early Tavey imports!

The Tavey affix (later transferred to Julia) was first granted to Fred Curnow in 1947, the year of arrival in the UK of the kennel's first imports. The Dutch-bred bitch Pia v.d. Dobberhof came to England in whelp to Benno v.d. Schwedenhecke, a leading stud dog of that time and a descendant of Blitz v.d. Domstadt. The puppies were born in quarantine but only two dogs survived, and at the age of six weeks these were taken into the Tavey kennels. They were Don and Bruno of Tavey. Bruno (sometimes given as Brunno) was retained for stud purposes; Don (later Vyking Don of Tavey) went to Mrs Pamela Korda and eventually to the Durham police. Pia v.d. Dobberhof was a grand-daughter of Dutch Ch. Waldo v.d. Wachtparade (a son of Troll v.d. Engelsburg) through her dam Alie v.d. Heerhof. She was thus related to Britta v.d. Heerhof, whose dam Alma was litter-sister to Alie.

Imported from Germany also in 1947 was Derb v.d. Brunoberg, and a bitch Beka v.d. Brunoberg followed a few months later. Like Pia a year earlier, Beka was imported in whelp, but none of the litter survived. Derb and Beka were half-brother and sister, their dam Unruh v. Sandberg being sired by Artus v. Furstenlager from World Ch. Alfa v. Hollingen (daughter of Troll v.d. Engelsburg). Beka was sired by Frido v. Rauhfelsen, and Derb by a son of Frido. Their first litter in 1948 included Adel of Tavey, sire of Margaret Bastable's foundation bitch Ch. Xel of Tavey, Wanda of Tavey, dam of my Vyking Drum Major (not a show winner but very success-ful in obedience and working trials), Shern of Tavey (later re-registered as 'Anna Wanderer') who bred several good litters, and Alpha of Tavey, the foundation of Eva Would's Cartergate line. They were all steady, outgoing and reliable, with good conformation and substance, and proved excellent basic breeding stock.

Before vaccines were available to give protection against the worst canine diseases, distemper, hardpad, hepatitis and kidney infections could strike suddenly and wipe out an entire litter, or so damage young stock as to make it worthless for showing or breeding. Many such losses were incurred by the early breeders of Dobermanns, who lost promising young stock both in quarantine, as indicated above, and in their own kennels. Even with present-day vaccines and a wide choice of antibiotics to combat infection, importing dogs from abroad can still prove expensive and risky. Six months in quarantine can spoil both physique and temperament unless each dog is given individual treatment, personal attention and some human companionship every day, and too few owners of quarantine establisments appear to bother with this aspect of the job. Quarantine is an essential safeguard against the introduction of rabies to this country and kennel conditions and management are very strictly controlled. In fairness it should be said that dogs can arrive from overseas in poor condition and noticeably improve in health during their term in quarantine but, undoubtedly, some brought in with high hopes of improving a breed's existing stock do lose condition or become withdrawn, unsure, unpredictable or aggressive after a period of confinement.

Dogs can and do leave quarantine in good condition, alert and happy, and ready for the show-ring, a course of training or for breeding. Such was the case with Prinses Anja v't Scheepjeskerk, who produced two champions, Elegant and Empress of Tavey, in her first litter by Bruno, the resident Tavey stud dog. After some months of training and successful competition in obedience and working trials (reported later in the appropriate chapter), Anja returned to the Tavey kennels. In 1952 she produced two more champions from a repeat mating to Bruno: Juno of Tavey, the foundation of the Sonhende kennel, and Jupiter of Tavey, who added the title of Obedience Champion as well after training with Bob Montgomery. Later that same year, Prinses Anja was mated to the next Tavey import from Germany, Tasso v.d. Eversburg, and as well as a champion, Lustre of Tavey, this litter contained Lyric (sold abroad after winning two c.c.s) and Lorelei, whom it was my privilege to own, train and handle in working trials, obedience and the show-ring, in all of which she consistently proved herself a winner.

Prinses Anja's intelligence and working ability, and her success in breeding five champions and a number of other puppies of excellent type and temperament, derived from her inheritance. She consolidated the bloodlines already in the country, and added another important line back to Troll v.d. Engelsburg through his son, Dutch Ch. Waldo v.d. Wachtparade. Anja's sire was the great International Champion Graaf Dagobert v. Neerlands Stam (a son of Waldo), her dam a daughter of Dutch Ch. Bucko v.d. Heerhof, who was litter-brother to Birling Britta v.d. Heerhof. Anja was also related to Pia v.d. Dobberhof, as both of them were grand-daughters of Waldo v.d. Wachtparade.

Tasso v.d. Eversburg's quality and breeding were appre-ciated both by supporters of the working type of Dober-mann and by those breeding for show. A litter-brother of the 1950 German Sieger Troll v.d. Eversburg, most of his forebears had working qualifications. His dam, Christel v.d. Brunoberg, was a full sister to Beka v.d. Brunoberg, so he carried the same line from Frido v. Rauhfelsen (and Troll v.d. Engelsburg and Jessy v.d. Sonnenhoehe) while introducing new blood through his sire, Alex v. Kleinwal-dheim, a dog line-bred to Muck v. Brunia through Blitz v.d. Domstadt. Tasso v.d. Eversburg was of standard size, compact and strong, and without coarseness. His steady temperament and proud, alert bearing carried through to his progeny, and his contribution to the breed in the UK went far beyond the five champions he sired.

For the next five years the bloodlines already in the country were developed and intermingled, and numbers increased as new enthusiasts acquired their first Dober-mann and started showing and breeding. Bernard and Dorothy Horton built up their Trevellis line from Ch. Satin of Tavey; Philippa Thorne-Dunn and her husband developed their Sonhende line from Ch. Juno of Tavey and a Cartergate champion. Greg and Jane Parkes bought

Anna of Catharden (daughter of Ch. Precept of Tavey) from Mrs Eileen Cathcart, and continued breeding under their Annastock affix for many years.

Soon the demand for police dogs was such that the breeding of Dobermanns for police work was transferred from the Surrey Constabulary to Mary Porterfield, whose Bowesmoor kennels became the maternity unit for Mountbrowne stock. Puppies surplus to police requirements were sold with the Bowesmoor affix, and were always of strong working type and steady temperament. Mary Porterfield sometimes had other bitches on breeding terms, and was able to add fresh bloodlines to the Bowesmoor stock. Shern of Tavey, and the imported bitches Centa v.d. Emsperle, Helga v. Kleinwaldheim and Frigga v. Romberg contributed in this way, as did the brown dog presented to the Dobermann Club, Mountbrowne Joe, and Bill v. Blauenblut, an imported dog that was a half-brother to Mountbrowne Joe's dam, Donathe v. Begertal.

In 1956 Mary Porterfield imported Treu v.d. Steinfurthohe, a son of the 1950 German Sieger Troll v.d. Eversburg. Welcomed at the time for introducing a bloodline strong in working ability as well as show potential (which he did), Treu v.d. Steinfurthohe in fact reinforced the line already established by his uncle, Tasso v.d. Eversburg of Tavey, a brother of Sieger Troll. Treu v.d. Steinfurthohe was a lively dog of excellent character, and was used by breeders of both show and working type Dobermanns. His only champion offspring, Bowesmoor Mona, was from a daughter of Birling Rachel. Mona became the foundation of George Thompson's Wyndenhelm line which aimed at breeding Dobermanns of substance that could work and show. Those that George kept himself were successful in the show-ring and later took part in working trials and the Dobermann Club working tests.

One person who skilfully combined the best lines of inheritance was Miss Eva Would, MBE, a wise and talented lady whose affix was Cartergate. She was a founder member of the Dobermann Club and a committee member for many years and later became President of the Midland Dobermann Club. In more than twenty years of breeding and showing, Eva kept only three Dobermann bitches, bred only three litters from each, and reared a maximum of six puppies per litter. From Cartergate Alpha of Tavey she bred four champions: Claus and Caprice were sired by Birling Roimond, and Day and Daybreak were sired by Tasso v.d. Eversburg. Ch. Day went on to sire Faust of Cartergate, an excellent police dog, and from Caprice came the Popladene line which, unfortunately, was not to continue for long. Ch. Claus of Cartergate, a dog of substance and handsome appearance, went to Philippa Thorne-Dunn and was her house-dog and companion as well as stud dog of the Sonhende line. He is probably best remembered as the grandsire of the great Ch. Iceberg of Tavey.

Lola of Cartergate had been brought to England by a family returning from service overseas. When her owner died, his widow was unable to keep the bitch, who eventually found a home with Eva Would, and was registered under her pet name and the Cartergate affix. Some time later details of Lola's breeding were obtained from Germany. She had a champion daughter, Helena, who, for all her life, was Eva's constant companion. Mated to Claus of Cartergate, Helena's litter contained a champion dog, Jove of Cartergate (who sired Lionel of Rancliffe, a brown dog that won two Obedience Certificates) and Juno of Cartergate, who later bred three champions: the great Iceberg of Tavey and a year later Oberan and Opinion of Tavey. Opinion became the foundation bitch of Mrs Jean Ryan's Nayrilla line and Oberan, soon after winning his title, went abroad with his owners.

At that time, when an apparently pure-bred dog was found or obtained, it could be entered in the Kennel Club Breed Register after its breed type had been certified by three championship show judges. Besides Lola of Cartergate, mentioned above, two other bitches obtained their KC registration in the same way. One was found wandering in Gloucestershire, and when unclaimed was given a

home by Mrs Eileen Blair, who registered her as Anna
Wanderer. Later, when Anna was taken to be mated to
Bruno of Tavey, she was recognised and identified by the
Curnows as being Shern of Tavey. It is as Anna Wanderer,
however, that she is recorded as foundation bitch of the
Dissington line and among her descendants were two
police dogs, Goliath of Dissington and Mountbrowne
Peter, both listed in Appendix I or mentioned in a later
chapter. Similarly, a Dobermann bitch found running wild
in the hills of southern Scotland, was taken in by Mrs
Brandon and subsequently registered as Ampherlaw
Gretel, under which name she appears in breed records
as the dam of a champion dog.

A Dutch-bred dog that deserved wider use at stud was
Alex v. Rodenaer. Imported in 1954, he was the grandson
of Int. Ch. Graaf Dagobert v. Neerlands Stam (sire of
Prinses Anja) and of Dutch Ch. Tomm v.d. Eversburg
(litter-brother to Tasso and the German Sieger Troll v.d.
Eversburg) and carried the lines which were already
proving so successful. From a daughter of Ch. Daybreak
of Cartergate owned by Mario Migliorini, Alex v. Rodenaer sired a bitch owned and registered by Peter Clark.
This was Carrickgreen Walda Nagasta, winner of ten
challenge certificates and the dam of Ch. Carrickgreen
Confederate. Because of these two great Dobermann
champions Alex v. Rodenaer has earned his place in the
breed's history.

The first challenge certificates for Dobermanns were on
offer at ten championship shows in 1952, starting with
Crufts, where Leo Wilson chose Elegant of Tavey and her
half-brother Ingot for the top awards. Elegant became the
first British champion, remaining unbeaten and winning
seven more c.c.s that year, three of them under judges
from overseas: Mrs Crane from the USA, Julius Selikowitz
from Norway and the great Philipp Gruenig, who came
from Germany to judge at a general championship show.
Herr Gruenig's choice for best dog was Wolfox Birling
Rogue, who became the first male champion in that same
year. Ch. Elegant of Tavey's champion son, Precept of
Tavey, won eleven c.c.s (seven of them in 1955) and sired

some exellent stock; her daughter Satin of Tavey became a champion and foundation bitch of the Trevellis line. Unhappily Elegant's full potential as a brood bitch was never realised; accompanying Fred Curnow one Sunday morning on a walk through the woods near home, she picked up a chicken carcass that was baited with poison, and died almost immediately – a tragedy for her owners and for the breed.

Two successful lines of breeding were based on bitches that gained their title in 1957. Margaret Bastable's Xel of Tavey was already a winner in top obedience competition when she became a breed champion, and as a brood bitch she was the foundation of the Barrimilne line. Elizabeth Hoxey was a breeder of Dachshunds with the Tumlow affix when her first Dobermann, Baba Black Pepper, gained her title by winning a third c.c. at the Dobermann Club's first-ever championship show. Fred Curnow, the Club chairman, was the judge, and he chose Syd Taylor's Ch. Daybreak of Cartergate as the dog c.c. winner.

Twenty-nine of the breed champions listed in Appendix E are derived entirely from the dogs and bitches imported from Europe from 1947 to 1956. Others with some success at shows also did well in obedience and working trials, as described in later chapters. The breed's achievements on the working side, as well as its appearance and behaviour in the show-ring, attracted attention and favourable comment. Dobermanns were seen to be strong and well-made, reliable in character, and capable of being trained to a competitive standard even by a novice handler.

In whatever activity their Dobermann was engaged, owners were encouraged and supported by the breed club. The importance of a club to promote the interests of the breed was realised by a group of enthusiasts as early as 1947. They sought, and obtained Kennel Club approval, and the Dobermann Pinscher Club was registered in 1948. It became the Dobermann Club in 1960, after 'Pinscher' was dropped from the breed's name. In its early years the club was active in guaranteeing breed classes at shows and the individual success of a member's dog received mention in the breed notes of the weekly dog papers. Any special achievement was rewarded with a club prize or a trophy which was competed for annually on a points basis. Inevitably club meetings, rallies, matches and shows took place in or near London, but membership gradually spread nationwide, and today includes a number of members living overseas. To serve the interests of owners and breeders north of the border, the Scottish Dobermann Club was established in 1959 and was also active, in its early years, in guaranteeing classes for Dobermanns at Scottish shows. Two branches of the Dobermann Club, formed in 1958 for the benefit of members living in the north of England and in the Midlands, sought and achieved independent status some years later. Today they operate very successfully as the North of England and the Midland Dobermann Clubs respectively. As the breed's popularity has increased, new clubs have been established in Wales, Northern Ireland and in different areas of England; the current list is given in Appendix B. Every breed club holds at least one open show each year. When a club qualifies for championship status its show becomes an event of special importance for exhibitors. As will be seen later, specialist judges from overseas have been a frequent choice by the breed clubs for their championship shows.

May 1956 saw the birth, in quarantine, of the first Dobermanns of American breeding. Pictures of American Ch. Rancho Dobe's Storm, and news of his Best in Show win two years running at the prestigious Westminster show in New York, had excited interest among Dobermann fanciers everywhere. When the strict post-war currency regulations were relaxed, Fred and Julia Curnow, on a business trip to the USA in 1955, purchased a champion bitch, Rustic Adagio, and arranged for her to be mated to the great 'Storm' and flown over to England when she proved to be in whelp. It was a considerable investment to make, and again the bloodlines were carefully chosen. Like the earlier imports from Europe, Rustic Adagio was directly descended from two sons of Muck v. Brunia: Troll v.d. Engelsburg and Blank v.d. Domstadt (litter-brother to Blitz), and from the great bitch

Jessy v.d. Sonnenhoehe. An earlier section described how in America these three, together with Kurt v.d. Rheinperle and the brown bitch Ossi v. Stahlhelm, had between them produced the so-called 'Seven Sires' that proved such a dominant force in developing the American type of Dobermann. Four of the 'Seven Sires', and champion bitches carrying Westphalia, Kilburn and Dow affixes, were behind Rustic Adagio. Rancho Dobe's Storm, a great-grandson of Muck v. Brunia and of Sieger and American Ch. Ferry v. Rauhfelsen, also came from the best German stock. Rustic Adagio's six puppies, four dogs and two bitches, were born in quarantine and taken to the Tavey kennels when they were six weeks old. One dog, Accolade, was exported and became an Australian champion. One of the bitches, Aminda, although she gained entry to the KC Stud Book through a championship show placing, was outshone by her sister and brothers, and was not further campaigned. The four other puppies made breed history; they were the Tavey's Stormy 'A' litter: Achievement, Abundance, Acacia and the bitch Adagio. They entered the show-ring in 1957.

Tavey's Stormy Abundance, aged nine months, won the reserve c.c. at Crufts. He went on to become a champion, winning a total of seven challenge certificates in that year. His brother, Tavey's Stormy Achievement, shown once, was awarded his first c.c. Tavey's Stormy Adagio took the bitch c.c. on each of the three times she was shown, so she too became a champion in 1957. In the following year Abundance won seven more c.c.s, and Adagio two. They were awarded best dog and best bitch when Herr Willi Hirscher from Germany judged the Dobermann Club's championship show that year and repeated this success twelve months later, in 1959, when the judge was Monsieur Marcel Demangeat. This was Adagio's sixth c.c., after which she was retired. Abundance won three c.c.s in all during 1959, and was withdrawn from further competition. His total of challenge certificates was seventeen. Last of the trio of brothers, Tavey's Stormy Acacia made his show début in the autumn of 1958 and won two c.c.s. Awarded a third early in 1959 he too became a champion, and afterwards was at stud in the north-east of England at Mrs Gladstone's Brief kennel. Tavey's Stormy Achievement had been held back and given time to mature. Having won his first c.c. as a junior in 1957, he was not shown again until 1959, when he won five c.c.s. He was the first Dobermann to win Best in Show at an all-breed championship show, which he did in 1960, the year he was awarded eight c.c.s. Two more certificates won in 1961 brought Ch. Tavey's Stormy Achievement's total to sixteen.

These three dogs, Tavey's Stormy Abundance, Achievement and Acacia, were not unbeaten in their show career; each in his turn had been placed reserve to a c.c. winner. But their undoubted quality and excellent conformation were recognised by all-rounder and specialist judges alike, and their combined total of thirty-six certificates out of fifty on offer in the years 1957–1960 inclusive was proof of the value of this new bloodline. Any criticism levelled against them was due to their lack of sharpness. From the best German stock of the 1930s, American breeders had developed a Dobermann that combined substance with a greater elegance than before, and was slightly taller, had good angulation and free flowing movement, a proud head carriage and a more equable temperament. The three sons of Rancho Dobe's Storm did not look for trouble but would stand their ground when provoked. On one occasion when being shown, Achievement was seen to react sharply to a sudden loud noise close behind him, which would probably not have been tolerated in Germany, but he was no coward and faced any known hazard. Established breeders quickly recognised the potential of these dogs, and the first champions to carry the affixes of Trevellis, Tumlow and Barrimilne came from each kennel's foundation bitch when bred to Stormy Achievement or Abundance.

Alf and Eleanor Hogg, whose first show bitch was Bandeau of Tavey, a daughter of Ch. Jupiter, used the American stud dogs in a most skilful breeding programme that made their Triogen Dobermanns a dominant influence for many years, as show winners and, more importantly, as foundation stock for later breeders.

Two bitches that made notable contributions to the breed when mated to an American dog were Tamara and Utopia, both of Tavey. Tamara was from Prinses Anja, Utopia from Birling Rachel, and both were sired by Tasso v.d. Eversburg. By Ch. Tavey's Stormy Achievement, Tamara had one champion daughter (who herself bred a champion) and another that was the dam of six champions. Already the dam of Bandeau of Tavey mentioned above as being the foundation of the Triogen line, Utopia bred three champions when mated to Ch. Tavey's Stormy Abundance and was also the grand-dam of Hawk of Trevellis, the winner of one working trials certificate.

Orebaugh's Raven was the next Tavey import from the USA. A daughter of Rancho Dobe's Primo, she was half-sister to the great Rancho Dobe's Storm, and her dam combined Rancho Dobe breeding with lines to Alcor v. Millsdod, one of the 'Seven Sires' and a grandson of Jessy v.d. Sonnenhoehe. Orebaugh's Raven was imported in whelp to Stebs Top Skipper, a grandson of Rancho Dobe's Storm and of Delegate v.d. Elbe, and was Fred Curnow's choice for best in show when he judged in Chicago in 1957. Raven's litter was born in quarantine in July 1959, but only two puppies survived. They were Arcadian (later Dirksby's Arcadian of Tavey) who went to Audrey Woods in Northern Ireland, and Acclamation of Tavey, who became a champion while still a junior and proved quite outstanding as a sire. Most of his twenty British champion offspring were from the daughters or grand-daughters of his cousins, Stormy Abundance and Achievement; but his most successful show-winning son, Iceberg of Tavey, was from Juno of Cartergate, who is mentioned previously as combining the earlier Tavey and the original Birling lines and who was a grand-daughter of the German-bred bitch Lola.

For twenty years the show record of Ch. Iceberg of Tavey remained unequalled by any British-bred Dobermann. The correct height for a male, he was strong, well-made and elegant, with a good head carried proudly, and a keen alert expression, and he caught the eye whenever he entered the ring. He was a perfect showman, who responded to Fred's sensitive handling and to the acclaim of the crowd, and would move round and across the big ring with great power and drive. He loved attention and had a delightful character. His total of best of breed and working group wins at general championship shows, and overall total of twenty-two best in show awards, made him Dog of the Year in national competition in 1965, and he was the runner-up in 1966 and 1967. In all he won thirty-five challenge certificates in a show career that spanned five years. Credit for maintaining this superb dog in peak condition, and keeping him happy and mentally alert throughout, goes to Len Charles, described by Fred Curnow in his introduction to this book as his partner at the Tavey kennels. Len was a master in every aspect of dog management, and the continuing success of Tavey dogs and bitches as breeding stock and show winners in the 1960s and 1970s owed much to his experience and skill. No matter how far the journey to a distant show, nor the duration of a period of competition, Len Charles had Ch. Iceberg of Tavey in optimum condition whenever Fred Curnow took him into the ring, where this team deserved every one of their many hotly contested awards.

While Iceberg was his outstanding son, the best daughter of Ch. Acclamation of Tavey was Tavey's Stormy Wrath, the winner of eighteen challenge certificates. Wrath was one of six champions bred in two litters from Tavey's Stormy Governess, a daughter of Achievement and Tamara of Tavey. The bitch was jointly owned by Julia Curnow and Elizabeth Hoxey, and half of each litter was registered with the Tavey affix, half with the Tumlow. Regardless of which affix they carried, the progeny of Acclamation and Governess made an outstanding contribution to the breed's success, both in the show-ring and as producers of good stock. From the first litter, Tumlow Fantasy became a champion and bred a champion daughter, and her brother, Tavey's Stormy Nugget, won ten c.c.s and sired a champion son. The second litter, whelped in 1961, contained two champion males: Tumlow Impeccable, a strong well-built dog who won nine c.c.s and sired eight champions, and Tavey's Stormy Wonder, a sound and handsome dog whose services at stud were unfortunately limited owing to the demand for the other dogs available at the Tavey kennels. In 1962 Julius Selikowitz of Norway judged the Dobermann Club's championship show, and he chose as best dog and best bitch the brother and sister Tavey's Stormy Wonder and Tavey's Stormy Wrath. Their litter-sister, Tavey's Stormy Willow, in Charlie Starn's ownership, gained her title and when mated to her grandsire, Stormy Achievement, produced a champion son, Tavey's Stormy Medallion, who proved an influential sire. Medallion was owned by Mrs Dorothy Parker; he was a wise dog of excellent steady temperament, and lived amicably as a house-dog with his champion son. Olive Neave's successful Chevington line was based upon Medallion. He was also the grandsire of my Koriston Pewter Strike, T.D.ex.

Although showing is the hobby of a minority of dog-owners, the show-ring is the shop window for any breed, and from 1957 onward the success of the American-type Dobermann attracted attention and brought new enthusiasts to the breed. The number of annual registrations steadily increased, as did show entries, and by 1966 the allocation of challenge certificates for each sex was twenty. The skilled handling and presentation of their exhibits by Fred Curnow and Elizabeth Hoxey became the model for newer exhibitors, and competition in the show-ring was keen. Dobermanns bearing new affixes such as Dirksby, Dolina, Edencourt, Gurnard, Heidiland, Tickwillow, Tramerfield, etc. either bred a champion or became champions themselves; all of them derived from at least one parent of Tavey, Triogen or Tumlow stock. Breeders well known today as specialist judges, and who have produced top-quality Dobermanns over many years, either started with the American line or added it with great success to the stock they already had. Among these were Margaret and Harry Woodward (Achenburg), Andy and Flora Auld (Auldrigg), Jean Ryan (Nayrilla), Jimmy Richardson and his mother (Roanoke), Pat Quinn (Royaltain), Thelma and Vic Lowe (Siddley) and Jean Scheja (Tinkazan).

A dog and two bitches brought from the USA by Fred and Julia Curnow in the mid-1960s widened still further the range of American bloodlines available to British breeders. Their effect was not as dramatic as the original imports, but each made a worthwhile contribution by producing new champions, or individual dogs and bitches whose progeny became winners and the foundation of successful lines of breeding carrying affixes such as Borain, Chater, Flexor, Koriston, Phileen, Saxonhaus, Zeitgeist, etc.

The first to arrive, in 1964, was Westwinds Quintessence, a young bitch that, when Julia was judging a breed show in California, had so impressed Fred Curnow at the ringside that he made an immediate offer for her. Bred locally at the Westwind kennel, Quintessence was a granddaughter of the great sire Ch. Delegate v.d. Elbe, who was from Westphalia and Marienland stock, and traced directly back to Blank v.d. Domstadt, Kurt v.d. Rheinperle, Ossi v. Stahlhelm and Jessy v.d. Sonnenhoehe. His descendants were therefore highly suitable for reinforcing the bloodlines already established in the UK, and besides producing two champions in one litter Westwinds Quintessence proved a valuable brood bitch. Her first litter by Tavey's Stormy Achievement contained two bitches that proved excellent broods. Tavey's Stormy Pepita at the Tumlow kennels (now in the names of the former Elizabeth Hoxey and her husband Raymond Harris) bred Tumlow Green Highlander, a dog many consider unlucky not to have gained his title. He was a handsome dog and a great character, and the sire of Flexor Flugelman, owned by David Crick. Flugelman won fifteen c.c.s in a show career that lasted over six years; he was the first Dobermann to win the working group at Cruft's, and he has proved an important sire, his name appearing on the pedigree of many later winners. Another bitch in the same litter born to Westwinds Quintessence in 1964 was Tavey's Stormy Pride, who, in the joint ownership of Jane Parkes and Mike Bradshaw, bred a champion son, and through him a champion grandson. Two champion bitches, Babette and Baroness of Tavey, were in a later litter from

Quintessence sired by the newly arrived American dog Vanessa's Little Dictator. Babette (later Royaltains Babette of Tavey), jointly owned by Pat Quinn and Pat Gledhill, was handled at shows with great skill by the latter and became a champion. She was the foundation bitch of the Gledhills' successful Borain line. Her sister, Baroness of Tavey, went to Vicki Killips (now Mrs Syd Philip) who breeds under the affix Chater. A brown puppy from the same litter, Bayard, was retained at the Tavey kennels for stud purposes.

Imported jointly by Julia Curnow and Elizabeth Hoxey (although later registered with the Tavey affix), a bitch, Distinctive Daneen, introduced MarksTey breeding to this country. A grand-daughter of Ebonaires Gridiron and Brown's Eric, Distinctive Daneen traced back to the Damasyn line and Dictator v. Glenhugel. Unfortunately however a period of illness that ultimately required surgery affected her breeding potential. Though she bred only two litters, one contained a bitch, Nieta of Tavey, who became the dam of four champions, and a dog, Nuance of Tavey, notable as the grandsire of Vyleighs Valerian, who won ten c.c.s during a show career that lasted five years.

Imported in 1965, Vanessa's Little Dictator was an alert and lively dog, short-coupled and of the correct square proportions. A double grandson of Ch. Alemaps Checkmate, his breeding traced back mainly to the great Delegate v.d. Elbe but, through Brown's Eric, he brought in a line going back to Dictator v. Glenhugel. Although used extensively at stud he sired only four champions from two bitches (two of them mentioned above). However, his influence could be seen in later generations of Dobermanns in the UK and many of his progeny were sold overseas and proved notable show winners.

The overall quality and rich coat colour of brown Dobermanns in America had always been admired by the Curnows, and Vanessa's Little Dictator, although black and tan himself, carried the gene for brown coat colour. This was due to the presence of Delegate v.d. Elbe in the breeding of both his parents. A detailed and extended pedigree of American Champion Delegate v.d. Elbe lists his fifty-four champion offspring and gives their coat colour: thirty-nine were black, fourteen were brown (called 'red' in the USA) and two were blue. Although none of them became champions, Am.Ch. Delegate v.d. Elbe also sired five fawn Dobermanns. While Vanessa's Little Dictator never sired a blue puppy, it is possible that he inherited the gene for dilute coat colour as he had Delegate v.d. Elbe in the breeding of both his sire and dam, but that was not a reason for choosing to import him to England. The Curnows hoped that he would not only improve the quality of future brown Dobermanns in Great Britain, but also that his vivacity and outgoing character would enliven the quieter and gentler temperament which came from the early American dogs. Sadly, this dog was the subject of controversy. He had a cowlick along the nape of his neck, referred to in the breed standard as a 'ridge' and classed as a serious fault. A number of his puppies also had a cowlick along the back of the neck, but this defect of the coat is rarely, if ever, seen today.

Increasingly a number of owners of the earlier type of Dobermann felt that, although the American dogs had greatly improved the overall quality, stature and confor-mation of Dobermanns in the UK, the breed was in danger of losing some features considered essential in its country of origin. The first doubts expressed were that the American type of Dobermann was not a working dog. The committee of the Dobermann Club acted promptly. They obtained, from Germany, the schedule of tests approved for the breed and, as a result, the Dobermann Club working tests were drawn up and came into operation in 1961, as described in Chapter 10. Details of the breeding of all Dobermanns that have qualified in a two-day stake in championship working trials, or have gained a diploma in the Club's working tests, are given in Appendices G and H respectively. A study of these will show that, from the time of the earliest imports to the present day, a Dober-mann bred from sound stock, of whatever origin, can still qualify as a working dog.

The strongest criticism made against those dogs that

were all, or partly, of American blood was that their temperament was faulty, and that they lacked the proper boldness and firmness of character. On the other hand, supporters of the American type could claim that their dogs were companionable, alert and protective, and efficient guards when required. They were easier to live with and ideal as family dogs as they were steadier and not permanently ready to challenge or give chase to anything that moved. Both points of view were sincerely held, and are still argued to this day. There have, of course, been other points on which loyal supporters on each side have stoutly defended their preferred type against critics with opposing views. Controversy over type is not confined to the Dobermann breed; argument frequently rages in other breeds too. It was, however, due mainly to dissatisfaction with the way the breed was developing, and a wish to counter some effects of the American bloodlines, that the move towards fresh imports from Germany was started.

Among the first to arrive was a bitch, Kitty v. Wellborn, imported by David Kingsberry in 1960 in whelp to Bary v. Kellergrund. David's interest in the working side of the breed, and the success of his previous Brumbies Dobermanns in obedience and working trials, are reported in later chapters. From Kitty's litter, born in quarantine, a bitch, Brumbies Black Bramble, was bought by Bernard and Dorothy Horton. Her first litter by a son of Tavey's Stormy Abundance contained two dogs of proven working ability: Hawk and Havildar of Trevellis. Hawk passed all grades in the Club working tests and won one working trial certificate; his brother Havildar worked for a time with Harry Appleby as a police dog, and was also successful in the Club tests. A repeat mating from Black Bramble produced Inga of Trevellis, whose daughter Helroy Lady Courage of Graybarry was the dam of four good working Dobermanns carrying the Helroy affix of Mrs Jill Glossop. Foremost among those who widened the choice of bloodlines available to British breeders, by introducing German dogs from the leading post-war kennels, was Margaret Bastable. Specialist judges – Fred

Curnow, Rex Hodge and John McManus among them –
have sometimes been invited to judge the breed at
European shows. However, only Margaret Bastable from
the UK has achieved a place on the élite German panel of
championship show judges, whose numbers do not exceed
twelve or thirteen at any one time. This status follows a
successful and rigorous apprenticeship, first as a learner
judge under supervision, then judging under the scrutiny
of senior examiners and reporting on all exhibits, and
finally, an oral examination, where in Margaret's case the
judges were Francis Fleitmann (Westphalia), Willi Rothfuss (v. Rauhfelsen) and Ernst Wilking (v. Forell). At the
time of writing, through seniority, Margaret's name heads
the list of judges, and she remains the only woman and
the only judge from overseas to have attained this honour.
Two occasions serve to illustrate the high esteem in which
Margaret Bastable is held on the Continent. When the
International Dobermann Club, fully operative again,
held its first ch. show in Strasbourg in 1963, Margaret
(with 'Hermy' Fleitmann as her steward) judged bitches,
and Herr Willi Rothfuss judged the dogs. Margaret
herself admits that her most treasured memory is of being
the guest of honour at the I.D.C.'s eve-of-show dinner in
Munich in 1982. A worthy tribute to a very talented lady.

Having studied lines of breeding in Europe, Margaret
decided that the Germans, with their strict control on
breeding and their insistence on correct temperament as
well as good conformation, were once more producing
Dobermanns of the required quality. At their country
home, she and her husband had a range of quarantine
kennels built to the latest requirements, where the inmates
received individual attention and were maintained in show
condition. Similarly, those that Margaret imported for
herself were given individual attention, and were made to
feel at home even while confined within the quarantine
unit for six months.

Over a period of fourteen years, Margaret Bastable
imported a total of ten Dobermanns from Germany. In
her own words, she found that 'Dobermanns in the UK,
especially those in the second and third generation of

breeding after the introduction of the American bloodlines, were too light in bone and over-long in loin, pale in
both eye colour and tan markings, and often insufficiently
firm in character'. For her, the essential features of any
Dobermann that she imported or kept herself were
shortness in loin, a level topline and good tailset (no falling
croup), rich tan markings, a dark eye and a good head.
They must also be firm in character but not vicious,
'honest' but not 'mean', and while short-coupled and
compact in body must have elegance, but without exagger-
ation in either length of neck or bend of stifle.

The lines of breeding from which Margaret chose her
Barrimilne imports were mostly those mentioned earlier
in the German section of this chapter. The first of her four
imported bitches was Iris v. Wellborn, who arrived in 1960
in whelp to Urian v. Mandurahof, a son of the Dutch ch.
Graaf Iskander v. Neerlands Stam and of Loni v. Hagenstolz, litter-sister to World Ch. Lump v. Hagenstolz (a
double grandson of the great post-war champion Alex v.
Kleinwaldheim). Iris was half-sister to Kitty v. Wellborn
mentioned already, and the elder by two years. As Iris was
registered in the joint names of Margaret Bastable and
Peter Clark, her litter of eight puppies was shared between
them. A dog puppy registered as Carrickgreen Cordon
Bleu later sired Pompie Seaman, a brown dog that was the
foundation of Hilary Partridge's well-known Pompie line.
A bitch, Carrickgreen Colette, when bred to a later
German import, appears in the pedigree of several show-
winning bitches carrying Margaret's Barrimilne affix. In a
later litter from Iris v. Wellborn sired by Tavey's Stormy
Achievement was Barrimilne Genghis Khan, a handsome
and well-made dog that made a promising début in the
show-ring before being sold abroad.

1962 saw the arrival of Gin v. Forell, the dog above all
others that was Margaret's special favourite. Herr Ernst
Wilking had succeeded his father in breeding under the
von Forell affix, and he made it famous. Both Gin's
parents had Schutzhund qualifications, his sire being
German champion Dirk v. Goldberg, his dam Diana vom
Oelberg. Trained and handled by Margaret, Gin qualified

U.D. in a ch. working trial, and passed the basic Dobermann Club working test. He was short-backed, compact and elegant, an alert dog and quick to act; his look was keen and his dark eyes missed nothing. He was quite sharp, but as Margaret herself has said, 'he was my devoted friend to the end'. Gin v. Forell was used extensively at stud, and two bitches in the Durham Constabulary were bred to him to sharpen up the character of the police dogs in that force.

The Germania kennel of Herr August Schneider had been established before the war, and Dobermanns of good quality that made excellent foundation stock were bred by Herr Schneider right up to his death in 1964. From him Margaret bought Vilja Germania, a bitch she describes as being large and kind. Her puppies by Gin v. Forell were particularly good; many were exported and proved successful in competition overseas. One of Vilja's daughters, sired by a son of Tavey's Stormy Abundance, became the grand-dam of Barrimilne the Signorina, the winner of two c.c.s in this country. After Vilja Germania, the next arrival from Germany was Angela v. Kastanienhof, the daughter of Blanka v. Hohenwurzburg, a bitch that Margaret admired greatly and had given high placing when she judged in Germany. Unhappily Angela proved to be a non-breeder.

Two dogs and a bitch brought from Germany in 1967 further reinforced the Barrimilne lines of breeding. Timo v.d. Brunoberg has been described by Margaret as a tall dog of good physical standard and a delightful character, being happy, extrovert and full of fun. His name appears in the breeding of some good present-day Dobermanns who have inherited his steady temperament. As a stud dog, Timo was overshadowed by Wilm v. Forell who was imported at the same time. Bred by Ernst Wilking, Wilm was by the International and German champion Cliff of Fayette Corner (a son of Int. and German ch. Arco of Fayette Corner) from the German ch. Cita Germania. Margaret has described Wilm as being short-backed, with strong topline and quarters and a good turn of stifle; he had a well-chiselled head and a dark eye. He proved a dominant sire, his influence on the breed extending far beyond the three champions he sired. He can be seen as the grandsire and great-grandsire of Dobermanns that have done well both in the show-ring and on the working side. Ken Frankland of the Linhoff affix bred Wilm v. Forell to his Triogen bitch, from which mating a bitch Linhoff Pearl Diver became a champion, and her brother, Linhoff the Pagan, proved a useful stud dog.

Wilm v. Forell's best-known son was Ch. Hillmora the Corsair, owned by Mrs Jean Baird and bred by Ben Johnson from Triogen Torcella, litter-sister to the great Ch. Triogen Tornado. In the same litter as Corsair, a bitch Hillmora the Capri later became the dam of Andy More's Ch. Hillmora the Explorer, winner of eight c.c.s and successful in working trials and the Club working tests. The Explorer's brother, Hillmora the Extremist, sired a champion dog, Chevington Royal Black Magic, who won five c.c.s and who was also a good worker, qualifying in the Club tests and in working trials. The influence of Wilm v. Forell was clearly apparent in later generations.

Third in the trio of imports to Barrimilne in 1967 was a bitch, Ditta v. Scholzback, whose sire, German ch. Arco of Fayette Corner, was the grandsire of Wilm v. Forell.

Baron v. Bavaria joined the Barrimilne stud force in 1970. His breeder was Herr Hans Wiblishauser, President of the International Dobermann Club when it was revived and re-formed. Baron combined two excellent lines of breeding; his sire was Odin v. Forell and his dam Mascha v. Furstenfeld, another good bitch carrying Herr Palmer's affix. Although used less often at stud than Wilm v. Forell, Baron v. Bavaria had a very good head, dark eye and rich dark tan markings; he was a hard dog, and a determined character. This was not surprising since both his parents had the Schutzhund III qualification. He passed on his excellent colouring and firmness of character to his offspring, and strengthened still further the German influence on the breed in the UK. He was the sire of Barrimilne the Signorina, mentioned above as the grand-daughter of Vilja Germania, winner of two c.c.s.

Bonni v. Forell and Dona v. Eichenhain were both

winners at the German National All Breed Show, and thus carried the title of Bundessieger and Bundessiegerin respectively. From a litter planned from them in 1970, Margaret Bastable had booked a brown puppy that was pick of the litter. Owing to a mix-up, however, the brown puppy was sold and Margaret took a black dog puppy instead. He was Gero v. Hagenstern. Whilst visiting Germany in 1972, Margaret saw the brown dog she had originally wanted, Greif v. Hagenstern, win the Sieger title. His appearance in the ring, excellent conformation and firm character impressed her greatly. She was able to buy Greif and bring him to England. After his release from quarantine there was an instant demand for his services and bitches from the Auldrigg, Baronstern, Heathermount, Kaybar, Metexa and Pompie kennels, among others, were bred to this German champion. Sadly, one day he found his way out to the main road adjoining the kennels and was killed. A great loss to his owner, and to the breed. Though he sired only one champion, Greif v. Hagenstern's influence is still apparent. Two well-known champion grand-daughters of his, Pompie Alcyone and Metexa Miss Brodie, have proved excellent brood bitches, and his name appears in the breeding of several other winning dogs and bitches of the present day.

The Barrimilne affix also appears on the name of another imported dog, but he was not from Germany. Admiral de Sophie was acquired by Margaret in lieu of quarantine fees owed to her by the family who had brought him back with them from Kenya in 1964.

Margaret Bastable's foundation bitch, Xel of Tavey, has already been mentioned as the dam of a champion, Caliph of Barrimilne. In the same litter, which was sired by Tavey's Stormy Achievement, was Canasta of Barrimilne, who, when bred to Acclamation of Tavey, produced Barrimilne the Moonraker and Barrimilne the Minx. Both had considerable success in the show-ring in 1963, and proved themselves the producers of good stock.

It is, of course, not possible to include in this book the name of every breeder who has had a share in developing the Dobermann in Great Britain. Some were involved for only a short time; others continued longer and, building on the stock available to them at the time, helped to consolidate the bloodlines. A few kept their kennel name to the fore for many years, repeatedly bringing out youngsters of show quality, providing breeders with good foundation stock, and sometimes producing that extra special dog or bitch that stood out from the rest, whether in show competition or for the consistent excellence of its progeny. While the names of all the breed champions are listed in Appendix E, most of those that have won more than the three challenge certificates (c.c.s) required for the title are mentioned in this chapter, starting with the breed's first champion, Elegant of Tavey. Where appropriate, if it is not clear from the name of their sire or dam, an indication is given of the particular bloodline from which the champions derived. Of course every winner has its critics – the perfect dog has yet to be born – but it should be pointed out that, besides being repeatedly found worthy of the top award on account of their conformation and physical condition, all the best winners have had a special quality of character – some call it showmanship, others call it style – which may be a sparkling presence enhanced by the public's acclaim or the excitement of competition, or a particular bond between dog and handler that enables both to rise to the big occasion, and time after time take the eye of specialist and all-rounder judge alike. However many certificates are on offer annually, the multiple winners have met and beaten the very best exhibits of that year, and the next year, and sometimes the year after that.

From 1965 on, the breed steadily gathered momentum. Registrations passed the one thousand mark in 1966, exceeded two thousand in 1975 and three thousand in 1979. They then doubled in just three years, with over six thousand registrations recorded in 1982. The number of challenge certificates on offer annually for each sex rose from the original ten in 1952 to twenty in 1966, then to thirty in 1975 and will reach thirty-seven in 1991. By 1975 five breed clubs had gained championship status for their annual show; the sixth soon followed, and judges from overseas continued to be invited to officiate at these prestigious events. The Dobermann Club's last overseas judge to be mentioned was Julius Selikowitz from Norway in 1962. The Club invited Professor Bodingbauer from Austria in 1971, Peter Knoop (the renowned professional handler from the USA) in 1972, Willi Rothfuss (breeder of the von Rauhfelsen Dobermanns) in 1973, and Hans Wiblishauser (von Bavaria) in 1978. The North of England Dobermann Club had Ernst Wilking (von Forell) to judge their ch. show in 1968, followed by Francis Fleitmann (Westphalia) in 1970, Peggy Adamson (Damasyn) in 1973, Marcel Demangeat from France in 1977 and Avi Marshak from Israel in 1984.

The Midland, Welsh and Northern Ireland Dobermann clubs all chose breeders whose years of service merited special recognition as judges of their first championship show. Greg and Jane Parkes (Annastock) judged the Midland Dobermann Club's show in 1970. Lionel Hamilton-Renwick (Birling) was the judge for the Welsh Dobermann Club's first ch. show in 1973 and Jane Kay (Kay Hills) came from the USA to judge in Wales in 1978. The Northern Ireland Dobermann Club first had championship status for their show in 1981, and they invited Julia Curnow. She was then eighty-four and had been judging Dobermanns every year since 1957. It was, of course, her final judging appointment but it was a great compliment to a wonderful old lady.

The Scottish Dobermann Club invited Jan Berggrav from Norway in 1976 and Monsieur Jean Mezières from France in 1983, but the judge of their first championship show in 1971 was Mr R. M. James who, in 1952, already owned and was exhibiting a Dobermann himself. He always had a special interest in the breed and became one of the country's top all-round judges, whose experience is acknowledged worldwide. His choice as best exhibit at the Scottish club's show was Donald Montgomery's champion Clanguard Cadet, then halfway through a dazzling show career. Bred from a daughter of Acclamation of Tavey, Clanguard Cadet won twenty-four c.c.s in all, a total exceeded by only four other male Dobermanns to date.

Proof of the overall excellence and superb showmanship of this dog is that, having already won eighteen certificates from 1968 to 1971, Cadet won four more in 1972, including Best of Breed at Cruft's under Fred Curnow and Best in Show at the Dobermann Club's show under Peter Knoop (the handler of Rancho Dobe's Storm). In 1973, entered as a Veteran at two breed club shows, he took the dog c.c. and was Best in Show on both occasions. The judge of his last show (Bobby James again) said he could find no other exhibit to beat Cadet, even as an eight-year-old.

The success of Clanguard Cadet tended to overshadow that of his brother, Clanguard Comanche. Similarly bred but a year older, Comanche too was a champion, and he won nine c.c.s. For breeders living in Scotland, the choice of a stud dog is limited to what is available within reach, so Cadet, Comanche and their champion sire, Carrick-green Confederate, were used extensively at stud. Other good sires brought to Scotland were Cubist of Tavey (by Tavey's Stormy Wonder), Tumlow Imperial (litter-brother of Tumlow Impeccable), Indigo of Tavey (litter-brother to the great Iceberg) and Tryst of Tavey (by Acclamation from Westwinds Quintessence). The top winning Scottish-bred bitch was Lachie Galbraith's champion, Rioghal Raquel, who won six c.c.s. Auldrigg, Clanguard, Orbiston, Rioghal and Whistleberry were the affixes of some of the breeders who first helped to establish the breed in Scotland. The kennel names of Ruskie, Swanwite, Kin-raith, Varla, Koriston, Metexa and Edcath followed, with newer affixes – Barztova, Fairbrigg, Kilmuir, Knecht, Krieger and others – also linked with present-day winners.

Flora and Andy Auld were keen exhibitors and skilful handlers who started breeding under their Auldrigg affix in the early 1950s. They always kept pace with new developments, and never hesitated to introduce a dog or bitch carrying the latest bloodline. They bred William Gallagher's champion Auldrigg Corsair, the winner of five c.c.s. They later acquired Dolina Naiad, a daughter of Acclamation of Tavey, and made her a champion. Their most successful home-bred champion was Auldrigg Pinza, who won eleven c.c.s in a single year, and sired a champion daughter. The Aulds turned to the German imports Wilm v. Forell and Greif v. Hagenstern for their later Auldrigg litters, and shortly before going to live abroad they imported a Dutch dog, Salvador v. Franckenhorst. However he proved too sharp for them to handle, and had several owners before being taken back to Holland, but during his brief stay in the UK Salvador v. Franckenhorst sired an English breed champion from a grand-daughter of Greif v. Hagenstern.

When Alf and Eleanor Hogg retired and their remaining stock was dispersed, their famous Triogen affix was handed on to John and Irene McManus, leading breeders in Scotland today. While litters bred directly from Triogen dogs and bitches were registered with that affix, the McManus Dobermanns more recently have been of German origin, and they carry the Metexa affix. A dog of all-German breeding, Quanto vom Haus Schimmel, was imported by them from Canada in 1979. His sire, Rico v. Hagenstern, was a full brother to Margaret Bastable's imported Sieger Greif v. Hagenstern, being from a repeat mating of Int. Ch. Bonni v. Forell and Int. Ch. Dona v. Eichenhain. His dam, Sally v. Hagenstern, was sired by Nero v. Hagenstern and on her dam's side was a grand-daughter of Bryan v. Forell (a Norwegian, Swedish and Finnish champion). The full potential of young Quanto was unhappily never realised, his physical condition being irreversibly impaired by six months' confinement in quarantine. He did, however, sire the first Metexa breed champion.

Although after gaining his title Tavey's Stormy Acacia was at stud in the north-east of England, this American line did not appear to find favour in that region; the Dobermanns of Sonhende, Annastock and Cartergate breeding were preferred. Most were house-dogs and family pets, and at the end of their life were usually replaced by another from the same bloodline. There were few breeders in the north of England who did not use one of Margaret Bastable's stud dogs – Timo, Wilm and Greif in particular. Lucifer of Cartergate (by Tavey's Stormy Achievement from Helena of Cartergate) proved an important sire in the north, mainly through his daughter, Heathermount Festive. She was the dam of David and Carol Brown's Heathermount Urvana of Moorbridge (who was sired by Greif v. Hagenstern), and of Ann Davies' Heathermount Flitzenjaeger (by Flexor Flugelman), a dog that was unlucky not to win his title. Heathermount Festive was also the grand-dam of one of Hazel Jones' Sigismund bitches, and of Bremenville Miss Sonya, on whom the currently successful line of Dolbadarn Dobermanns is based. Another stud dog based in the north of England, whose influence on the breed went far beyond the three champions he sired, was Gerry Young's Ch. Flexor Adonis, a double grandson of the great Flexor Flugelman.

Several long-serving committee members of the North of England Dobermann Club had considerable success in both showing and breeding. Jim Hall's first champion, Tramerfield Dubonny Princess, won five c.c.s and was the dam of Rita Anderson's devoted companion, champion Ecstasy of Tramerfield. Kathy Kennaman chose Heathermount Grenadier as a puppy; he gained his title and proved an influential sire. Before buying her first Dobermann, Joan Crowe studied the American bloodlines carefully, and has bred three champions to date. Her Jasmere line is based on Borains Born Free and a Tavey grandson of Iceberg and Nieta of Tavey. Her first champion, Jasmeres Royal Melody, owned and handled by Pat Judge, won six c.c.s and was the dam of three champions. Also bred in the north, by Adrienne Lonsdale and her mother under their Perihelia affix, Perihelia Madame Rochas won six c.c.s and in her only litter produced Ch. Perihelias Resolution, winner of six c.c.s and a dog that promises to be one of the great sires of our time. He is owned and handled by Mary Bartle.

Richard Jackson's contribution to the Dobermann world cannot be overlooked. He became part of their history through thirty years of unfailing support of the breed, at club rallies, meetings, shows and matches, and in competitive obedience (in which his accounts of the antics of his own Dobermanns make hilarious reading). He served as chairman of the Dobermann Breed Council for eight years, and latterly was the president of the North of England Dobermann Club. His wise counsel, freely given and based on his legal experience, helped many an individual owner and breed club committee, whilst his devotion to each of his own dogs was total.

Two Yorkshire-based breeders have made a significant contribution to the breed. Terry Lamb bred his own champion, Highroyds Avenger, an influential sire who won five c.c.s and was in great demand as a stud dog. Terry was the first to bring north the Nayrilla bloodline from Vanessa's Little Dictator and Jean Ryan's champion, Opinion of Tavey. In 1976, needing an outcross bitch for the next stage of Highroyd breeding, Terry Lamb chose Studbriar the Fortune Gal from a litter bred by Margaret King. Mated to Avenger, the Fortune Gal's first litter contained Highroyds Corry Belle, a bitch that, in Nick Naylor's ownership, became a champion and was the foundation of the currently successful Jenick line. Two years later, Studbriar the Fortune Gal was mated to Pat Woodcock's Jacade Mercedes of Mantoba, a son of Highroyds Avenger (and bred from a daughter of Achenburg Delilah), and in that litter was Highroyds Man of the Year, an aptly-named Dobermann if ever there was one. Bought as a puppy by David and Edith Bamforth, carefully reared and trained, and expertly handled by David, Man of the Year in four full years of showing won twenty-five c.c.s, thirteen of them in a single year, a total exceeded only by his great-grandfather, Iceberg of Tavey. Tall but not oversize, Man of the Year was of the correct square proportion, balanced, sound and elegant, and always shown in peak condition. He won the Working Group at three of the biggest all-breed championship shows, including Cruft's in the final year of his show career, and at all times his appearance and behaviour in the ring brought credit to his owners and to the breed.

The sire of Man of the Year, Pat Woodcock's Jacade Mercedes of Mantoba, was bred from a daughter of two champions, Triogen Tornado and Achenburg Delilah. Like his sire Highroyds Avenger, Jacade Mercedes was strong and sound, with a beautiful outline, head and expression and a steady temperament. In the ring he was spirited and sometimes difficult for Pat to handle and so he was not campaigned for long. His reputation, therefore, was made as a sire of winners rather than as a title-holder himself. When Pat needed another bitch for her Mantoba line of breeding, she chose a daughter of Vyleighs Valerian sired by Chevington Royal Black Magic, UDex. This bitch, Chevington Royal Virtue, became a champion and won six c.c.s, and, to date, several winners and one champion have come from her two litters by Jacade Mercedes. Royal Virtue's litter-sister, Chevington Royal Virginia, remained in the south of England; she won seven c.c.s, and was owned and handled by Bob David.

Besides those already named, exhibits bearing affixes such as Bondend, Holtzburg, Kaybar, Mabaro, Magana, Moorbridge, Rheinbar, Sanjyd, Sophreta and Vickisfree, among others, are currently seen winning, both in the north and on the national circuit.

Since 1980 two new kennel names appear regularly in the show awards, both northern-based. A nationwide contest to find 'Top Breeders' based on a year's show results, and sponsored jointly by *Our Dogs* and the makers of Pedigree Chum dogfood, was won by Mick and June Higgins of the Dolbadarn Dobermanns in 1985 and 1986. In 1987 the same title was awarded to Graham Hunt and his mother of the Sallate kennel. The success of both kennels has come through recognising the potential of their foundation bitch, and carefully choosing the most suitable sire for each or any of her litters. The foundation bitch of the Dolbadarn line was Bremenville Miss Sonya, a bitch of Heathermount and Jasmere breeding, her grandsires being Flexor Flugelman and Highroyds Avenger. She is the dam or grand-dam of five champions to date, with others of her progeny still competing for their title. Foundation of the Sallate line was Sigismunds Ice Cool Kate, a daughter of Ch. Dizown the Hustler that proved herself a winner in both obedience and show classes, as well as an excellent brood. She produced winners to two of today's top sires, her best-known son being Sallates Ferris, owned by Yvonne Bevans. Handled in the ring first by Graham Hunt and later by Dave Anderson, Ferris became a champion in 1986, won sixteen c.c.s the following year, and fifteen in the next two years. He won the working group at Cruft's in 1987, and again in 1990 on the day he was awarded his thirty-sixth c.c., thereby exceeding Iceberg of Tavey's total, and becoming the top-winning British Dobermann. Besides Ferris, the Sallate affix is also carried by an increasing number of dogs and bitches currently winning in the show-ring.

The Midland branch of the Dobermann Club, formed in 1958, drew support chiefly from Dobermann owners in the Nottingham area of England. Harry and Margaret Woodward were active members and, with others, they became founder-members of the Midland Dobermann Club when this was later established as a breed club in its own right. For over twenty-five years their Achenburg affix has been associated with good Dobermanns which are always black-and-tan. Margaret's skill as a handler in the show-ring is justly admired; she learned in tough competition against Fred Curnow and Elizabeth Hoxey, both masters in the art of presentation. Few exhibitors today will know that Harry Woodward was in obedience competition in the mid-1960s with Katina of Trevellis, a bitch bred by Dorothy Horton from Brumbies Black Bramble and sired by Gin v. Forell. In those days Harry trained with Jim Bramley and Brian Pole, both of whom were handlers in the Nottingham police force (and mentioned in a later chapter), and it was from an Achenburg bitch that, in 1965, Jim Bramley bred his champion dog Delmordene Buccaneer. The Woodwards' first home-bred champion was Achenburg Delilah, a daughter of Katina of Trevellis and already mentioned as the great-grand-dam of Highroyds Man of the Year. Following the retirement of Alf and Eleanor Hogg, their great stud dog Ch. Triogen Tornado found a home with the Woodwards, and so came within easier reach of breeders in the Midlands and the north of England. In 1974, a son of Triogen Tornado, registered as Kenstaff Tornado of Achenburg, won the first of a total of fourteen c.c.s. Campaigned in Ireland, he became an Irish champion, and then with a new owner he went abroad and became an Australian champion. The next stud dog at Achenburg was Von Klebong's Solar Encore, which the Woodwards had imported from Malaya. Solar Encore won twelve c.c.s and sired a champion son that won seven c.c.s, but more recent show winners have come through an Achenburg stud dog line-bred to Triogen Tornado.

After a few years' residence in London, during which she served a term as chairman of the committee of the Dobermann Club, Pat Quinn returned to the Nottingham area, where she had originally lived when she started to breed Dobermanns carrying the Royaltain affix. Her foundation bitch was Barrimilne Helga, whose dam (with the unusual name of New Line Flor) was bred from Ch. Day of Cartergate and a daughter of Jupiter of Tavey, who, under the ownership of Margaret Bastable, won two c.c.s in 1961. Helga's sire was Ch. Caliph of Barrimilne, so she was also a grand-daughter of Tavey's Stormy Achievement. She proved to be an outstandingly successful brood bitch. In each of the two litters sired by Tumlow Impeccable there was a champion bitch that won six c.c.s. From a litter of Helga's by Acclamation of Tavey, Kassel of Royaltain became a champion in 1967. When mated to Ron Selbourne's Ch. Heidiland Trouble Spot (a son of Tavey's Stormy Achievement and the winner of nine c.c.s in a show career that spanned six years), Kassel produced Royaltains Reluctant Hero, a dog that won five c.c.s and sired some very good stock indeed. Besides being the sire of two breed champions, Royaltains Reluctant Hero can now be seen as the grandsire or great-grandsire of ten or more champions, and may be ranked among the breed's most important stud dogs today. His best-known son was Merrist Reluctant Knight, whose dam was a daughter of Iceberg of Tavey. Owned and skilfully handled by young Robert Scott, Merrist Reluctant Knight won twelve c.c.s in the years 1975 to 1978. There have been seven Royaltain champions to date, and several others unlucky not to gain their title, and yet the Royaltain kennel has remained a small one. Its success, for more than twenty-five years, is

Julia and Fred Curnow

German and American Ch. Jessy v.d. Sonnenhoehe, 1934

American Ch. Rancho Dobe's Storm

Ch. Tavey's Stormy Achievement

Ch. Tavey's Stormy Abundance

Ch. Tumlow Fantasy

Ch. Tavey's Stormy Wrath

due to the quality of its bitches, and Pat Quinn's careful choice of stud dogs who carried the early European and American bloodlines.

Royaltains Babette of Tavey was mentioned earlier as being bred from two of the Tavey American imports, Vanessa's Little Dictator and Westwinds Quintessence, and is owned jointly by Pat Quinn and Pat Gledhill. Originally chosen as an outcross bitch for the Royaltain line of breeding, Babette lived at the Borain kennels, won six c.c.s in the show-ring and proved to be a valuable brood bitch. Because ownership was shared, puppies from her two litters were registered with either the Royaltain or the Borain affix, and brought credit to both. In Babette's litter by Royaltains Reluctant Hero was Borains Born Free, the foundation bitch of Joan Crowe's Jasmere line. A litter-sister, Borains Born Forth, was the dam of Pat Gledhill's superb bitch Borains Raging Calm, who won seventeen c.c.s in five years of showing, pausing halfway through her show career to breed a champion daughter. Half-sister to Raging Calm was a brown bitch, Borains Hot Chocolate, unlucky not to win her title too, but remembered today as grand-dam of Borains Night Watchman, winner of nine c.c.s from 1980 to 1983. Like the Royaltain Dobermanns, Pat Gledhill's Borain line has been based on a combination of the earlier European and the Tavey American blood-lines. Dobermanns carrying the Royaltain or Borain affix are still doing well today.

Babette's litter-sister, Ch. Baroness of Tavey, was owned by Vicki Killips (now Mrs Syd Philip), whose Chater affix can be seen in the breeding of some important winners. A dog, Chater Icy Storm (sired by Iceberg of Tavey), was bred by Vicki and owned by Noreen and Trevor Simmons, as was the bitch Chater Moon Queen, who was sired by Heidiland Trouble Spot. From them, the Simmons bred Vicki's handsome champion Javictreva Brief Defiance of Chater, who sired three champions, one of which, the bitch Maxtay Meritorious, won nine c.c.s. A grandson of Brief Defiance, Chater the Ferryman, is Vicki Philip's latest champion.

Another famous son of Chater Icy Storm (and therefore

a grandson of Iceberg) was Chornytan Midnite Mark, Thelma Toole's great stud dog. For almost twenty years a succession of show winners and some good working Dobermanns have carried Thelma Toole's Chornytan affix. Two Chornytan dogs have served with the police, and besides several c.c. winners Thelma has bred three champions to date, of which the best-known is Chornytan Dinahawk, the winner of five c.c.s. Dinahawk's dam, Kittyhawk of Chornytan, was a grand-daughter of Royaltains Reluctant Hero.

The Roanoke affix is shared by Mrs Daisy Richardson and her son Jimmy, well known to showgoers and admired by all for his handling skill, sportsmanship and profound knowledge of the breed. The stated aim of this kennel has always been 'to breed Dobermanns of high quality with sound health and good temperaments', and the large number of owners that over the years have shared their homes with a Roanoke Dobermann can confirm attainment of this objective. Show success has also been achieved. A photo of the first three Roanoke champions was in the Dobermann Club's 1972 Year Book: Triogen Tuppenny Feast (who won six c.c.s), Cadereyta of Roanoke and her daughter Roanoke Bobadilla (who won eight c.c.s). In kennels that are models of their kind, litters have been carefully planned and puppies reared in the best possible conditions. The home-based stud dogs have carried the best bloodlines available at the time (mostly of American origin), but judicious use of current winners has added further quality. Good browns have been a feature of this kennel: one most successful line of brown winners was based on Ch. Delmordene Buccaneer through his son Roanoke Goldfinger, who sired Rosie Hedges' Sandean Aquarius, winner of seventeen c.c.s and the top-winning brown Dobermann to date. Terry Tyler's Roanoke Marigold of Boreamond, a daughter of Sandean Aquarius, was the breed's top-winning bitch in 1980, taking six c.c.s in all. From their knowledge of genetics and study of background, particularly of the later American imports, the Richardsons, in the 1980s, bred a number of blues and fawns. Sharing the same interest in colour inheritance, Bernard Spaughton of the Frankskirby Dobermanns bred, in 1977, the 'Jubilee' litter that contained two black, one brown and two blue puppies. One of the blues, Frankskirby Jubilee Blulad of Roanoke, was successfully shown by Jimmy Richardson, and won a challenge certificate. The first fawn Dobermann to be shown in this country was also owned and handled by Jimmy Richardson; he was Twinglo the Silver Wraith of Roanoke. Bred by Marion and Derrick D'Cruze, he was with Jubilee Blulad part of the Roanoke team of stud dogs of all four colours which this kennel advertised in the 1980s.

Olive Neave always considered good temperament and sound character to be the first priority in breeding, and her Chevington Dobermanns were, above all, family dogs and proved good ambassadors for the breed. Although her first Dobermann was of Triogen breeding, it was a son of Tavey's Stormy Medallion that was Olive's special favourite, and his physical type and character were apparent in later generations of her Chevington line. Olive herself always loved showing, and for years she fought ill-health to be in the ring. She took showing very seriously but always had a smile and a word of congratulation for other winners and, win or lose, she loved her dogs. Trevor Ager lived in the same village and became a successful junior handler in national competition. When he grew up he accompanied Olive to shows and handled her Chevington exhibits with increasing skill and unfailing sportsmanship. When Olive bought Ch. Vyleighs Valerian, Trevor was in his early teens. He handled Valerian in the show-ring during his holidays, and had the thrill of winning the challenge certificate at three shows in ten days, bringing the bitch's total up to ten c.c.s. As the affix implies, Vyleighs Valerian was bred by Heidi Vyse. She was a grand-daughter of Nuance of Tavey and a great-grand-daughter of Iceberg, and her sire was the Australian champion Bonniedale Dougal, a dog imported by Tony Irvin that combined English, American and Australian bloodlines. With her first owner, Roger Skinner, Vyleighs Valerian became a champion and was Best in

Show at the Dobermann Club show in 1973. From a litter
of hers by Triogen Tornado, Roger Skinner retained a
dog, Ikos Valerians Valor, and showed him very successfully, winning a total of seven c.c.s. Later, in the ownership
of Olive Neave, Vyleighs Valerian became the dam of two
champions already mentioned, and her name can be seen
in the breeding of other Chevington winners.

The greatest concentration of show-winning Dobermanns has always been found in the south and east of
England. Besides the Chevington, Ikos, Roanoke and
Vyleigh Dobermanns just mentioned, many other winning
dogs and bitches carry affixes such as Chrilise, Corvic,
Damocles, Dartrian, Elroban, Essenbar, Gekelven, Jatra,
Jowendy, Linzella, Merryn, Nyewood, Pampisford, Petrax, Sataeki, Tanbowtra, Twinglo, Valmara, Vivluc, Vonmills and others. These kennel-names are the present-day
successors of those of earlier breeders. Building on the
bloodlines currently available, or introducing new imports
themselves, they, in turn, are making their contribution to
the breed in the 1980s.

Further west in England, and in Wales, there are also
some very successful kennels but, with fewer local opportunities for showing, campaigning a dog is costly and can
involve many long journeys. There have however been
worthy champions and some very important sires bred in
this part of the country. Raymond and Elizabeth Harris
(*née* Hoxey) lived for a short time in Wales. Tumlow stud
dogs and puppies of Tumlow breeding were thus more
easily available in the west. Two of their later champions
were Alan Barnard's Tumlow Whiplash and George
Collins' Tumlow Satan, a dog that proved a very important
sire indeed. Alan Barnard had always favoured the
American type of Dobermann, and supported both the
show and the working side. His first champion, the bitch
Gurnard Gemma (jointly owned with Daphne Billing-
ham), won seven c.c.s in the 1960s, while her litter-
brother, Gurnard Gloomy Sunday, successfully passed all
four of the Dobermann Club's working tests and also
qualified T.D.ex. in working trials. George Collins' champion Tumlow Satan was the sire of Alan Mulholland's

Welsh champion Davalogs Crusader (winner of six c.c.s), and also of Alma Page's first-ever champion, Mitrasandra Gay Lady of Findjans. Tumlow Satan is therefore important as being one of the two great stud dogs on which the famous Findjans line of Dobermanns was originally based.

Two dogs bred in the west that proved outstanding show winners in the 1970s, but differed widely in their breeding, were Demo's Skipper and Major Marauder. Demo's Skipper was bred, owned and handled by Mike Turner. Sired by Tumlow Whiplash, he won a total of ten c.c.s in all, nine of them in 1974. Major Marauder's sire and a litter-sister were both champions. His dam was a daughter of Royaltains Reluctant Hero and a grand-daughter of Iceberg of Tavey. Marauder's owner, Tegwyn Jones, campaigned him with skill and enthusiasm for four years, winning the working group several times at general championship shows, and also gaining several Best in Show awards. He won a total of twenty-five c.c.s in all, twelve of them in 1980. Like Highroyds Man of the Year, whose total of c.c.s was also twenty-five, Major Marauder was a much-loved family dog, handled with skill and sensitivity by his owner. He was sound, handsome and well made, moved and showed superbly and had great ring presence.

Also bred in the west of England, Jean Scheja's Tinka-zan Dobermanns had great success in the 1960s and 1970s. Their breeding was based on American and Canadian bloodlines. The foundation bitch of this kennel was Ch. Triogen Tuppenny Treat. Bought as a puppy, Triogen Tuppenny Treat grew to become the winner of five c.c.s, and was the grand-dam of Jean Scheja's home-bred champion Tinkazan Serengetti, who won six c.c.s and herself bred a champion daughter, Tinkazan Shinimicas. The sire of Shinimicas was Camerons Snoopy, a brown dog that Jean Scheja imported from Canada. Snoopy, a son of American Champion Tarrados Chaos, was bred from vom Ahrtal and Highbriar lines. Another of his daughters was Sheila Mitchell's champion, Ashdobes Brown Berry, T.D.ex., who won five c.c.s and whose all-round success is featured in later chapters. Camerons

Snoopy was also a grandsire of Ch. Roanoke Marigold of Boreamond and of Thelma Toole's great stud dog, Chornytan Midnite Mark. Like so many stud dogs, whose true worth can be assessed only after a lapse of several years, Camerons Snoopy is now seen as having made a worthwhile contribution to the breed.

David Crick lived near to the Welsh border and so the name of his great champion, Flexor Flugelman, appears in the pedigree of several Welsh-bred Dobermanns. Besides Flugelman, other dogs and bitches from the Flexor kennel have proved to be both show winners and sound breeding stock. Kennel-names achieving show success in the 1980s include Bledig, Crossridge, Halsband, Heimdall and Lynfryds, etc. Recent champions carrying these affixes are seen in Appendix E, while other winners from the same kennels are still being campaigned. One notable winner however is the brown bitch Ch. Halsbands Redwing, who took the challenge certificate at Cruft's two years running and has won six c.c.s to date. The Halsband kennel of Roger James and June Lewis bred four champions in three litters from their foundation bitch, Halsbands Manhatten (a daughter of Ch. Dizown the Hustler), and by using stud dogs carrying American bloodlines.

When Fred and Julia Curnow again decided to bring in fresh stock from the USA they were joined in this venture by two enthusiasts from Wales. Phil and Eileen Edwards, who owned Yucca of Tavey, had tasted show success with her (winning five c.c.s in all), and were themselves keen to import a bitch from America. On a joint trip to the States, the Curnows and the Edwards carefully co-ordinated their choice of dog and, in 1972, this resulted in the arrival in the UK of three bitches who were mainly of Kay Hills breeding, thus tying in with bloodlines already established and introducing new ones of proven quality.

Phil and Eileen Edwards' purchase was Kay Hill's Outrigger, a black bitch of substance and great elegance (and a gentle feminine character) that was carefully line-bred. Her sire was the American champion Dolph von Tannenwald (a grandson of Borong the Warlock CD), and her dam Kay Hill's Kat a Maran who was bred on similar lines. Before leaving America, Outrigger was mated to the American champion Tarrados Corry, a dog that combined vom Ahrtal and Highbriar lines. He could also be traced back to Stebs Top Skipper and Rancho Dobe's Storm, and was the sire of twenty-three American champions. (Corry's litter-brother, Tarrados Chaos, has already been mentioned as the sire of Camerons Snoopy, the brown stud dog imported to the Tinkazan kennels.) In May 1972, Kay Hill's Outrigger whelped in quarantine kennels which were within reach of the Edwards' home in Wales. At six weeks of age, two black bitches and two dog puppies, one brown and one black, went home with Phil and Eileen, and the other brown dog pup joined the Curnows' Tavey kennels. He was registered as Phileen's Duty Free, the 'of Tavey' affix being added to his name later. His litter-mates similarly carried the Edwards' Phileen affix, and were registered as Phileen's Travellers Cheque, Plane Jane, Airborne and American Express.

An early litter sired by the last-named contained a few surprises. A black bitch, Inge aus München, had been imported from America to the Triogen kennels in 1967. She later went to live with Audrey and Peter Kelly, who had moved to the West Country and whose Rathkeel Dobermanns were based on Triogen stock. From a litter of Inge's sired by Bayard of Tavey (litter-brother to the champion bitches Babette and Baroness) the Kellys kept a brown bitch, Rathkeel Red Pepper, and in due course mated her to Phileen's American Express. The sire of American Express, Tarrados Corry, was a son of the famous blue American champion Felix vom Ahrtal, line-bred on his dam's side to Delegate v.d. Elbe who is mentioned earlier in this chapter. Tarrados Corry was black, but records in America show him as the sire of a fawn bitch that became a breed champion. The litter born to the Kellys' brown bitch contained puppies of all four colours. This was the first litter bred in Great Britain known to have puppies of all four colours. Audrey said later it was a lesson in genetics! She had not realised that, like Phileen's American Express, the American bloodlines behind Rathkeel Red Pepper also carried the gene for dilute coat colour. American Express was a black dog, but he was the carrier of the genes for brown and dilute coat colour and could therefore sire puppies of all four colours to bitches of the required genetic potential. He was also the sire of the Frankskirby 'Jubilee' litter already mentioned, which contained black, brown and blue puppies.

Fred and Julia Curnow aimed at producing good black or brown Dobermanns, and never claimed that their Phileen's Duty Free carried the gene for dilute colour. It should however be pointed out that the first British-bred fawn Dobermann to be regularly campaigned, Twinglo the Silver Wraith of Roanoke, was a grandson of Duty Free on his sire's side, and a great-grandson through his dam. It is for a geneticist and not a historian to establish whether the presence of Phileen's Duty Free on both sides of the pedigree of this fawn Dobermann was coincidence, or a contributory factor to his colouring.

In America in 1972 the Curnows chose two brown bitches, one of which, Arawak Perfecta, was a daughter of the American champion Dolph von Tannenwald. Before leaving America she was mated to Kay Hills Dealers Choice, a son of Dolph von Tannenwald and a full brother to Kay Hill's Outrigger. From the litter, which was whelped in quarantine, one dog, Tavey's Satellite, later became an important stud force, while a brown bitch, Tavey's Sandra, joined the Edwards' household in Wales. Their business commitments and a growing family prevented Phil and Eileen from campaigning Sandra as she deserved, and though usually well placed at shows she failed to gain the third certificate she needed to win the title of champion. From their imported bitch, Kay Hill's Outrigger, the Edwards did breed a champion dog. He was sired by Tavey's Satellite.

The last of this trio of imported bitches was Camereich Day Trip, a brown bitch bred from generations of American champions and also related to Kay Hill's Outrigger and Arawak Perfecta. She later became the dam of Eric Steggle's Tavey's Ladyship of Shaheen, the winner of nine c.c.s from 1977 to 1980. June Briscall's champion,

Tavey's Ovation of Tancrey, was a grand-daughter of Camereich Day Trip.

Phileen's Duty Free and Tavey's Satellite were the last stud dogs born in quarantine to be owned by Fred and Julia Curnow. When Herr Willi Rothfuss judged the Dobermann Club's 25th Anniversary Show in 1973 Duty Free was chosen as Best Puppy, but he was not further campaigned and has earned his place in the breed's history through his progeny. As well as the seven champions he sired, Phileen's Duty Free's physical quality, overall balance and soundness were carried down to later generations.

One of his most important litters was the basis of Sue Wilson's Olderhill line. Her first bitch, a daughter of Iceberg of Tavey, had a litter by Phileen's Duty Free in 1974. Sue kept two puppies: Olderhill Sheboygan, a powerful, well-made dog with an extrovert character, became a champion, won six c.c.s and was always Sue's particular favourite and companion. His sister, Olderhill Sioux, was unlucky not to win her title, but she bred a champion (by Tavey's Satellite) and several show winners. Two other bitches from the same litter were Olderhill Seattle and Olderhill Salvador, on whom Diane Patience based her successful Dizown line. In her ownership, Olderhill Seattle became a champion and the dam of a champion, Dizown Razzamatazz. Olderhill Salvador bred three champions in one litter by Tavey's Satellite: Dizown the Hustler, Di's famous stud dog; Dizown Bedazzled, foundation of Rosie Lane's Chaanrose line, and Dizown Georgie Girl, who won eight c.c.s in 1978. Later, in the ownership of Rosie Lane, Olderhill Salvador became the dam of John Fleet's working trial champion, Chaanrose Night Queen, whose achievements are recounted in a later chapter.

Diane Patience's talent as a handler in the show-ring has been matched by a skilful breeding programme. Based on the three Olderhill bitches mentioned above, the Dizown Dobermanns have remained predominantly American in type. The sire of Dizown Razzamatazz was Ferrings Mike Victor, a dog born to an American bitch of Marks Tey breeding that was imported by Mr R.H. Walker. Both The

Hustler and Razzamatazz sired good stock, as will be shown later, and there has continued to be a steady demand by discerning breeders at home and abroad for Dizown puppies. At the time of writing the Dizown affix is seen in the pedigree of successful winning dogs bred in the Crossridge, Halsband, Holtzburg and Sigismund kennels.

Roy Gazley's early success in the breed was on the working side, his dog gaining a diploma in the Dobermann Club's working tests. His next dog, Findjans Hawk, was a son of Gurnard Gloomy Sunday, T.D.ex. and he showed great promise in both tracking and obedience. Unfortunately, having once been attacked and badly bitten during an exercise he became unreliable when among other dogs, so his working potential was never fully developed. Roy bred him to a grand-daughter of Tavey's Stormy Wrath (the bitch that he admits came nearest to his ideal Dobermann), and kept a daughter, Jatra's Blue Star. She later produced a champion, Jatra's Raven. Of greater importance to the breed however was a bitch from an earlier litter of Blue Star's which was sired by Phileen's Duty Free. Registered as Jatra's Commanche Princess, she proved an outstanding brood in the Studbriar kennels of Derek and Margaret King.

Margaret is the holder of the Studbriar affix and Derek is noted for his expert handling in the show-ring. The foundation bitch of the Studbriar line was Eikon Jests Amazon, a daughter of Barrimilne the Minx (who was sired by Acclamation of Tavey), and she gave the Kings their first champion, Studbriar Chieftain. Continuing to build on Tavey bloodlines, the next Studbriar champion was by Phileen's Duty Free from a daughter of Bayard of Tavey. But it was from Jatra's Commanche Princess that the subsequent Studbriar winners were bred. In her first litter by The Chieftain was Studbriar Dark 'N' Sassy, who was owned by Mike Jones and won ten c.c.s. A repeat mating produced three bitches of great importance: Studbriar the Fortune Cookie was exported and became a Brazilian champion (her son Cadmus da Fazenda was later imported from Brazil by Margaret King as their next stud dog); Studbriar the Fortune Gal went to Terry Lamb and became the dam of Highroyds Man of the Year, and Studbriar the Fortune Seeker bred a champion daughter and several other winners. By Studbriar the Red, Jatra's Commanche Princess later produced another champion, and she is also seen as the grand-dam of Peter Carroll's working trials dog, Studbriar Royal Sentinel, T.D.ex., who also holds a diploma in all grades of the Dobermann Club's working tests.

The most consistently successful breeders of top-winning Dobermanns throughout the 1980s have been Alma and Martin Page (Findjans) and Hilary Partridge (Pompie). Both kennels can claim over twenty years' involvement in the breed. Each has, from time to time, introduced into their own line an individual from the other kennel, but the Pompie Dobermanns have developed by continuing to use stud dogs imported from Germany and Holland, while the Findjans success (which was based on two dominant sires) has come from building on the American bloodlines already established in this country.

Like the others who were first interested in the working side of the breed, Martin Page appears in Appendix H as the handler of two Dobermanns that qualified in the Club working tests in the 1960s. They were Pompie the Bosun (son of Hilary Partridge's Pompie Seaman, who was a grandson of Margaret Bastable's first import, Iris v. Wellborn) and the Bosun's grand-daughter, Pompie Sunset Shell, whose paternal grandsire was Vanessa's Little Dictator. From her litter by Heidiland Trouble Spot, Sunset Shell gave Alma and Martin Page one bitch, Fair Allyne, that was the dam of their first champion, and another that produced Valerie Harle's champion, Arkturus Valan's Choice. Sire of their first-ever champion, Mitrasandra Gay Lady of Findjans, was Tumlow Satan. For Gay Lady's first litter the Pages used Phileen's Duty Free, which gave them Findjans Poseidon, not only a champion who won eight c.c.s but who became the sire of nine champions and grandsire of many more, among them the top-winning dog and bitch of the 1980s. Findjans

Poseidon has proved to be one of the breed's greatest stud dogs.

Alma Page acknowledges the help and advice given to her in those early days by the Curnows and especially by Len Charles. Having established her preferred type of Dobermann through using Tumlow Satan and Phileen's Duty Free with good bitches of compatible inheritance, Alma has maintained type and continued to breed winners for herself and for other enthusiasts. While Poseidon was her original and best-loved home-bred stud dog, his son Findjans Chaos is proving similarly successful at the present time, having won twelve c.c.s and now proving a dominant sire in his own right. The Findjans bitch line, founded on Pompie Sunset Shell and her daughter Findjans Fair Allyne, was further strengthened by bringing in Pompie Dione, a bitch bred by Hilary Partridge that was a grand-daughter of Findjans Poseidon and Heidiland Trouble Spot, and carried a line back to Greif v. Hagenstern. In the Pages' ownership Pompie Dione bred three champions in successive litters by her grandsire Findjans Poseidon; one of them was Findjans Chaos, and another was Mary Bartle's champion Perihelias Resolution, who is also proving an important sire, his best-known son to date being the breed's top winner Sallates Ferris. The success of this kennel continues, with Findjans dogs and bitches consistently among the winners at shows and proving themselves producers of good stock for other breeders.

The Pompie kennel's strength lies in its bitches. In choosing a stud dog, Hilary Partridge has always looked for one with substance and good bone, a good head and rich tan markings, and she found these qualities combined most often in dogs of German or Dutch breeding. Litters have been bred from Wilm v. Forell, Timo v.d. Brunoberg, Baron v. Bavaria and Greif v. Hagenstern. The Pompie line is not however wholly German, and Hilary has used British champions with similar qualities, such as Heidiland Trouble Spot, Arkturus Valan's Choice, Flexor Flugelman and Findjans Poseidon. Hilary was one of the first to use Margaret Bastable's Greif v. Hagenstern after his release from quarantine. In the litter that resulted (from a daughter of Baron v. Bavaria that was also a grand-daughter of Wilm v. Forell) was Pompie Sea Aphrodite, a bitch who is behind the best-known Pompie winners. Hilary's first champion, Pompie Alcyone, was from Sea Aphrodite and was sired by Findjans Poseidon. Alcyone in her turn bred two champions, and a bitch Pompie Idylla who was the dam of Pompie Dione of Findjans (mentioned above) and of other winners.

It was stated earlier in this chapter that a dog imported from Holland, Salvador v. Franckenhorst, had later been taken back to that country. Hilary Partridge mated her champion Pompie Alcyone twice to Salvador. A dog that won a challenge certificate and several reserves was in the first litter. In the second was the champion Pompie Dutch Leiveling, who won six c.c.s and was Hilary's special favourite, but who sadly died at five years of age. She did however breed one litter by a dog imported from Holland by Heidi Vyse; he was Quinto v.d. Kunnemaborgh. Sired by a double grandson of International Champion Guys Hilo v. Norden Stamm, Sch.H.III, Quinto's dam was line-bred to Int. Ch. Don Dayan vom Franckenhorst, Sch.H.I. The Pompie line and its breeding policy is therefore set to continue.

The breed's best-known show bitch, and the top winner to date, is Pompie Sea Jade of Chancepixies, bred by Hilary Partridge from her champion Pompie Alcyone and sired by Ch. Flexor Adonis (a double grandson of Flexor Flugelman). Owned by Jean Frost and Dave Anderson, and expertly handled at all times by the latter, Sea Jade won no less than twenty-four c.c.s in a concentrated show career. She also gained the title of Irish champion. This show record surpasses that of any other Dobermann bitch in the UK. Her overall quality, conformation and character brought credit to both her breeder and her owners. Like the current top Dobermann dog, Sallates Ferris, Pompie Sea Jade of Chancepixies was selected to take part in the sponsored annual Contest of Champions.

After making up three champions in 1973 (Tavey's Icypants, Gridiron and Yachtsman) Fred and Julia Curnow were able to add only one more to their kennel's impressive total. Tavey's Encore won five c.c.s and in 1976 was retired for breeding. At the kennels the number of dogs kept was steadily reduced and Len Charles retired and went to live in Cornwall. In the late 1970s Fred and Julia were often abroad, where they had many judging engagements, and at home Fred felt the need to cut down on his activities. One of champion Encore's sons, Tavey's Diploma, was retained for showing, had considerable success as a puppy and later won two c.c.s, but he never gained the title of champion. After Fred's death Diploma and his sire, Phileen's Duty Free, made their home with Mary and Reg Barton, to whom the Curnows transferred the Tavey affix. Although not long established in the breed, the Bartons had shown great kindness and proved good neighbours when Fred's health was failing.

In the hands of Mary and Reg Barton Tavey Dobermanns are still in contention for prizes in the show-ring, and the traditional policy of Tavey breeding is being maintained by the addition of dogs imported from America. The first of these, Marks Tey Magnam, was bred by Joanna Walker. He came out of quarantine when still a junior, and was able to enter competition under KC rules as his ears had been left uncropped. In the show-ring he has held his own against the top males of the day, and his many awards have included at least two reserve challenge certificates. Chosen for his overall balance and sound construction, good head and steady temperament, Marks Tey Magnam is now proving of benefit to the breed.

A dog bred by Mary Rodgers was recently released from quarantine to join the Tavey kennels. Registered as Marienburg Firedanza he is carefully line-bred to the American and Canadian champion Marienburg Sun Hawk CD, who sired eighty-five champions in the USA. A full sister to Sun Hawk, Marienburg Apache Warbonnet, is also in the breeding of Firedanza's sire and dam, making him a potentially dominant stud force.

It is interesting to note that the names of the great American champions Gra-Lemor Demetrius v.d. Victor, and Derek of Marks Tey appear in the pedigrees of both of these recent imports and also in the pedigrees of the four Dobermanns brought from America between 1970 and 1982 by R.H. Walker and Mike Bradshaw. On his dam's side Demetrius was a grandson of Stebs Top Skipper and his sire was of Damasyn breeding. He sired more than fifty American champions, thus ranking with Dictator v. Glenhugel and Delegate v.d. Elbe as one of America's most influential stud dogs. Derek of Marks Tey was bred by Joanna Walker from her foundation bitch (a double grand-daughter of Dictator v. Glenhugel) and was sired by Brown's Eric (a Dictator son). The breeding potential of their four descendants imported earlier – Gra-Lemor Freebooter, Walkaway Wildfire and Echo of Marks Tey, and the bitch Amsel Andante of Marks Tey – has apparently gone unrecognised by exhibitors, except for Diane Patience, who used the British-born Ferrings Mike Victor (a son of Amsel Andante) to sire her champion Dizown Razzamatazz.

Fresh imports from America and Canada, and from Germany and Holland, are still being introduced by individual enthusiasts who admire the qualities of one or other type of Dobermann, and who wish to improve further, or to consolidate, the bloodlines already established. For health reasons Mark Ladd has recently had to curtail his showing activities, but previously he had enjoyed success in the ring with Vijentor Seal of Approval, a black daughter of Dizown the Hustler. An admirer of the American type of Dobermann, Mark decided to import one, and chose a brown dog, Montess Defender vom Ahrtal, that was line-bred to the American champion Phillida vom Ahrtal, a daughter and grand-daughter of the great Cassio vom Ahrtal, sire of thirty-eight champions. Demand for Montess Defender's services has so far been slight, but his good head and topline, and strong well-angulated rear quarters, so characteristic of the vom Ahrtal line, have been passed on, and are seen in the puppies bred by Mark and his wife under their Valmara affix.

A young brown dog, Tri-Lees Stuff 'N' Nonsense, was imported from Canada in 1981 by Hazel Jones, the

Yorkshire-based breeder of the Sigismund Dobermanns. His dam was of close Tedell breeding, his sire and grandparents were Canadian champions that traced back to Gra-Lemor Demetrius v.d. Victor and to well-known winners from Marienburg, vom Ahrtal and Highbriar lines that excelled in body and topline and moved with a strong driving action. His breeding potential should interest the owners of bitches with compatible bloodlines. From a bitch of her own breeding, Hazel had already bred a c.c. winner, Sigismunds Ice Cool Kate. She was sired by Dizown the Hustler, and, as already mentioned, in the ownership of Graham Hunt and his mother became the foundation bitch of their currently successful Sallate kennel. A repeat mating using Dizown the Hustler gave Hazel two more good bitches, Pretty Cyprian and Happy Hooker, who have done well in the show-ring, and with her Canadian import are set to carry on the Sigismund line.

The first of Samantha and Bill Gover's Bilsam Dobermanns was sired by Dizown the Hustler from a daughter of Tumlow Whiplash. Registered as Princess Our Pride, she was bred by Roger James and June Lewis and was litter-sister to their Halsbands Manhatten (the dam of so many show winners). In 1982 the Govers imported a brown dog, Rosecroft By The Way. Strong in Kay Hills and Highbriar bloodlines, he was a grandson of Am. Ch. Liquorish The Ron Rico CD, a great dog that was a champion in four countries and earned a working qualification in three, and was himself a grandson of Dolph von Tannenwald. On his sire's side, the Govers' Rosecroft By The Way is similarly bred to the Curnows' brown import, Camereich Day Trip. To date he has sired one champion and several good winners that are still being campaigned. In 1985 two bitches from America joined the Bilsam kennel. They were litter-sisters, sired by American Ch. Ragnar vom Ahrtal (a double grandson of the great Phillida vom Ahrtal) from a bitch carrying Tedell and vom Ahrtal lines. These three American imports would seem to back up and reinforce the proven winning American-based lines already established here.

A brief mention of the principal line of breeding behind these latest Transatlantic imports shows them to be descendants of the many famous Dobermanns that Fred and Julia Curnow and other enthusiasts admired so greatly on their trips to the States. In the same way, descendants of the great German champions that Margaret Bastable studied, and came to know when she judged abroad, have been brought to England in the 1980s by those who prefer the European type of Dobermann.

As yet there has been just one breed champion bearing the Vonmac affix, but this kennel of all-European blood-lines has already had some influence on the breed in Great Britain. Stan Macdonald's first import was an eight-week-old puppy registered as Graaf Wodan v. Neerlands Stam, bred in Holland in 1975 by the great Mrs Knijff-Dermout, and sired by her Dutch and Int. Ch. Graaf Questor v. Neerlands Stam. Six months' confinement in quarantine seriously affected the physical development of this puppy, but not his temperament or character. Four bitches from a litter born in quarantine to Pamela v. Hagenstern, and sired by Nero v. Hagenstern (a grandson of Bonni v. Forell), had already been retained in England by the Macdonalds. Their dam and two other puppies continued on their journey to Australia with their owners, Mr and Mrs Rudi Foggenberger. Some time later, when the Foggenbergers bought Iwo v.d. Westfallenhalle in Germany, he was at stud and used on the Vonmac bitches between release from quarantine in England and being sent on to Australia. From one such mating to the Macdonalds' Schutzhund Anya came Vonmac Brianna, the dam of Lyn and Dave Griffiths' champion, Dorusta Lutzow, a dog that has proved successful on the working side as well as in the show-ring. Brianna's sister, Vonmac Bonnie, became the dam of Ch. Vonmac Keegan, and in a later litter by the Macdonalds' own 1979 import Ibsen Jingo v. Ferrolheim (another grandson of Bonni v. Forell), she produced Vonmac Nero, sire of David Stafford's champion, Heimdalls Ero.

Vicki Cuthbertson has owned and bred Dobermanns for

more than twenty-five years. Her first bitch, Birchanger Dawn, a grand-daughter of Tasso v.d. Eversburg, was the dam of Ian Inskip's Heiner Rustic, C.D.ex., a brown dog that won an Obedience Certificate. Disappointed with the Dobermanns of later British breeding, Vicki carefully studied different strains in Europe, and was greatly impressed by the van Neerlands Stam dogs of Mrs Knijff-Dermout. The Dutch have always skilfully combined physical substance with elegance and balance in their Dobermanns, retaining intelligence and firm temperament without aggression. Vicki's choice for import to her Milperra kennels in 1981 was a bitch, Gravin Cita v. Neerlands Stam, and two litter-brothers, Graaf Citto and Graaf Carlos v. Edele Stam. Upon release from quarantine Citto was found to have a broken leg, while Carlos had sustained a broken back and broken hindleg, injuries incurred some four or five months earlier which had been left untreated and were not reported to the Cuthbertsons. Legal action was taken and ultimately resolved. The quarantine kennels concerned have ceased to operate. Carlos's indomitable spirit and great character were a tribute to his illustrious forebears; his sire Graaf Aristo v. Neerlands Stam being by Guys Hilo v. Norden Stam (by Bryan v. Forell) from Gravin Wietske v. Neerlands Stam (a daughter of Graaf Questor, and litter-sister to Stan Macdonald's first import, Graaf Wodan v. Neerlands Stam). Carlos has sired one champion and several good winners to date.

Heidi Vyse (Vyleigh Dobermanns) always admired the German dogs brought to England by Margaret Bastable, and has herself now imported two males from Holland. The first, Quinto v.d. Kunnemaborgh, has already sired a British champion. Heidi's second import, Xantos v.d. Kunnemaborgh, arrived early in 1987. Both Quinto and Xantos are line-bred to Norwegian Ch. Bryan v. Forell through his famous sons Int. Ch. Guys Hilo v. Norden Stam and Int. Ch. Don Dayan v. Franckenhorst. Heidi chose them for their good heads and overall physical balance, and desired German characteristics of alertness, firm character and working ability.

In 1983 Tony Winter of the Sorkie kennels imported a dog and a bitch from Holland. They were Drusus v. Weimar-Eisenach, a son of Ero v. Franckenhorst (the sire of Vicki Cuthbertson's Gravin Cita v. Neerlands Stam), and Beryl v. Weimar-Eisenach, a daughter of Don Dayan v. Franckenhorst.

The latest reported import from Holland is Jim and Marty Burrell's bitch, Laika v.d. Rameler Marke, who is a daughter of Graaf Aristo v. Neerlands Stam (the sire of Vicki's Graaf Carlos v. Edele Stam). Laika's progeny will be registered with the Burrells' Jimarty affix.

The skill of the early British breeders, and the foresight and dedication of those who brought in important bloodlines from Europe and America, have enabled breeders of the present day to establish and maintain their kennel-type. Which of the show winners and the imports of the 1980s will prove the most important in their influence on future generations is for a later historian to recount. Philipp Gruenig wrote that the quality of a breeding dog could not be properly assessed until his descendants 'appeared in public view in sufficient numbers to permit of a well-reasoned and conclusive judgment of his hereditary qualities'. This principle has served to guide the writer, whose study of pedigrees and Kennel Club Stud Books has revealed that behind leading winners of the day the same names or lines of inheritance occur over and over again. It is not just the name of sire and dam in a show catalogue that proves why So-and-So is a champion. His (or her) real worth probably derives from the careful breeding of earlier generations, with one or more forebears of potent quality. In this connection, characteristics of temperament and personality are equally as important as physical attributes. The appendices to this book provide an up-to-date record of Dobermann success both in the show-ring and when trained for championship working trials and obedience, and for the breed's special working tests. It is gratifying to find individuals proving successful in more than one of these activities.

The writer has tried to indicate successive trends in breeding, to highlight those champions that were the most successful in their day, and to build on and extend the account of the breed's early development which Fred Curnow wrote in 1970/71. The omission of any notable kennel is regretted and quite unintentional.

In any account of the breed's history it is most fitting to leave the last word with Philipp Gruenig who, writing in 1931 for publication of his book in the following year, pointed out that 'the dogs of 1927 and the following years have performed no hereditary transmissions by which we are enabled to pass judgment upon their qualities as breeding dogs . . . we must wait for the future to disclose the rest'. He goes on, and it is as appropriate in the mid-1980s as when he was writing: 'Many of the dogs which are now unknown may force their entry into our list of progenitors of the higher class by their powers of hereditary transmission in the future, and they have our best wishes in this respect.'

2

Conformation and Character

The conformation of the ideal Dobermann is described in the breed standard. A breed standard has been defined as a guideline, a general description of a breed set out for someone who already knows a bit about the breed, and where he can find certain characteristics that make that breed unique and distinct from other breeds. The official standard of every breed registered at the Kennel Club is under the control of that ruling body. After consultation with the breed club of the time, the British standard for the Dobermann was first published in the early 1950s and remained virtually unchanged for more than thirty years.

Following the first World Conference of Kennel Clubs in 1978, at which the desirability of an international unification of breed standards was agreed, the Kennel Club in London undertook to achieve uniformity in the format and style of all the British breed standards. The aim was to achieve greater clarity and conciseness of definition, and to cut out unnecessary verbs and definite articles. There was consultation with the breed clubs, and in 1986 the breed standard of the Dobermann was finally approved and published by the Kennel Club, and is quoted here with their permission. As one distinguished breeder has aptly written, this is the blueprint by which everyone should breed, show and judge. Let us look at the standard and try to see what exactly is required.

General appearance

Medium size, muscular and elegant, with well set body. Of proud carriage, compact and tough. Capable of great speed.

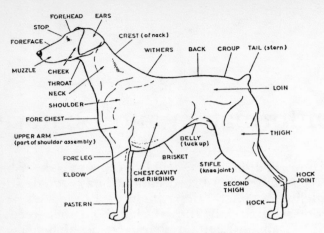

Figure 1 *Anatomy of the Dobermann*

'Medium size' means exactly what it says. Dogs palpably over or under size should be penalised. Judges who assess the Dobermann only as a working dog may prefer a heavier type of animal, forgetting that the standard asks for elegance. An elegant dog can still be muscular, with a well-set body; some with very heavy muscle are far from elegant. Nor can a compact and tough appearance be achieved by a dog with weak and spindly bone formation. The proud erect carriage of a Dobermann, and his ability to move with great speed, derives from a proper balance of the desired physical qualities.

Characteristics

Intelligent and firm of character, loyal and obedient.

A summary of the qualities that endear a Dobermann to his owner. His intelligence and loyalty make him a splendid companion and family dog. Firmness of character denotes steadiness and remaining resolute under pressure. Being classified as a working breed, a Dobermann is not subservient and does not lack initiative, but is co-operative and trainable, accepting discipline from an owner he trusts and who is worthy of his respect.

Temperament

Bold and alert. Shyness or viciousness very highly undesirable.

A bold dog is not aggressive or fierce; his poise and energetic expression show courage and determination. Alertness is absolutely essential in a dog of a working breed, but must not be confused with viciousness, mentioned as highly undesirable. In the show-ring there is no test of temperament, and a judge can assess a Dobermann's temperament only by seeing how the dog stands up to examination, with no flinching and no fear in his eyes. Retreating from the judge, or showing fear and running behind the handler, would certainly indicate that the animal is not bold.

Head and skull

In proportion to body. Long, well filled out under eyes, and clean cut with good depth of muzzle. Seen from above and side, resembles an elongated blunt wedge. Upper part of head flat and free from wrinkle. Top of skull flat, slight stop; muzzle line extending parallel to top line of skull. Cheeks flat, lips tight. Nose solid black in black dogs, solid dark brown in brown dogs, solid dark grey in blue dogs and light brown in fawn dogs. Head out of balance in proportion to body, dish faced, snipey or cheeky very highly undesirable.

As in every breed, we find Dobermanns with various forms of head. Some are too heavy, usually because of thick cheek formation; others are too fine, mainly because of weak, thin and snipey muzzles. The standard best sums up the ideal by asking for an elongated blunt wedge, when seen from the side and above, as shown in Figure 2. Incorrect head types are shown in Figures 3 and 4, Figure 3 being too snipey and Figure 4 too heavy in skull, and Figure 4 also showing a lot of dewlap, meaning excess of skin from the chin to the neck.

The slight stop referred to is that part of the head where the skull meets the upper jaw. There should be no distinct stop but rather a slope as shown in Figure 1, and the top

Figure 2   *Correct head: 'blunt wedge'*

Figure 3   *Incorrect head: too snipey*

Figure 4   *Incorrect head: too heavy in skull*

line of the skull should be parallel to the top line of the muzzle. The length of skull when measured from the occiput to the eyes should be approximately equal to the length of muzzle when measured from eyes to tip of nose. Quite a few Dobermanns carry too much loose skin around the mouth, which gives a sour and sad expression to the head.

Eyes

Almond-shaped, not round, moderately deep set, not prominent, with lively, alert expression. Iris of uniform colour, ranging from medium to darkest brown in black dogs, the darker shade being more desirable. In browns, blues or fawns, colour of iris blends with that of markings, but not of lighter hue than markings; light eyes in black dogs highly undesirable.

It has sometimes been claimed that a light-eyed dog of a working or gundog breed works better than does a dark-eyed dog, but of the Dobermanns that have proved themselves good workers and are listed in the relevant Appendices to this book, none is remembered as having a noticeably light eye, whether their coat colour be black or brown. Light eyes spoil the expression, as do the pinkish eye-rims seen sometimes in brown dogs. Round and staring eyes too are detrimental to an alert expression. The eyes of a Dobermann of whatever coat colour should show vigour and courage.

Ears

Small, neat, set high on head. Normally dropped, but may be erect.

This part of the standard was expressly kept in this form because British-bred Dobermanns have natural ears, whereas in Germany, the USA and some other countries the ears are cropped. As so much of the Dobermann's character is seen in his head, it is obvious that long, pendulous, heavy and low-set ears are not desirable, whereas small high-set ears, well used, add much to an alert expression. The standard allows for an erect ear, and although it is the wish of every breeder to produce puppies with this asset, I doubt very much whether it will ever be attained. In Norway there was a bitch with natural pricked ears, and although she was mated back to her father in an attempt to fix this trait, the experiment failed.

Mouth

Well developed, solid and strong with a complete dentition and a perfect, regular and complete scissor bite, i.e. the upper teeth closely overlapping the lower teeth and set square to the jaws. Evenly placed teeth. Undershot, overshot or badly arranged teeth highly undesirable.

A detailed and very clear description of the correct mouth, a full set of teeth and a strong 'bite' being essential in a working and guarding breed. The scissor bite, illustrated in Figure 5(a), gives a very powerful grip. An overshot or undershot lower jaw is indeed highly undesir-

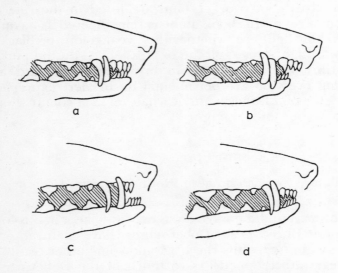

Figure 5   *Dentition: (a) Correct scissor bite   (b) Overshot jaw
(c) Undershot jaw   (d) Pincer bite*

able; both faults are illustrated in Figures 5(b) and (c), and a further faulty tooth formation is shown in Figure 5(d) and referred to as a pincer bite. Judges examine the mouth of each exhibit in the show-ring, to check the even placing of the incisors which gives the complete scissor bite, the correctly placed canine teeth (the strong fangs that hold and grip), and the presence of four premolars on both sides of the upper and lower jaw. A faulty bite is sometimes found in a Dobermann, and one or more missing teeth is not uncommon. Missing premolars used to be a fairly common fault; today it is more often incisors that are missing. The full dentition of a dog is forty-two teeth, and in Germany these are very carefully checked and counted, as unless all are present a dog is disqualified from a major prize.

Neck

Fairly long and lean, carried with considerable nobility, slightly convex and in proportion to shape of dog. Region of nape very muscular. Dewlap and loose skin undesirable.

A good neck can add to or detract from an elegant appearance. A Dobermann is a working and a tracking dog, and needs both a good reach of neck and strong muscular development in the region of the nape, but 'fairly long' does not mean over-long; breeding to achieve too long a neck can lead to unsoundness and physical handicap. The standard calls for the head and neck to be in proportion to the whole shape of the dog.

Quite a few Dobermanns which appear to have a good neck are spoilt because upright shoulders give the appearance of a 'stuck on' neck, with a distinct break where it meets the top line of the body. (*See* Figures 5(a) and (b).) Bagginess of the skin under the neck also spoils the graceful line, as shown in Figure 4. Stuffy necks, that is to say, short and thick, are most ungainly and show a lack of elegance. A graceful, fairly long and slightly arched neck flowing into the top line of the body in one rhythmic sweep is not only pleasing to the eye but proves correct shoulder placement.

Forequarters

Shoulder blade and upper arm meet at an angle of 90 degrees. Shoulder and upper arm approximately equal in length. Short upper arm relative to shoulder blade highly undesirable. Legs seen from front and side, perfectly straight and parallel to each other from elbow to pastern, muscled and sinewy, with round bone in proportion to body structure. Standing or gaiting, elbow lies close to brisket.

The upper part of the shoulder blades extend above the chest cavity, and between them at their highest point are the protuberances of the vertebrae that form the withers. The 90 degrees stipulated as the angle at which the shoulder blade meets the upper arm should be taken as the ideal. Some judges (Philipp Gruenig and Julius Selikowitz among them) have claimed that in a squarely built dog such as the Dobermann good angulation at the shoulder-joint is more usually found to be 100 or even 110 degrees. It can be argued that the angle depends on just how you measure it. Assessment of the exact angle of the shoulder is less easy to make accurately on a living animal

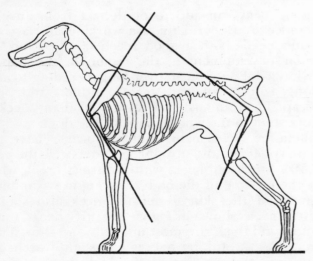

Figure 6 *Straight in shoulder, too long in upper arm*

than by measurement of a diagrammatic sketch on a flat sheet of paper. But however the shoulder angulation is estimated, a right angle or a near right angle is what judges look for, and is essential if the dog is to move freely and correctly. Upright shoulders will most certainly give an incorrect gait.

A Dobermann must be well muscled along the shoulder and upper arm, but not to a degree that gives a coarse overloaded appearance. A dog with soft muscles, especially those between the elbow and brisket, does not move soundly, giving the well-known 'loose elbows' effect. A Dobermann in good hard condition will have its muscle formation clearly visible, whereas a soft or over-fat animal will not.

Good forequarters, and the strong straight legs called for in the standard, can be clearly seen in the photographs of some of the champions used to illustrate this book. Figure 7 shows legs that are parallel and straight, with the elbow close to the brisket, and Figures 7(b) and (c) illustrate two types of faulty leg structure.

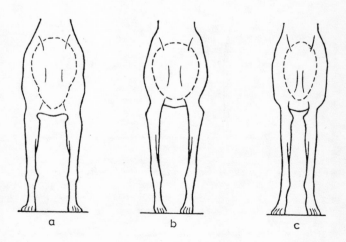

Figure 7   *Legs: (a) Correct   (b) Bow-legged*
            (c) 'Chippendale' legs

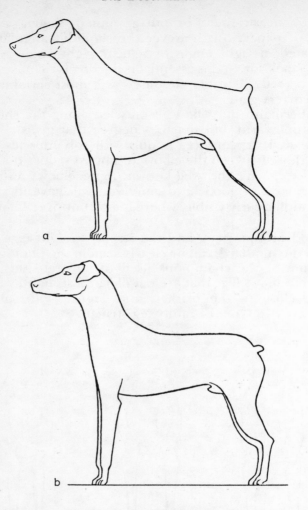

Figure 8   *(a) Ideal Dobermann   (b) Faulty in structure*

Body

Square, height measured vertically from ground to highest
point at withers, equal to length from forechest to rear
projection of upper thigh. Forechest well developed. Back short

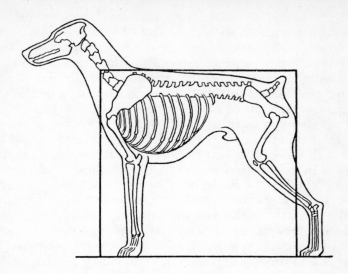

Figure 9   *Squareness*

and firm, with strong straight topline sloping slightly from withers to croup; bitches may be slightly longer to loin. Ribs deep and well sprung, reaching to elbow. Belly fairly well tucked up. Long, weak, or roach backs highly undesirable.

Here we come to what makes or mars a real Dobermann. Figure 8(a) demonstrates the ideal, showing the flow of neck into the topline which, while sloping away a little from shoulder to tail, must be strong and straight, with no dip or hump, usually referred to as a saddle or a roached back. Figure 9 demonstrates the proper squareness of a Dobermann, although some judges do not penalise a slightly over-long female, claiming that she needs the extra space to carry her litters. The animal illustrated in Figure 8(b) may fit the description of squareness, but lacks layback of shoulder and the correct topline.

With a well-developed forechest the point of the breastbone should stand out in front of the chest a little, but not be so exaggerated that it gives the appearance of a chicken breast. A Dobermann with no chest prominence is usually straight in shoulder. The ribs must be deep and reasonably well barrelled, with width at the upper line and midline of the chest to give room for the heart and lungs, narrowing at the lower end as shown by the dotted line in Figure 7(a) so that the elbows are not impeded by the rib formation. A point of conformation that is mentioned by Philipp Gruenig as important (and one checked by most judges) is that the lower point of the breastbone should be level with the elbow. It is important that the depth of the chest is in proportion to the height of the body. This is generally taken as meaning that the distance from the withers to the elbow should be not less than half of the height from the withers to the ground.

Most judges talk about a Dobermann as being 'compact'. This of course is really saying that the body is square as described in the standard. Perhaps the best way to describe a compact Dobermann is by quoting an American authority some years ago when he said: 'A compact dog will give the impression of motion caught in an instant of suspended action and one whose ability to move will not belie the impression made when standing.'

Hindquarters

Legs parallel to each other and moderately wide apart. Pelvis falling away from spinal column at an angle of about 30 degrees. Croup well filled out. Hindquarters well developed and muscular; long well-bent stifle; hocks turning neither in nor out. When standing, hock to heel perpendicular to the ground.

The angulation of the hindquarters should balance that of the forequarters, as shown in Figure 9. The thighs should be well developed, with muscles that are firm and supple, clearly visible to the eye but not cloddy. Lack of muscle in the second (lower) thigh is generally due to insufficient exercise. Upper and lower thighs meet at the knee-joint, or stifle; a well-bent stifle is clearly seen in profile. When the dog is standing naturally the hocks should be perpendicular to the ground, as in Figure 9.

The desired angulation in the hindquarters is unlikely

to be achieved if the pelvis is either too steep or too flat. A steep pelvis is very often accompanied by straight stifles and hocks, while too flat a pelvis can bring about over-angulation of the hindquarters, which is often accompanied by extra length in the lower leg. A vertical line from the rear of the thighs to the ground should strike the toes of the rear feet. Over-angulated dogs, which when standing with the hocks perpendicular to the ground have their hind feet 6 to 9 inches behind this imaginary line, have an unbalanced appearance. Should this be a natural stance, and not one exaggerated by the handler trying to 'stack' the dog by lifting and holding up the tail, the gait will be affected, and the hind legs will be trying continually to catch up with the forelegs.

Feet

Well arched, compact and cat-like, turning neither in nor out. All dewclaws removed. Long, flat, deviating feet and/or weak pasterns highly undesirable.

Cat-like feet, with strong toes tightly bunched, are essential. Slack pasterns and splay feet are a handicap to an active or working dog.

Tail

Customarily docked at first or second joint; appears to be a continuation of spine without material drop.

The addition of the word 'customarily' to the present standard indicates that docking is optional, not compulsory. As the breed clubs and nearly all owners still support tail-docking, Dobermanns will continue to be seen with tails neatly docked at either the first or second joint.

A fault once prevalent in earlier years was the falling croup, or low-set tail, shown in Figure 8(b). This has been largely bred out, but can still sometimes be found. The ideal is still that the tail should appear as a continuation of the spine without material drop.

Gait

Elastic, free, balanced and vigorous, with good reach in forequarters and driving power in hindquarters. When trotting should have strong rear drive, with apparent rotary motion of hindquarters. Rear and front legs thrown neither in nor out. Back remains strong and firm.

'Elastic' does not mean 'bouncy', but a free-flowing effortless movement that is light, easy, free and vigorous. Great emphasis is placed on correct movement because an incorrect gait means the dog is faulty in at least one part of his body structure. Ribs barrelled right to the bottom of the brisket will cause the dog to plait, as will also a badly angulated shoulder blade and upper arm. Weak elbows or pasterns give a peculiar paddling action, while splay feet cause the dog to flop along in a most ungainly fashion. Cow hocks will cause weaving in the hind legs, as will hindquarters that are bandy, or, in other words, with the feet turning inwards.

The front legs should reach well forward when the dog is in motion, but with no semblance of a high-stepping or Hackney action. At the trot, the hindlegs which are the driving power should move strongly with what is aptly described as an apparent rotary motion. Good drive is achieved by a reaching under and propelling forward movement of the rear legs and not a kicking out and up behind. When seen from front, rear or side, the whole action of a Dobermann must give the impression of rhythmic power.

Occasionally a Dobermann is seen to move with what is known as a 'pacing' action, which is similar to that of horses bred and trained for trotting races. When pacing, a dog moves the front and hind foot on the same side simultaneously, and the resulting sway gives a peculiar rolling, waddling action. This condition is undesirable, and can be easily corrected if sufficient attention is given in early training, and if the dog is properly exercised and moved in the show-ring at the right speed.

Much has been written and argued about whether a Dobermann should move on a single line, or what is termed single-tracking. Having attended lectures on this subject and having studied the movement of some of the best-proportioned Dobermanns in England and the USA, I have come to the conclusion that when a Dobermann is correctly built and moved at a normal walk, the front and hind legs must work in parallel. As the speed is increased, and particularly when the dog is moving at a very fast pace, single-tracking is automatically adopted. The speed at which dogs are moved in the show-ring is such that exhibits which single-track are probably weaving both in front and at the rear, an action caused by incorrect shoulder placement and malformed hindquarters.

Coat

Smooth, short, hard, thick and close lying. Imperceptible undercoat on neck permissible. Hair forming a ridge on back of neck and/or along spine highly undesirable.

The shiny coat of a well-bred and fit Dobermann is one of its most valued assets. The coat is short, smooth and glossy, but the individual hairs are hard in texture. Philipp Gruenig has stated that this type of hair is best suited to dogs exposed to frequently changing weather conditions. It dries quickly and is always clean. A soft silky coat is never quite weather-hardened. Certainly a Dobermann is able to work in extremes of weather. Black-and-tan Dobermanns carry a more dense coat than do the browns, while blues and fawns have a less dense coat still. A sparse coat on any Dobermann certainly detracts from the overall appearance. The early brown Dobermanns seen in the UK often had a coat with yellowish patches showing through, but later imports from the USA and from Germany have improved the coat colour of their brown British descendants, which now mostly carry a deep rich coat of an even colour.

Short hair is dominant over the long or rough varieties, and although one or two long-haired dogs were used in the evolution of the Dobermann, it was cross-breeding with the short-coated Manchester Terrier that helped to produce the lovely short coat we admire so much these days. Philipp Gruenig said that in 1902 an experimental cross with a Gordon Setter was made to improve the colour of the Dobermann. Although the long hair of the Setter was recessive to the short hair of the Dobermann, even now an older dog may occasionally develop a slightly curled coat, usually on the neck and along the back. Occasionally too we come across a Dobermann with a longish, slightly wavy coat. This is a throwback to the Rottweiler and is undesirable.

Other experiments in cross-breeding have left us with an undesirable cosmetic fault known as a ridge or a cowlick. This is occasionally seen as a raised section of hair, usually a couple of inches in length, appearing on the neck and along the back, and sometimes on the muzzle. Philipp Gruenig stated emphatically that 'fringes, manes, bristling whorls, etc. cannot be tolerated in the Dobermann'.

Colour

Definite black, brown, blue or fawn (Isabella) only, with rust-red markings. Markings to be sharply defined, appearing above each eye, on muzzle, throat and forechest, on all legs and feet and below tail. White markings of any kind highly undesirable.

J.F. writes: The first British standard of the Dobermann ruled that the colours allowed were black, brown or blue with rust-red markings. The wording was amended by the Kennel Club in December 1981 to include the fourth colour, fawn. Fred Curnow relates how in South Africa in 1963 he saw a litter of ten puppies of which three were black, three brown, three blue and one fawn. More recently in this country too a litter has occasionally included puppies of all four colours. The emergence of the fawn Dobermann became a matter of concern to many breeders and representation was made officially to the Kennel Club, asking that the German standard be adhered to and the fawn Dobermann disallowed. At the Kennel Club's request, a consultant geneticist prepared a short paper explaining the mode of inheritance of the four colours. This said, briefly, that coat colour in the Dobermann is controlled by two pairs of genes. The first in its dominant form produces the black coloration, and in its recessive form the brown. The second is concerned with the *density* of the colour. In its dominant form this pair of genes 'confirms' the black or brown colour, while in its recessive form the 'blacks' appear as 'blue' and the 'browns' as 'fawn'. On this evidence the Kennel Club considered it illogical to accept three of the colours and exclude the fourth. Accordingly they decided to add fawn to the permitted coat colours. This has now ceased to be a subject of controversy within the breed, and the Kennel Club acted entirely within its rights in deciding to legislate. It is interesting to note that the American Kennel Club a few years previously had made the same ruling for exactly the same reasons.

A few white hairs are sometimes found on the chest of Dobermann puppies, and occasionally a white toenail on one foot. This is a throwback to whatever dogs were used by the original breeders in the very early days of the Dobermann in Germany. Sometimes these markings disappear as the puppy matures but they are an undesirable characteristic.

In Germany, where breeding is very strictly controlled, an official of the German Dobermann Club visits every litter to see whether there are any puppies with white markings on the chest or toes. If these are found the breeder is told to have such puppies destroyed, otherwise no official pedigrees will be issued by the Club. Furthermore all puppies in excess of six in a litter have to be culled.

Size

Ideal height at withers:

Dogs	69 cms	(27 ins)
Bitches	65 cms	(25½ ins)

Considerable deviation from this ideal undesirable.

Faults

Any departure from the foregoing points should be considered
a fault and the seriousness with which the fault should be
regarded should be in exact proportion to its degree.

NOTE Male animals should have two apparently normal
testicles fully descended into the scrotum.

Character

Many things, good and bad, have been said about the
Dobermann, sometimes because of loving blindness and at
other times because of ignorance. Let us look at the
character of this great breed, so that those who already
know and love Dobermanns may understand them better,
and those contemplating ownership may have a better idea
of what is in store for them.

The breed standard requires a Dobermann to be bold
and alert. Indeed alertness should be his dominant
characteristic, his eyes, his mind, action and appearance
all revealing this quality. André Wilhelm, a President of
the International Dobermann Club, wrote that a Dobermann is faithful and fearless, has strong nerves, and is
alert and courageous. Any individual showing timidity or
cowardice would not be considered by the authorities in
Europe to be worthy of a prize in the show-ring, or classed
fit for breeding. He added that the very aggressive
temperament of the Dobermann in the initial years of its
development had been considerably mellowed by cross-
breeding with the black and tan Manchester Terrier and
the English Greyhound, from which it gained in sociabil-
ity. As mentioned too in the previous chapter, the policy
of breeders in Holland and America was to select individuals possessing qualities of character more suited to the
lifestyle of a house-dog and companion, whilst maintaining intelligence and natural keenness, energy for work
and an excellent nose.

Those who already own a Dobermann know of the great

loyalty inherent in the breed, which is evident from the moment the puppy enters your home. He loves to be near or beside you, to ride in your car, accompany you on walks or outings, live in your house, run in your garden, be a friend of the family and a guardian to your children. At least, that is what you may think! Actually, it is you who share *his* home and ride in *his* car; he romps in *his* garden and he greets, plays with and protects *his* family. Your responsibility is to provide the amenities and, more importantly, the companionship, leadership and guidance he looks for. His sense of ownership endears the Dobermann to his family, and most owners enjoy the stimulating company of such an intelligent and affectionate dog. It is indeed a breed that takes you over, and it has been said that to own a Dobermann is to be disappointed with all other breeds.

During the 1939–45 war, the Germans used Dobermanns in the Middle East to carry messages, as sentry dogs and as guardians of ammunition depots. British troops who came up against these guard dogs realised their qualities and learned to respect them. They returned home with stories proving the reliability, stamina and steadfastness of this breed, and it was no doubt partly due to their enthusiasm that serious importation into England of adult stock was started. When first introduced into Britain some 'know-alls' described the dog as vicious and unsafe, and even today this prejudice may persist among people only seeing a Dobermann acting the part of a 'killer dog' on film or television. A Dobermann trained to attack is certainly a sight to deter the most hardened criminal, but in the hands of professional trainers or police handlers they remain normal and well-behaved animals. A dog that is teased or persistently provoked to show aggression, becomes like a loaded revolver without a safety-catch: liable to go off at any moment. The training of dogs for manwork is not a job for the unskilled handler.

Hank, a Dobermann bred in England from show-winning stock and trained by Harry Darbyshire, starred with Lloyd Nolan and Kenneth More in the film *We Joined the Navy*. He attended the film première in London and obviously enjoyed all the attention. On later occasions, Harry Darbyshire would put on a demonstration of 'manwork' with Hank, when his toughness and determination in locating, chasing and detaining a 'criminal' delighted the crowd. Once off-duty, Hank would seek out the children in the crowd and settle down happily among them, where he enjoyed much petting and attention. He was neither aggressive nor dangerous. Trained and handled by a professional he remained a sociable and lovable dog.

Peggy Adamson has stated emphatically that a Dobermann is an 'honest' dog, and Harry Darbyshire used the same term in assessing a suitable individual for training. The Dobermann's direct and open look is not deceptive. Honesty of character is apparent in the loyalty he gives to his immediate human family, to whom he is a devoted companion. The solitary owner out walking, or alone at home or in the car, can feel safe with a Dobermann at their side. He has an uncanny insight into human character, trusting those friends who are readily accepted and distrusting strangers or those who are not welcome. He stands aloof from those outside his circle and will accept them into his home only if accompanied by one of the family. Even then he will invariably keep one eye on the visitor, just to make sure nothing untoward happens. When the visitor rises from his chair preparing to depart, the dog will get up immediately (sometimes with a short bark) and escort him to the door.

A Dobermann craves affection. He loves to lean against you while you stroke him, put his head on your knee or your hand when you are seated, and curl up beside (or on) your foot. Contact is a sign of his affection; it reassures him and strengthens the bond between you. When you come home from the office or from shopping his greeting is enthusiastic. He may welcome you with a toy, a shoe, or the nearest object he can pick up and bring to you, his whole rear end wriggling with joy. He can be boisterous and exuberant, or restrained and quietly delighted, but his eyes always sparkle with pleasure. Some Dobermanns 'smile' when they are pleased, their lips parted in a grin; some have a sense of fun and love a game of hide-and-seek with you, or tug-of-war with a toy; others are more serious and sedate in their behaviour. Some wag their short tail very fast and very frequently, others are less demonstrative but equally loving. The Dobermann may give a noisy greeting, bark a welcome, or make happy whining sounds that are a response to your own voice; he may make no sound, but express his delight at seeing you with all his body. The vitality and energy of the dog, combined with its intelligence, adaptability and loyalty, make a Dobermann a very special dog to own and live with. He is honest not only in character, but also in conformation. There is no long coat to hide imperfections in build, and no trimming is required to improve his appearance. A Dobermann has been likened to a thoroughbred horse, and when you see the elegance, grace, dignity, strength and balance of this breed the comparison becomes obvious.

Of course not every Dobermann has all the desired characteristics, and some owners would be better suited to another breed of dog. Although the vast majority of owners enjoy a happy relationship with their Dobermann, it is usually the sad cases that attract publicity. Any dog, of whatever breed, *may* bite and become untrustworthy even with its owner or family. Failure is a result of human error – in breeding from unsuitable or poor stock, in bad rearing, or incorrect handling and treatment. A tendency to sharpness in the Dobermann can be inherited, but almost always the fault lies with those who, consciously or not, have ill-used or bewildered the dog. An intelligent dog learns fast, and remembers well. Treated badly, confused by inconsistent treatment, chained up, neglected, beaten or shouted at, some dogs become vicious through fear and sheer desperation. Alternatively, when a dog has been excessively spoilt by being given its own way and indulged in every whim, it grows up unaccustomed to obey, and, when its will is thwarted, may bite. This behaviour is characteristic of any dog, not just a Dobermann. Toy dogs and small terriers may get away with being labelled snappy, but a Dobermann ends up in the newspapers. When a Dobermann has learned through cruel experience to distrust the human race, it needs loving care, sympathetic handling and very careful rehabilitation.

When defending its master, a Dobermann has no thought for danger, and many cases have been reported of a dog confronting intruders and suffering injury. One owned by a farmer near Cambridge gave its life in defence of his owner's property. A shot was put into the dog, who continued to defend the house until several bullets killed him. Again, a bitch called Hanna, belonging to the landlord of a public house in London, challenged two men who forced an entry after the pub had closed. She leapt at the man who raised a gun, and was shot and very badly injured (ultimately losing a foreleg). In spite of her injury she drove off the intruders. Many publicans, sub-postmasters and petrol-station owners in rural areas have purchased a Dobermann as a deterrent to vandals, and report that while the dog will tolerate and even become friendly with customers on the right side of the bar or counter, he will immediately challenge anyone who leans over or steps behind it.

Zak was the pet of a family living in a coastal town in Scotland. When the eleven-year-old son got into difficulty swimming in the sea, Zak, who was on the beach, heard his call and swam out to the boy and towed him back safely to shore. But for the dog – a Dobermann that was a normal family pet – the boy would certainly have drowned.

Though strongly built, a Dobermann will play safely and happily with smaller dogs or young children and never be rough with them. He is not a bully, nor does he have a mean character, but should he be attacked his fighting spirit is immediately roused and he reacts accordingly. Thereafter he will never forget the aggressor should they meet again.

The efficacy of the Dobermann as a house-dog is well known at every level of society. In the 1950s, when living at Colwood Court in rural Sussex, Harry Darbyshire, then working with the Surrey Constabulary, telephoned to say that house-breakers were operating in our district. He warned me to lock away all ladders, because the thieves generally used them to gain entry. With a couple of adult Dobermanns in the house I felt no unease, previous attempts at burglary having been forestalled by our dogs. A week or so later, Harry telephoned again, saying the thieves had been apprehended. One of the thieves had on him a list of houses that had been or were to be robbed, or were to be left severely alone. Against Colwood Court was the entry: 'Keep away. Dobermanns.'

It should now be clear that a Dobermann's physical strength, energy and vitality are matched by his alertness, intelligence and loyalty. To his admirers, his character appeals as much as his appearance, and both deserve the right environment and adequate outlet for their full development. The breed's skill, courage and trainability is shown in later chapters, but it is above all as a companion and family dog that the Dobermann excels. Philipp Gruenig wrote: 'The Dobermann is by nature a protector, guardian and companion. Kept in a home and in intimate touch with people he will display his inherently watchful, willing, obedient and brave character.'

3

Choosing a Puppy

You are sure a Dobermann is the breed of dog for you, and you want to buy a puppy. Please take your time, and think carefully about what is involved. A dog is yours (and your responsibility) for its life, maybe ten years or more.

If you already have dogs in kennels at your home, then the addition of a Dobermann puppy will make little difference; an extra dish at feeding-time, another run to clean, a new breed to study and to bring up in your ways. If however, like most of us, your Dobermann is to live in the house and share in the activities of the family, then a little reflection and a few words of advice may help to prevent difficulty and misunderstanding later. More and more families get a dog on impulse or to follow a trend, without much idea of what they are taking on or what it means, and within a few weeks find they cannot cope. Sad proof of this is the number of young adults (particularly males) that require re-homing before they are one year old, and which are either taken in by the National Canine Defence League or the breed Rescue services, or are passed from home to home and are eventually put down as unwanted animals. So, reflect a little before you buy a puppy and bring a Dobermann into your home.

Are you really sure it is the breed for you? Is every member of the household happy about your choice? If not, if there is mistrust or disapproval within the family, then proceed no further. An intelligent dog is acutely sensitive to emotional upset or controversy within the family, and you may end up with a canine as well as a human problem.

Have you room in your home for an active and growing animal? Has he access to a backgarden or yard which is safely enclosed, where he can relieve himself, and from which he cannot escape? Is there a park within walking distance, or an open space where dogs are allowed to be exercised or to run free? Have you the time (and the energy) to exercise your dog every day, on the lead for most of the time? (A dog must not be allowed to run wildly around on its own in park or field until it is under control and will come back when called.) Are you prepared to take your puppy with you to see and learn about what goes on outside its home, and become accustomed to people, traffic, noise and bustle? Do you know how much it will cost per week to feed your dog properly? Can you afford the fees for inoculations and the annual 'boosters', and the veterinary attention that may be needed in the event of an illness or mishap? When you go on holiday, are you prepared to take him with you, or to pay the cost of boarding him at a good kennels?

Will you take him to a training-class where he can be among other people and dogs, and where you will learn the proper way to handle and control him? When you first get him, are you prepared for several weeks (or months) to devote the time needed to settle him into a human environment, and to teach him what he needs to know to be a happy family dog – i.e., to be clean in the house, to be quiet at night, to sleep in his bed when playtime and meals are over, to lie quietly in the car when you are driving, to play with you and the family without showing aggression, to accompany you on a walk without pulling on the lead, to become a companion and a valued member of the household?

So far the intended addition to your family has been referred to as a 'he'. But it is essential to decide whether you want a dog or a bitch. Many breeders will not sell a male puppy to a family with small children and will insist that a bitch is best as a family pet. Many people are still prejudiced against a bitch as being a 'nuisance' because she is in season for three weeks twice a year, and has to be protected from male suitors who may arrive on the doorstep or in the garden. But a male dog is sexually aware at any time once he is mature. He will follow a bitch that seems attractive, or try to get out if a bitch is in season nearby, or tend to wander in the neighbourhood if he has been allowed to get out on his own as a youngster. There are many exceptions either way, but generally speaking a bitch is more placid and tolerant of children, is very affectionate, and usually more easily handled and trained. A dog can show defiance as he reaches adult size and needs an owner who can control him; he responds well to training if he is handled correctly, and he will have tremendous character; he will grow larger and tougher than a bitch, but he can be very gentle and loving and loyal.

Having considered all these points carefully, and still being sure that a Dobermann is the right dog for you, you are now prepared to buy one. There are several ways to find out about litters of puppies for sale. If you have studied the different lines of breeding, and are attracted to a particular type of Dobermann, then you probably already know who are the principal breeders, and can approach them at a show, or write and ask what puppies they have available. If you intend to buy one with the intention of showing it yourself, the breeder can advise you as to which puppy in the litter will probably turn out to be suitable. You must be prepared firstly to pay a higher price (as several buyers may be seeking the same dog), and later, when it is old enough, and looks good enough to be shown, to have sufficient time and money and patience to campaign it. Showing a dog is an expensive and highly competitive sport, though it is an enjoyable hobby too.

If you are wanting your Dobermann purely as a companion and a family dog, then you still need to get a good one. A well-reared puppy from an experienced breeder will cost no more to feed, and will cost much less in veterinary fees and owner-anxiety, than one from poor stock. 'Buy from a Breeder' is a slogan seen on car stickers today, and it is good advice. What is a breeder? How do you find one? The Kennel Club defines a breeder as the registered owner of the dam at the time the litter is born, and they can supply you with a list of breeders whose kennel name is advertised each month in the *Kennel*

Gazette. (The address of the Kennel Club is 1–5 Clarges Street, Piccadilly, London w1y 8ab.) The secretaries of the breed clubs whose addresses are given in Appendix B can also tell you of any of their members likely to have puppies available. One advantage of seeking out a breeder who is a member of one of the breed clubs is that he or she will have agreed to observe the club's Code of Ethics before they can be accepted as a member. Adherence to their club's code should ensure that puppies are bred only from adult, healthy and KC-registered parents, that they get proper attention and care, and that you will receive the proper documents and the information you require upon purchasing a puppy.

The two weekly dog papers, *Dog World* and *Our Dogs*, carry advertisements of litters for sale. The local veterinary surgeon will know of breeders who are clients of his, and he can maybe tell you of litters available. Finally, since the Dobermann has become a popular breed and production of puppies has tended to exceed demand, the local paper will probably include under 'Pets for Sale' the telephone number of people anxious to dispose of puppies. They may be bona-fide breeders – i.e., people who have a good bitch which has been mated to a stud dog of good character and suitable breeding, and from the resulting litter they have a few well-reared puppies still unsold. In that case, it would be worth your while to go and see the puppies.

More likely, an advertisement in the columns of the local paper that appears week after week above the same telephone number can be that of what is termed 'a backyard breeder'; that is, someone with more than one bitch, and often several bitches of different breeds, who produces puppies as a 'cash crop'; rearing them in dirty conditions, and with minimum feeding and care, from parents of poor physical quality and unknown character. Such a supplier may also be a dealer, one who buys in whole litters of puppies from backyard breeders in rural areas, and whose purpose is a cash sale as quickly as possible. Such a 'puppy-farm' may look smart from the outside, but the conditions under which the unfortunate puppies exist are dreadful, and stress, dirt and disease take their toll. From either a back-yard breeder or a puppy farm you will get no after-sale advice or help, and no sympathy or compensation when within a few days your puppy may become ill and perhaps die.

When you hear of a good litter of puppies within reasonable travelling distance, make an appointment with the breeder and go and see them. When you arrive, take your time. If the breeder has a real interest in the welfare of his dogs he will want to assure himself you are a suitable person to have one. So be prepared to have a talk with the breeder first, tell him exactly what you are looking for, and whether you want a dog or a bitch. Ask to see the dam (and the sire if he is in the same ownership). If either parent is aggressive or bad-tempered, nervous or cowardly, that tendency will be inherited by the pups. The temperament of the dam is particularly important and has the greatest influence, so be sure that you see her. If the breeder has other dogs of the same breeding, perhaps from a previous litter, ask to see them too. It will give you an idea of the sort of Dobermann the puppies will grow to resemble.

When you are taken to see the puppies, either outside in an enclosed run, or in the utility room or kitchen, note how clean and healthy and happy they appear to be; also how eagerly they come forward to greet their breeder and how they react to you, a stranger. Note their physical condition. Are they fairly even in size, active and playful? Are their coats sleek and shiny, with rich tan markings? Are their eyes clear and bright, with no discharge, and their nostrils clear of mucus? Watch them as they play together; see which is the boss, which are the most active, which first finds something to play with (a twig, ball of crumpled paper, a fallen leaf). A confident puppy will be inquisitive, and come to look you over, and probably nibble your shoelaces. A shy one that turns away or hides, or retreats from your hand, is not suitable for you. Character and temperament are the most important things to assess when choosing a puppy.

Watch each puppy standing, or ask the breeder to hold

it in a stand position (to 'set it up' as show people would
say) for a few moments. Is the topline straight? Is the tail
neat and carried level? Is the head carried proudly on a
strong neck? Are the forelegs and hindquarters firm and
strong for the age of the pup? Are the feet cat-like with
bunched knuckles? Are the eyes dark? Does the puppy
look well-balanced, in proportion? If the litter includes
puppies of different coat colours, assess each one in the
same way for temperament and physical attributes, and
don't choose one for its colour alone.

Take your time, study the puppies carefully, and watch
them. Knowing the individual character of each puppy in
the litter, the breeder may well suggest which one he
thinks will suit you best; sometimes it is the puppy himself
that decides you are the one for him; sometimes as you
look you know for sure which is the one you want (but it
must *never* be one you are sorry for because it looks
miserable or is shy). If you decide on one of them then
make arrangements as to when you can take it, and agree
the price. If you are not sure, and know of other puppies
elsewhere that you would like to see as well, don't be
rushed into a purchase that day, but be sure to let the
breeder know within a day or two whether or not you are
still interested in buying from him.

Prices vary, but a good Dobermann will never be cheap.
The cost of rearing a good puppy is high. Besides keeping
the dam in peak condition, paying the fee for a stud dog
of compatible breeding, feeding the bitch properly
throughout her pregnancy, paying veterinary fees for her
to be checked out after whelping, and for removal of the
puppies' dewclaws and the correct docking of the tail,
providing extra food for the bitch while she is nursing the
puppies and giving them the meat and cereal and milky
feeds they need after weaning, a good breeder will also
register the litter at the Kennel Club, advertise the puppies
for sale, and insure them as an after-sale service. You
should find out the present rate for a well-bred Dobermann puppy before you go to choose one, and then agree
the price with the breeder after making a choice. One final
word of warning: when you have chosen your puppy,

never be persuaded to take a second one as well – even if it is offered at a throw-away price or so as 'to keep each other company'. Whether of different sexes, or worse still of the same sex, two puppies can mean disaster. Take the one of your choice, bring him up as an individual in your home, to be the companion, house-dog and friend you wanted, and if he's a good Dobermann you'll not regret it.

The new puppy in your home

Most breeders today like their puppies to go to their new home when aged between seven and eight weeks. Twenty or thirty years ago four months was a more usual age. Since then however research into animal behaviour has shown that a dog goes through several distinct stages in its development, and it is important that a puppy experiences the right treatment and conditions during each of these critical periods. Of course a puppy needs its mother, primarily for food, warmth and protection, later for leadership and discipline as well, for the first four weeks of its life. It should have human contact, both seeing people and being talked to and handled gently, from the time its eyes are open and when it starts to move around. During the fifth and sixth weeks a puppy starts gradually to explore the area where it lives. The company of litter-mates at this time is important, and each puppy finds its own level within this basic canine pack. At this time too (between four and six weeks of age) a puppy becomes aware of people, will recognise them and respond to voices. Probably the best time to study a litter and to choose your puppy is around five to six weeks of age.

Puppies should remain with their litter-mates until they are seven weeks old, and the bitch should be allowed to be with them too whenever she chooses. Between seven and eight weeks puppies are ready to go to their new homes, and a wise breeder will suggest you collect yours at this age, when he will socialise best with people, and learn most easily how he must behave in his owner's household. He will also quickly become deeply attached to you, his owner.

So, your puppy is ready, and off you go to collect him. (Though you may have chosen a bitch and not a dog, it is convenient still to refer to the puppy as 'he'.) You will already have decided where he is to sleep, and have ready at home his bed and a blanket, a feeding dish and bowl of water, and a supply of the same food that he has been reared on. If you go by train to fetch the puppy, he can come back with you either in a travelling box of suitable type, or on your lap in the carriage with you if the journey is a short one.

Most probably you will go by car to fetch him. Take with you a cardboard box large and deep enough to contain him, and put it on the floor by the front passenger seat. Put a small piece of blanket or folded material in the box, and have with you a roll of kitchen paper and an old towel, for mopping-up in case he drools or is sick. If the journey is a long one, take newspapers to put in the box if the blanket has been soiled.

Knowing when you will arrive, the breeder should have ready all the documents you need. Besides a receipt for the price of the puppy, you should be given a three- or four-generation pedigree, and the Kennel Club green-and-white certificate of registration, the breeder having already registered and named your puppy. You should also receive a diet sheet, a certificate of vaccination for any inoculation your puppy may already have been given, a note of when he was wormed and the type of medication used. If the breeder has arranged for insurance under Pet Plan's Puppy Cover, you will receive a certificate to that effect; this is generally valid for six weeks after purchase. A caring breeder will probably also send you away with at least three days' food of the kind your puppy has been reared on, to minimise the chance of any tummy upset after all the excitement and strangeness of a journey and new surroundings. Optional extras provided by some breeders are an application form for membership of one of the breed clubs, and a good book about Dobermanns!

During the drive home see there is good ventilation and

that the car is not stuffy or over-heated. Have the puppy
in the box on the floor; he will then not be frightened by
seeing things going by (which is most often the cause of
car-sickness) and will be learning his first lesson, namely,
to travel quietly and sit still in the car. Speak to him gently
during the drive, and tell him he's a good boy. This is
reassuring, and makes him familiar with your voice too. If
he is sick, pull in and stop when it is safe, dry the puppy
and replace the blanket in the box with newspapers.
Should he be sick again, it is easy to remove soiled paper
and still leave him with several dry layers underneath him.
Don't feed him or give him anything to drink until you
reach home, unless the journey is so long you yourself
need to stop for several hours. A dog travels best when
empty.

When you reach home, carry your new puppy at once
out into the backgarden or yard, put him down on the
grass and tell him to 'pay penny' (or whatever you intend
to use when encouraging him to relieve himself). He'll
probably do so almost at once, in which case praise him,
pick him up and take him indoors to the kitchen – or
wherever he will sleep at night until he is house-trained.
Let him walk round and explore the room; his bed will be
there, in a corner and out of any draughts. When he has
had a good look round, let the family come in quietly and
meet him. To a small puppy in a strange environment
people are just legs and ankles and shoes moving towards
him; he will best make acquaintance with the rest of the
family if they sit on the floor and let him meet them at his
level. It is strange and exciting; the puppy must not be
frightened by being grabbed or pulled or shouted at. The
right approach is very important. Take your time; speak
gently, stroke him when he is beside you, tell him he's a
good boy.

The introductions being over, offer him a milky feed (of
whatever type he is used to having) and leave the dish
down for about five minutes, so he can decide whether
he's thirsty and needs a feed, or whether it is all so strange
he won't take anything yet. Pick up the dish either when
it is empty or after five minutes if it isn't. Carry the puppy

out to the garden, put him down and tell him to 'pay penny', or whatever you said before. He'll probably wander about for a little and will most probably relieve himself again. Praise him, pick him up, take him indoors and put him on his bed, saying 'Bed, good boy, bed!' Make sure he stays on his bed for a few moments, then go out and shut the door and leave him. He'll probably cry. Let him cry. Leave him on his own (you'll have to at night), and after all the excitement of the journey, the new surroundings he finds himself in, and a good meal, your puppy in due course will discover that his bed is a comfortable place and will settle down and go to sleep. Later, when put to bed and left for the night, he will find himself in a familiar spot and settle more readily.

If he wakes before you go back into the room about an hour later, you'll find a puddle or a mess, or maybe both, on the floor. If he only wakens when you enter the room, speak to him, tell him he's a good boy, pick him up and take him out to the garden. Tell him to 'pay penny' and he will, so praise him well. A puppy will relieve himself whenever he wakes up, after a meal and after (sometimes during) a game or period of play, so you must take him out when he is likely to need it. He will not know to ask to go out, and he has as yet little control of his bladder or bowels – he just feels the need for relieving himself and does it at once. So don't scold him if your puppy makes a puddle, but try to anticipate his need and until he is clean keep him in a room without a carpet! Whenever he is taken outside and is about to relieve himself, tell him to 'pay penny' (or whatever words you've chosen to use) and he'll soon associate the words with the necessary act. This is useful training for later on whenever your dog is in a strange place and you need to indicate where he may relieve himself.

At home with you there are now no other puppies to play with, so you must give yours some attention when he wants to play. An empty cereal carton makes a good toy, a hard rubber ball can be slowly rolled across the floor, and a knotted piece of towelling is easy to pick up and carry round, and you can gently pull it (as would another puppy) and then throw it for him to regain and carry proudly once more. Play strengthens the bond between you, and helps him accept you now as his 'pack-leader'. A puppy cannot concentrate for long, nor take formal training, but he can learn to associate with certain actions the words that will be used later for control. So, when he runs towards you, say 'Come'; when he sits, say 'Sit'; when he prepares to lie down, say 'Down'; and when he picks up anything, say 'Fetch'. It is all play at this stage, but it is also valuable basic training if a puppy is allowed to learn in this way. If you are too busy to spare time to play with your puppy, he will look around for something to interest him and will probably find something that is either forbidden or dangerous! Remember too that after leaving his litter-mates your puppy will be alone at night for the first time. It is therefore very important to make sure that, from the first day you get him, by the time you and your family are ready for bed, your little Dobermann is not just waking up after three or four hours spent sleeping happily on your lap, while you sat and watched television in front of a good fire in the sitting-room. For him, that ideally happy situation, warm and protected, and cuddled against his new owner, seems to be cruelly interrupted, and after being given a meal he finds himself taken outside yet again to relieve himself, and then put in his bed in the kitchen and left alone in the dark. Feeling abandoned and lonely, perhaps a little cold, and in an utterly strange situation, he'll cry. And having slept well all evening he'll continue to cry. The wailing of an unhappy Dobermann puppy is most disturbing, not only to you and your family, but to the neighbours as well, and it can go on for several hours. If you go downstairs to try and quieten him, he'll be overjoyed and very relieved to see you – and the wailing and yelps will start again as soon as you close the door and leave him.

By the time a puppy is seven weeks old it can sleep through the night, perhaps waking once if it needs to relieve itself. You can help your new puppy, and save yourself and your family from being badly disturbed, by giving him his last meal (and make it a meat feed, not a milky one) at bedtime rather than in the early evening, and by taking care to see he is really tired and longing for sleep at the time *you* wish to go to bed too. So, spend the evening in the kitchen (if it is there that he will be left for the night), or outside in the garden if it is summertime, and let your puppy play or wander round until bedtime. Puppies do need a lot of sleep, and it is vital they should have it, but unless you keep dogs in kennels, and are accustomed to occasional noise at night, a little over-tiredness in the evening is better for your puppy than feelings of anxiety and distress at finding himself alone all night in a strange environment. Keep him awake in the evening, especially for the first week, then when he's dropping with sleep offer him his meat, take him outside once more, and put him to bed. Give him a worn sock, or an old sweater, to cuddle against in his bed, make sure he is warm, protected from any draughts, and has a radiator or some source of heat nearby unless the weather is very warm, draw the curtains and put out the light. He should be asleep by the time you get upstairs, and everyone will enjoy a quiet night.

Next day try to be downstairs before the rest of the family, and take your puppy outside at once, telling him he's a good boy and sounding really pleased with him if you reached the kitchen before he woke up and began to make a noise. Keep to this routine until he is used to sleeping on his own.

To help your puppy sleep through the night without needing to wake up and relieve himself, it is a good idea to pick up the bowl of water about 7 p.m. and give him no more to drink until the next morning, when his first meal is a milky one anyway. A full tummy and a warm bed will encourage a restful night's sleep, so give him meat for his last meal.

Because it is easy to pick up and replace after being soiled or wet, most breeders put newspaper down on the floor of their puppies' kennel. Your youngster will therefore be accustomed to relieving himself on paper. Before you leave him for the night, cover the floor of the kitchen with newspaper. After a few nights you will see which area he tends to use, so gradually reduce the area until only a few sheets are required; usually this is by the door. A puppy has incomplete control, and is therefore not fully 'house-trained' until he is three months old. If by then he is not clean at night, or by day still makes a puddle or a mess on the floor before he gets to the door asking to be let out, it is most likely to be your fault, and not his. You have probably not maintained careful watch in the first weeks, and taken him outside regularly during the day, or whenever he showed signs of preparing to relieve himself. After he is three months old, finding either a puddle or a mess when you come downstairs in the morning can mean that something has woken him up earlier, or that his feeding timetable needs slight adjustment, with a meal being given either a little earlier or later, or that he is not sufficiently warm and comfortable in his bed. Don't ever blame him for any 'accident'. Be patient, and *never* scold him when you find a puddle or a mess. Blame yourself.

When he is clean by day, and knows to go towards the door to indicate that he needs to go out, your puppy can be allowed through to the rest of the house, but he should not have access to a flight of stairs until about five months old. Before that, coming downstairs puts a strain on his shoulders and elbows. Besides spoiling his front, a puppy can have a nasty fall trying to come downstairs when he is still small, so if you live in an upper flat, you must carry your puppy whenever he needs to be taken downstairs. For the same reason, arrange for a Dobermann always to eat or drink from a bowl or dish that is raised above floor level, so that he stands straight and reaches forward instead of bending down, which puts a strain on elbows and shoulders and will spoil a good front and correct conformation. At first, putting his dish on a box will raise it sufficiently, then as he grows, use a bigger box and when he reaches adult height have the water bowl permanently, and the feeding-dish at mealtimes, on a stand or a little shelf fixed in a corner of the kitchen.

As soon as possible after you get your puppy, make an appointment with the veterinary surgeon. You may already be a client of one of the local veterinary practices; if not, find out from dog-owning friends whom they can recommend. When you arrive at the surgery, go in and tell the receptionist you are there, but don't take your puppy into the waiting-room. Keep him in your arms, wrapped in a blanket, and wait outside or in the car until the receptionist tells you it is your turn and you can go straight into the surgery. The vet will take a quick look at your new young friend, and confirm that he is in good health. Having examined the vaccination certificate and any note as to the worming medication already given, the vet will recommend what further treatment for worms is needed, and when the remaining inoculations should be given.

Until vaccination is complete, your puppy will be very vulnerable to virus infections, particularly canine parvovirus. While immunity is building up, generally over a period of four weeks, your puppy should be kept away from all possible sources of infection. 'Don't take him out. Just keep him in the garden' is the advice usually given by breeders and veterinary surgeons alike. Unfortunately the recommended four-week period of isolation within the home environment, while his body develops immunity to serious disease, usually coincides with the period during which it has been proved conclusively that a puppy most needs to see and learn about the world *outside* his home. Between seven and twelve weeks of age is the critical time when he should be socialised and meet people, watch and meet (under controlled conditions) children, cats (and farm animals if you live in the country), travel in a car or be carried on a bus, watch traffic go by, pass prams and handcarts, see men going up and down ladders, or sweeping up leaves, and so on. He must never be frightened, but given time and gentle encouragement to look and learn. It is at this stage that his character and personality, and his attitude to people, develop to their best advantage. A dog's acceptance of discipline, his ability to learn, proficiency in training, desire to please, self-confidence and trust, all depend on what he has been allowed to learn before he is three months old.

Faced with such totally conflicting advice from those responsible for his health and those for whom character and temperament are of paramount importance, a wise owner must use both care and commonsense, and steer a course between the extremes of secluded isolation and exposure to risk. Carry the puppy to where he can safely watch what is going on; don't let him be sniffed or bullied by dogs, or put down and allowed to walk in areas they frequent. This is the policy adopted by the Guide Dogs for the Blind Association. They prefer their puppy-walkers to take a small risk with infection rather than spoil a puppy's chances of developing fully the outlook and temperament it will need for successful training later on. Similar sensible care can be used by any dog owner. As this is the time when a puppy learns most rapidly, do not shut him away and deprive him of the opportunity to see and become accustomed to the world he will have to live in. Depending on where you live, it should be possible to take the puppy out in the car. The car park of a supermarket can be quite interesting, and every household needs at least one shopping expedition per week, so take your puppy with you. Safe in the car he can see people of every type going by; some pushing trolleys, older folk walking with a stick, children in push-chairs, all kinds of movement and bustle. Keep him away from the local park or any area where dogs roam, and never walk him across ground that has been fouled by dogs. Anyone fearful of their new puppy picking up infection, and who keeps it at home for the prescribed four weeks, should remember that a virus can just as easily be brought into the house on shoes and clothing, or carried by the cat or any other dog that lives on the premises.

Lead-training starts well before your dog is old enough to be taken out for a walk. Let your puppy wear a round leather collar (*never* a slip-chain) for a short time every day. When he is accustomed to it, attach to the collar a piece of cord, long enough to reach the ground but not to become entangled in his feet, and let the puppy continue playing until he forgets it is there. Next day clip on a longer cord (an old show-lead does very well) and hold the end of it.

Don't pull it, or tug the puppy, but let him quietly get used to you holding it; then call him to you and praise him well when he comes. A few minutes like this for a couple of days, and when your puppy will come to you as you hold the light lead, he can be encouraged to walk for a few steps at your side. When his inoculations are completed, and at nearly five months old he is big enough to be taken out for a short walk, he will be used to a collar and lead, and with encouragement will walk beside you outside without pulling. If he stops, or jumps ahead, or tries to pull away, you must stop and reassure him. Don't pull him sharply, don't get cross, but don't let him pull you either. Speak to him, draw him gently in beside you and walk slowly. Take your time. As with everything else in training, be patient, teach him aright, and don't let bad habits develop. Pulling on the lead should never be allowed to start.

When the first teeth are shed and the permanent teeth are coming through, a puppy will tend to chew anything he finds. Provide him therefore with something suitable, and put away out of his reach shoes and clothing, children's toys or anything he must not have. A raw beef marrowbone that has been sawn by the butcher into three- or four-inch lengths is ideal; the marrow can slowly be licked and sucked out and the bone is of a type that will not splinter or be broken off and swallowed. *Never* give cooked bones to your dog, or bones of pork, mutton, poultry or game, only a length of raw beef shank. There are many products on sale at pet food stores which are made especially for dogs to chew. Some of them splinter dangerously when a Dobermann's strong jaws have worked on them, and these can cause serious trouble when swallowed, so choose carefully when you buy one. A product such as Nylabone is safer, being very tough and not brittle. Some Dobermanns go through a prolonged period of chewing again when they are adolescent; they may become quite destructive, so keep them busy with a raw beef bone and give them plenty of exercise and regular training too. A bored Dobermann can cause a great deal of damage if given access to unauthorised items in the home.

When he has outgrown the original cardboard box on the floor of the car in which he was brought home as a small puppy, and is accustomed to travelling by car, give your dog a place at the back where he can sit or lie comfortably, and is not able to jump around and interfere with the driver. Metal dog guards which are made to fit both estate cars and hatchbacks prevent a dog jumping over to the front. In time they may be made compulsory when dogs are carried in a car, just as seat-belts for adults and safety seats for young children have become statutory safety equipment. Alternatively a dog may travel safely and comfortably in a wire cage of sufficient size to allow him to stand up and turn round, as well as sit and lie down. These cages are known as crates in America, where they are used both for transporting dogs safely and as their bed at home. A cage that is suitable for a full-grown Dobermann is quite a costly piece of equipment, but it has several advantages, one of them being that the dog can be put into it, and the door closed, if visitors who dislike dogs are entertained at his home. Cages are also very convenient on holiday; the dog can be left safely in a hotel room without risk of his doing damage or jumping on to the beds. To anyone considering investing in a wire cage for their young Dobermann however, a word of warning: it is *not* a prison, nor must confinement therein ever be used as a punishment. At home the door should be left open. Your Dobermann must always feel that his bed (whether in a cage or not) is a refuge, and the most comfortable place to lie in. It cannot be stressed too often that every dog must feel secure and free to relax in his bed. He must *never* be teased, or poked, or pulled about when lying in his bed. If you want him to leave his bed, call him in an encouraging tone of voice and praise him when he comes to you.

When he is about four months old your puppy will begin to show some independence, and may start to challenge your authority, probably by ignoring your call and moving away as you go to him. Be firm but never rough; keep to the routine and rules of behaviour already laid down, and make sure he does what he is told. Never hit him, or kick him, or strike him with anything, and don't shout. When you need to correct your puppy for doing wrong, take him by the loose skin under the neck and give him a little shake, scolding him in a low, growling voice. Always remember to praise him warmly when he does the right thing and correct him when he errs. Use the same words every time, and the same tone of voice. It is inflection as much as the words that will help him to understand that you are praising him when he does well, or correcting him when he has misbehaved. A pat when he is good, and a shaking when he is bad, given at the same time as you speak to him, will emphasise the words and impress them on his mind. Always be as liberal with your praise as you are with your correction. Never give way to anger and do not let punishment for him come out of your bad temper; always be calm, temperate and swift. A young dog is unable to associate either a kind word and a pat, or a harsh word of correction, with an action that has already passed. If you have missed the act itself, forget all about it.

The same principles apply to everything your dog needs to learn: use a single clear word for each command, accompany it with the appropriate action, and praise when it is carried out. *Teach a good habit before a bad habit can develop.* Make a rule and stick to it, and make sure the other members of the family do the same. Any dog becomes bewildered and insecure if he is allowed to do something one day and is scolded next day for doing the same thing. Your Dobermann is an intelligent and sensitive dog. He will trust and respect you if he is shown clearly, patiently and firmly just what he may or may not do. Make him sleep always on his own bed, and not on yours. Let him know where he may sit or lie in each room in the house (put down a blanket, or a piece of Vetbed, and make him lie on that, whether it be on the floor or on a specially permitted armchair). Whether indoors or out in the garden, or later on when out for exercise, don't chase after him when you need him to come to you. Make him come to you, if necessary by running away from him and letting him chase *you*. Shouting at and running after a dog is the quickest way to teach him *not* to come when he is called. Don't allow him to bite, or snap, or chew at your hands or ankles or clothing. Don't let him jump up when he greets you; bend down and always pet and praise your puppy when he is standing on all four feet. At your mealtimes, don't feed him from the table, but insist that he lies quietly in his proper place. Keep to his regular diet and don't feed him titbits. If he doesn't eat his own food, pick up his dish after five minutes and give him nothing else until his next meal is due. An older dog can easily go for twenty-four hours without food, but if your puppy continues to refuse to eat, seek professional advice and don't try to coax him with little luxuries from your own menu.

If you have never trained a dog before, find a good book and follow the advice it gives. Once your youngster is old enough, take him to a training-class. There he will learn to behave in the presence of other dogs and people, and to concentrate on what you are telling him to do. Both ringcraft and general obedience training can be carried out at the same class, but experienced handlers insist on making a clear distinction between each activity, so that the dog does not become confused, by using a different collar and lead for showing and obedience, as well as a different command.

Proper training is absolutely essential for an intelligent and active dog such as a Dobermann. Ignored, and left on his own, he will learn bad habits and will soon be continually in trouble. Harsh treatment can turn him into a defiant and bewildered animal that runs away, and when cornered will either cower and squeal, or snarl and try to bite. Dobermanns are not born bad. Those that chase everything that moves, that fight and bite and never obey an order or come when they are called, are made that way by their owners and the home environment. Make sure you bring up your Dobermann properly. He deserves it, and with wise care is unsurpassed as a family dog, companion and friend.

4

Management and Feeding

The management and feeding of dogs has been dealt with hundreds of times by hundreds of breeders, many of whom differ widely in their experience and ideas. Nevertheless, advice based on many years' experience by owners of Dobermanns should be included in any book on the breed.

Where he is the only dog, and has been bought as a family pet, a Dobermann can live happily in the house provided his needs are catered for. Besides proper training and care, regular meals, access to an outside run or backgarden where he can relieve himself, and a box or suitable dog-bed where he can lie undisturbed, or sleep, a Dobermann also needs the companionship of his owner, loving care from the family, and daily exercise under proper control. The breed was after all evolved specifically to be a personal companion and guard. Too often nowadays the majority of people are out and away from their home during working hours. A strong, active dog will soon become destructive, noisy, dirty and frustrated if left alone for several hours, day after day. It is both ill-advised and downright cruel to leave a dog alone in the house. Let him have his own kennel and run outside, where he can be safely confined and do no damage, can go in and out as he chooses, or rest under cover in a warm, sheltered box. Most people who keep more than one dog consider it preferable anyway for them to live outside in a kennel and run during the day, and to come indoors in the evening and sleep in the house. This applies equally well to a single dog where the family is busy and out all day. A dog that is kept outside for most of the day treats his kennel as his home and refuge, and his run as an area in which part of his daily exercise can be taken.

The following recommendations have been made by breeders in different parts of the UK, which if followed will provide the best living conditions for a Dobermann.

He should have a 6 ft × 6 ft kennel made from weatherboarding, or tongue-and-grooved boards, on a strong 2 in. × 2 in. wooden frame. Sheets of polystyrene or similar insulating material should be fastened inside to the kennel frame, and this in turn must be faced with fibreglass or plastic sheets, or any similar smooth, impervious material. (A new material called Purlboard currently used for lining piggeries is found to be ideal.) Hardboard or plywood is not now considered suitable for lining a kennel as dogs can chew it. Also the surface is not waterproof and can harbour germs or bacteria. The roof too should be interlined with fibreglass wool, polystyrene or some similar insulating material, and again covered with plastic sheets. Such a triple layer on walls and roof keeps the kennel warm in winter and cool in summer; insulation like this is essential for a short-coated breed.

The outside of the kennel must be protected by regular painting with creosote or some other wood preservative. The ideal door for a Dobermann's kennel is one divided into two parts, like a stable door, so that in cold or stormy weather the top half can be closed, and just the lower half of the door left open to allow the dog free access to the run. If the door is to be left open, or partly open, at night, hang a sheet of heavy rubber over the gap; this acts as a flap, allowing the dog to go out and in as he needs, but keeping out draughts. The kennel should have a floor of cement or concrete which must be sealed. First use two or three coats of a water-repellent paint, and when these have dried paint over with a preparation such as Chlorisco Rubber. This is used in quarantine kennels, and is germproof and urine-proof. The dog's bed should be a wooden box approximately 3 ft square, raised a few inches off the ground, with walls about 12 in. high.

Wherever you live in the UK some form of heating in the kennel is necessary for your dog's comfort. Use a good electric kennel heater with a wire mesh cover (several are

Wilm von Forell

German Ch. Greif von Hagenstern

Anne Hewitt

Ch. Edencourt's Avenger

Anne Hewitt

Ch. Annastock Lance

Diane Pearce

Ch. Tavey's Stormy Medallion and (behind) his son, Ch. Hensel Midnight
Max

Sally Anne Thompson

Ch. Tumlow Whinlands Flurry and Ch. Tumlow Impeccable

Ch. Acclamation of Tavey at twelve months

Sally Anne Thompson

Vanessa's Little Dictator of Tavey

advertised in the dog papers), securely mounted high on the wall where the dog cannot reach it, with all wiring, switches and plugs also well out of reach. Electric heating in a kennel should be installed by a qualified electrician so that it conforms to safety standards. It should preferably be thermostatically controlled, so that a sudden drop in temperature by day or night does not mean the dog becomes chilled, and when the temperature rises the current is switched off automatically.

The kennel and kennel floor, installed as above, should be made ready before your Dobermann is acquired and is ready to go into it. Then put in his bed, not opposite the door but in a corner to one side. If your Dobermann is still a puppy, line his bed with newspaper and a strip of Vetbed cut to fit the box. Ideal bedding for an adolescent or adult Dobermann is shredded paper; it is cheap, warm and easily disposed of. Straw as bedding material is dangerous; wood wool (recommended when this book was first written) is expensive and not always easy to obtain; newspaper, which is cheap, easily obtained and easily disposed of, gives little comfort, and sawdust should never be used. Wood chips or shavings are suitable for bedding provided they come from seasoned timber and not green wood, or they will be damp. (If shavings are used as bedding, avoid any from a red wood; one kennel owner found such shavings stained the dogs' coats; two more found their dogs were allergic to wood shavings.)

The kennel should be installed as described at one end of a concrete run 6 ft wide and 18 ft long. The sides and end of the run should be made from 6 ft chain-link fencing, with strong corner irons and supports, and preferably set on top of 9 in. concrete blocks all round. This greatly facilitates cleaning. When the fencing goes down to ground level, faeces, mud, dirt, scraps of food, etc. can stick to the bottom wires and be difficult to clean off except by a high-powered hose. Some veterinary surgeons with experience of quarantine kennels recommend that a kennel run be covered with blue or other tinted plastic sheeting (never a clear plastic). This drains off the worst of the weather, and in hot weather keeps off the intense heat of direct sun. It also prevents a dog jumping out. The gate to the run should be strong, with two catches, placed at the top and bottom (and not a single sliding bolt halfway down). If several dogs are kept and runs adjoin, it is advisable to have a 3 ft wall of breeze blocks built along the shared side. This can minimise aggression, help to prevent the spread of any infection, and stops urine being sprayed by a dog through to his neighbour's run!

The floor of the run should be of concrete. As it can become quite hot in summer (and cold and wet in winter), it is advisable to have in the run a wooden platform, about 3 in. high and approximately 4 ft square, on which several puppies or a couple of adults can rest or bask in the sun. These wooden platforms are also an asset after rainfall because they dry out quickly. They should not be painted, nor covered with linoleum or anything similar, as puppies will probably chew them.

Whether living in the house or outside in his kennel and run, a Dobermann must have regular exercise. From the time you get him, take him out, in your arms when he is small, or in the car, so that he may see the world outside and watch what goes on. A puppy that is deprived of learning about the happenings beyond his home or kennel becomes timid and withdrawn. It has been proved by trainers of guide-dogs that social contact with people, other friendly dogs, traffic, country animals and noises, town bustle, etc. is essential for developing a steady, balanced temperament. So once his inoculations have given him some immunity to the dangerous infections that can strike down young growing dogs, your Dobermann should become used to wearing a light round leather collar, and then to having a leather lead attached. (See pages 138–9.) When he will walk beside you without panic or leaping about to play with or chew the lead (which must be quietly but firmly discouraged at all times), you can take the puppy out firstly for ten minutes, then for fifteen minutes' slow walking along the pavement or the side of a road. Let him stop and look at anything that he notices for the first time, and reassure him. Never let him be frightened, or rushed at by children, traffic or another dog. Gradually and gently he must learn about conditions outside his home. As he grows, exercise on the lead can be extended to twenty or thirty minutes twice a day (if he is a house pet), or once a day if he lives in a kennel.

When he has been taught (at home in the house, or in the garden) to come to you when he is called, take him to a park or empty field when it is quiet and free from distraction, and let him off the lead to romp and play with you as you yourself run about and keep his attention. *Never* let a fast-moving dog such as a Dobermann learn to take off, or to run around just out of reach, before he has learned to come when he is called. Whenever he does come to you, indoors or out of doors, praise him. If as adolescence approaches he shows signs of being defiant and deaf to your call, preferring to please himself, turn and run away from him as fast as you can, and when he runs after you praise him well and tell him he's a good boy. *Never* scold your dog when he comes up to you, even though you may be angry inside because he has not come at once. If you do, he won't feel it worth coming to you again and may start playing 'hard to get'.

Especially during the period when an adolescent Dobermann of either sex can become very wilful, it is a good idea to attach a length of light rope – such as an old washing-line – to his collar when you take off the lead to allow him his usual free run. He will be free to run, but the line acts as a (slight) brake and reminds him that he is not entirely free from your control. A useful lesson in teaching him to come when he is called, and to remind him that you *are* in control, is when you can get your foot on the end of the line and then call him. If he takes no notice, pick up the line and give it a tug as you call him again, and – most important – praise him enthusiastically when he reaches you. It takes time and patience, but if a Dobermann is to be allowed to run free anywhere he *must* be under proper control. Even with a free run of some fifteen to twenty minutes each day when he is fully grown, he should still have at least half an hour's walk on the lead, which will strengthen his muscles, improve his gait, keep the close bond between you as he shares your outing, and keep his feet tight and cat-like. Steady walking on a hard surface is the best conditioner for a companion or a show dog.

Feeding

Well-bred, carefully reared, properly housed and lovingly cared for, a Dobermann must also be fed correctly, his diet being adequate in quantity and its content properly balanced. No longer a wild animal that hunts for food alone or with the pack, a family dog is entirely dependent on his owner to supply his needs, and for good health throughout his life good feeding is essential. If your Dobermann has come from a well-known breeder he will have had a good start, and you will be given a diet sheet when you collect him, and full instructions about how to carry on so that he can grow strong and remain healthy. These instructions should be carefully followed, especially if the diet suggested obviously suits your puppy. Before considering making any changes, consult the breeder. It is unwise anyway to alter a puppy's diet until he has completely settled down in his new home. Any change in the type of food should then be made only gradually, over a period of several days.

When there were fewer dogs around, and little was known about nutrition generally, the family pet was usually fed on household scraps and dog biscuit, with extra meat added if it was available. Now it is known that dogs need a balanced diet containing protein, carbohydrate, fat, roughage and very small amounts of essential minerals and vitamins. A dog must also have fresh drinking water available at all times. While probably most dogs are still basically fed on meat and biscuit, a great deal of research to determine the correct balance of a dog's dietary requirements has been undertaken by manufacturers; the pet food industry has developed and expanded until it is now big business. Different types of food are being made with the ingredients in correct proportion. The products with well-known brand names are prepared under hygienic conditions and strict quality control, and are highly competitive in cost and content. With a wide choice of meat and cereal products, the preference for any particular natural or manufactured type of foodstuff depends initially on the advice given to the owner when he buys his dog, and then on convenience, and the availability of the product in his area.

Raw meat can still be obtained in small quantities from butchers who mince together scraps of offal (liver, lung, spleen, kidney, etc.) with fat, and the trimmings from joints prepared for sale in their shop, but the quantity available and the balance of the ingredients (although fresh and of good quality) can vary from week to week. Meat and tripe, bought in bulk by a local supplier and then minced and frozen, can usually be bought from a pet food shop, which may also be the agent for a larger firm which delivers different sorts of cooked meats or tripe, pre-packed, and either minced or as brawn, or mixed with cereals. Some such products are chilled, others are frozen; all need to be stored under refrigeration. Most handy of all of course is tinned meat, on sale everywhere, in small shops and supermarkets alike. The moisture content of a tin of dog meat is higher than in either fresh or pre-packed dog foods, so more is needed at each meal, but greater convenience often outweighs the extra cost. Tinned meat is obtainable in many flavours, and comes either mixed with soya or other cereal to a thick paste texture, or as chunks in meat jelly.

Dog biscuits originally were made in large cakes and fed whole for the dog to chew. Later the same mixture, baked and crushed, was sold as biscuit meal graded in puppy, terrier or hound size. Today dog biscuits come in different sizes, flavours and colours, and are given as a separate crunchy snack. Biscuit meal can be either plain, or reinforced with fish meal, dried meat, fat and flavouring, with some minerals and vitamins added. Both types, plain or enriched, are generally soaked in gravy or warm water before being mixed with the meat portion of a puppy's dinner. For a fully-grown dog, many owners prefer to mix the meat with dry, unsoaked biscuit meal. Opinions differ as to which is better, so once again ask the breeder, or your vet.

The growing demand for convenience foods has led manufacturers to enlarge their range still further by making cereal-based foods for dogs, in pellet form or as expanded, crunchy pieces, from a carefully balanced blend of cereal products, protein, fat, minerals and vitamins. This type of food is claimed to be complete in itself, no meat or other additives being required, the required amount for each meal being measured and poured straight from the bag into the feeding dish, where before being given to the dog, it must be soaked or moistened according to the instructions given on the bag.

When the importance of minerals and vitamins was realised, these were added in ready-mixed powder form, generally by the spoonful, and sprinkled over the meat. Calcium and vitamin D being essential for growth and strong bone, calcium tablets and halibut liver oil capsules were in the past fed to puppies and youngsters often in over-large amounts. Gradually it has become clear that too much is as detrimental to a dog's health and physical development as too little. As regards mineral and vitamin additives, more is *not* better. Indeed, too much can be dangerous.

With such a variety of foods on sale, it can be difficult for an owner to know which to choose for his puppy, particularly if no instructions about diet were given him by the breeder. Advice has therefore been sought from Dobermann breeders throughout the UK as to what they find suits their own dogs best, and which they would recommend to others. A generous response came from many who obviously care deeply about the breed, and is gratefully acknowledged. Their helpful suggestions and comments about diet are summarised below.

Milk and milky foods for puppies Fresh milk is recommended by most breeders; a few prefer to use goats' rather than cows' milk if it is available. Some suggest puppies continue with the same brand of powdered milk they were weaned on, Litterlac, Welpi and Lactol being most often used. To either type of milk add one of the breakfast cereals, Weetabix or ReadyBrek being recommended, while it is also suggested that rice pudding, semolina or scrambled eggs can be given as a change. A handy alternative is a special milk and cereal food product for puppies such as Laughing Dog Milk Food. While it is usual to include milk in a puppy's diet up to the age of six months, one well-known breeder gives no milk at all to puppies once the bitch has left them, feeding instead meat with breakfast cereal for the morning meal.

Meat   There has always been a divergence of opinion among dog owners as to whether they should feed meat raw or cooked. Today it seems that while almost all the breeders questioned feed raw meat to their puppies from three weeks of age, and continue throughout their life, some strongly advise using only meat that is cooked. The same advice applies to tripe; raw tripe can be added to a puppy's diet at five weeks and used with or instead of meat thereafter, while the supporters of cooked meat recommended giving tripe only if that too is cooked. A few owners find that, for older puppies and adults, tinned meat such as Pedigree Chum is convenient and of high quality.

One breeder with considerable experience in dealing with unruly or problem dogs at a large training-club has found that some Dobermanns who are hyperactive and restless, and tending to show aggression, can be helped dramatically as much by a change of diet as by firm discipline. If such dogs are given *no red meat at all*, whether raw or cooked, but are fed on rabbit, fish, chicken or any kind of white meat (cooked, never raw), with a plain wholemeal biscuit, they often grow calmer and easier to live with.

Biscuit   Dog biscuits are given to puppies to chew, and to youngsters and adults as a snack or bedtime treat. The brands recommended are Laughing Dog Milkwheat Biscuits or Spratt's Bonios. For mixing in with meat or tripe, a majority of owners use Laughing Dog 100% Wheatmeal Biscuit Meal; as the name suggests it is plain biscuit without additives. Other brands recommended are Pedigree Chum Mixer and Spillers Winalot. Biscuit meals enriched with other cereals, fat, flavouring, etc. and which are recommended, come from the Omega, Beta, Wafcol, Valumix or Febo range.

Opinion seems to be evenly divided concerning the expanded and crunchy biscuit meals that claim to be a complete food in themselves. The number of breeders totally against 'complete' foods exactly equalled the number who in giving advice recommended those from the Omega, Beta or Wafcol range. Most of those who regularly use one of the complete foods do however add some raw meat or tripe as well.

Concerning biscuit meals, three different breeders from widely separated areas added a comment based on their own experience and observation. Some Dobermanns have a marked allergy to any cereal product containing flaked maize, and can become restless, irritable and over-active, often with some skin irritation too. These breeders strongly recommend using either a plain biscuit meal, or Wafcol Betterflake, or one of the Omega blends.

Mineral and vitamin supplements, and other extras   Research into the problems of hip dysplasia (H.D.) and Canine Vertebral Instability (C.V.I. or cervical spondylopathy, or the 'wobbler' syndrome) has led many scientists, veterinary surgeons and breeders to believe that a major contributory factor to these skeletal abnormalities in dogs is the over-use of mineral and vitamin supplements for puppies. While a deficiency of calcium and vitamin D in particular inhibits growth and the development of good teeth and strong bone, these need to be properly balanced with other essential minerals, vitamins and 'trace elements'. To make sure a growing puppy is getting his proper share of all the essential elements it is recommended by almost all breeders that a prepared supplement is added to the diet, but as both meat and biscuit contain some minerals or vitamins the amount of supplement recommended by the manufacturer should never be exceeded. One breeder in fact emphasised that the prescribed amount should be halved. Two breeders insist that no supplements at all are added to a puppy's diet, but recommend nourishing, well-balanced meals, including plenty of milk and a little bonemeal to provide calcium. The remaining breeders who offered advice give a prepared supplement in powder or tablet form, the two preparations most often recommended being SA 37 or Canovel. Stress, favourite for many years, and VetHealth VH 100, a newer product, are good alternatives. Supplements in liquid form have some supporters, but other breeders advise against them because of their high concentration and the risk of giving too much.

An extra for puppies during the weeks of maximum growth is Dunlop's Bonemeal, a valuable source of calcium. For adult dogs, extras that are sometimes added to the diet by breeders include a dessertspoonful of Mazola Corn Oil, or a sprinkling of minced garlic (cheaper than garlic tablets or capsules and eaten readily by the dogs), or a level teaspoonful of Seaweed Powder, or a few Vetzyme tablets (yeast). These are claimed either to improve the coat or to increase resistance to infection, but opinion is divided as to whether these additions have much real value. Corn oil is however high in polyunsaturated fatty acids and these are essential for a balanced diet.

A puppy needs plenty of rest. Don't over-excite or over-tire him. After a meal, put him in his bed and let him sleep. Remember every dog is an individual, and you may need to adjust slightly the quantity of food recommended on a diet sheet. Keep your puppy looking nicely rounded, and give sufficient at each meal for him to finish it within five (or at the most, ten) minutes. If food is left, give a little less at the next meal. Never leave the food bowl down for longer than ten minutes. Pick it up and put it away. Never give titbits from your own dinner-table or between meals. Keep to a regular routine.

Appetite can vary with the time of year, dogs needing more food in cold weather to make up for loss of body heat, so adjust the daily amount of food if found to be too much (or too little), while always keeping a proper balance between the meat and biscuit content, and any supplement. At the time of maximum growth (up to six months of age), a puppy will eat as much as an adult dog. Do not underfeed at this vital stage.

Some puppies do not easily digest milk, and others do best with one milky meal a day, not two. See how your puppy reacts, and adjust his meals accordingly.

As mentioned earlier, for a puppy that lives in the house, a raw beef marrow bone (sawn by the butcher into 3-inch or 4-inch lengths) makes a good toy and helps when teething. As puppies will find something to chew anyway when shedding their milk-teeth it is better to have something suitable which you can give them. It bears repeating – *never* give cooked bones, and *never* give bones of pork, poultry, rabbit or game. Don't give your puppy soft or rubber toys; a raw beef bone is best, and is enjoyed at any age.

Feeding Chart

Use the following as a general guide to the different diets recommended. Remember your puppy is an individual. Adjust quantity according to his need, his rate of growth, the time of year, etc.

Always feed meat or tripe at room temperature, *never* chilled or straight out of the fridge.

Traditional diet

8 weeks of age　4 meals daily

8 a.m.　　At least ¼ pint milk (fresh or powdered) with Weetabix or ReadyBrek.

12 noon　4 oz minced raw meat or minced tripe, mixed with 2 oz Laughing Dog Puppy Meal or Winalot. Add vitamin/mineral supplement (SA 37, Canovel or VH 100) as instructed on the packet.

4 p.m.　　Milk and cereal.

8 p.m.　　Repeat midday meal. No supplement.

Increase daily meat content by 2 oz each fortnight and increase milk according to need.

12 weeks of age   4 meals daily

8 a.m.   ½ pint milk with cereal.
12 noon   6 oz raw meat *or* 8 oz raw minced tripe, with 3 oz
            Puppy Meal. Add supplement as directed and 1 level
            teaspoon bonemeal (Dunlop's).
4 p.m.   Milk and cereal *or* milky rice or semolina pudding *or*
            scrambled egg twice a week if liked.
8 p.m.   Repeat midday meal. No supplement.

*Increase daily meat content by 1 oz each fortnight or tripe by 2 oz each
fortnight.*

16 weeks of age   3 meals daily

8 a.m.   7 oz raw meat *or* 10 oz minced tripe, with 4 oz Puppy
            Meal. Add supplement and 1 teaspoon bonemeal.
1 p.m.   ½ pint milk and cereal *or* milky rice or semolina
            pudding.
8 p.m.   Repeat morning meal. No supplement.

*Gradually increase daily amount of meat or tripe, and biscuit in
proportion.*

6 months of age   2 meals daily

8 a.m.   12 oz meat *or* 1 lb tripe with 4–6 oz Laughing Dog
            Terrier Meal or Winalot.
1 p.m.   Give half a dozen Laughing Dog Milkwheat Biscuits
            or Bonios.
8 p.m.   Repeat morning meal. Add supplement as directed.

12 months of age   1 meal daily

8 a.m.   Give Milkwheat Biscuits *or* Bonios as required.
6 p.m.   1–1½ lb meat *or* 1¼–1½ lb tripe, with 10–12 oz
            Terrier Meal. Add supplement if required.

Diet based on tinned meat and enriched biscuit (with pre-packed tripe if liked)

Ensure your puppy always has fresh water available to drink

8 weeks of age   4 meals daily

Mix 1–1½ cans Pedigree Chum Puppy Food with an equal
   volume (5–8 oz approx.) of Pedigree Chum Mixer that has
   previously been soaked in milk.
Divide between 4 meals.

Give *half* the recommended amount of vitamin/mineral supplement once a day.

12 weeks of age   4 meals daily

Mix 2 cans Pedigree Chum Puppy Food *or* 1½ cans and 8 oz tripe with an equal volume of *dry* Pedigree Chum Mixer (8–10 oz approx.).
Divide between 4 meals.
Give *half* the recommended amount of supplement and 1 level teaspoon bonemeal once a day.

16 weeks of age   3 meals daily

Mix 2–3 cans Pedigree Chum Puppy Food *or* 2 cans and 1 lb tripe, with an equal volume of dry Pedigree Chum Mixer (10–15 oz approx.).
Divide between 3 meals.
Give *half* the recommended amount of supplement and 1 level teaspoon bonemeal once a day.

6 months of age   2 meals daily

Continue with Pedigree Chum Puppy Food and tripe with dry Pedigree Chum Mixer, and half recommended amount of supplement.

12 months of age   2 meals daily

Change to Pedigree Chum Original and add to equal volume of dry Pedigree Chum Mixer. Use less tinned meat and add tripe if liked.
Divide allowance between 2 meals.

Diet using complete foods

Ensure your puppy always has fresh water available to drink

General instructions

Use Wafcol Puppy Food, Omega Extra, Beta Puppy or Febo Professional Puppy Food.
Follow the instructions given on the bag.
Measure the amount recommended for the daily ration, according to the weight of your puppy.
Divide between the number of meals indicated below.
Feed moistened, soaked or dry as instructed.

No milk or supplements required

8 weeks of age   4 meals daily

12 weeks of age   3 meals daily

The manufacturers of Wafcol and Omega suggest that if liked one meal a day can be of meat or tripe with Wafcol Yeasted Wheatmeal Rusk or Omega Crunchy Dog Food.

Feed Beta Puppy or Febo Professional Puppy Food as before, also Wafcol Puppy Food and Omega Extra.

No milk or supplements required

16 weeks of age   3 meals daily

6 months of age   2 meals daily

Change from Wafcol Puppy Food to Wafcol 27.

At 8–9 months change from Beta Puppy to Beta Field.

Continue with Febo Professional Puppy Food or Omega Extra as before.

12 months of age   2 meals daily

Because of their high concentration, the manufacturers of these complete foods suggest that an adult Dobermann should continue to have his daily ration shared between 2 meals.

Change from Febo Professional Puppy Food to Febo Professional Dog Meal.

Continue with Wafcol 27, Omega Extra or Beta Field as before.

These foods are all prepared to suit dogs that are growing, or that lead an active, working life.

When fully grown, and living as a family dog, your Dobermann will require less protein. Give him Wafcol 20, Omega Tasty, Beta Pet or Febo Professional Dog Food for a balanced maintenance diet.

5

Breeding and
Puppy-rearing

So far your Dobermann has been referred to as 'he'. Now
it is time to consider what is involved in owning a bitch,
whether you should breed from her and, if so, how to raise
a litter. The comments and advice that follow are intended
for the one-bitch owner, or the first-time owner of a
Dobermann. Anyone already established as a breeder of
good quality puppies will have the knowledge and experience, as well as adequate accommodation, both for
safeguarding a bitch when she is in season, and for rearing
good stock properly. Indeed many of them, real Dobermann enthusiasts, have supported the revision of this
chapter by giving advice and information about the way
they rear puppies. Their help is most gratefully acknowledged.

A bitch is very often the preferred choice as a family
pet, being considered easier to handle and train, more
reliable with children, less boisterous and wilful, and more
affectionate than a male. A Dobermann of either sex
makes a loyal and devoted friend and companion, but
some owners are more suited to a bitch than to a dog. Only
when she is 'on heat' or 'in season' will a bitch need special
care, to protect her from unwanted suitors, and your
premises from intrusion by the local canine Romeos. With
careful management a bitch can be kept at home while she
is in season, and indeed exercised daily on the lead,
without the dogs in the neighbourhood being aware of her
condition. This requires care and vigilance, but is a small
price to pay for the pleasure of owning her.

If you have a kennel and run where she normally

spends part of each day, and it is secure and roomy as described in the previous chapter, then your bitch can safely be kept there while she is in season. If she normally lives in the house and is free to run in and out to relieve herself in a garden or backyard that is totally enclosed by a high fence or a wall, then the neighbours' dogs will not be able to intrude, and indeed may not even know that she is in season. But the boundary must be really secure; dogs can quickly find a way over, or under, or through a fence or a hedge. Don't let your bitch play in the front garden while she is in season; the local dogs will quickly get the message and gather at the front gate, or get over or through it. If your garden boundary is not secure against would-be intruders, so that your bitch cannot safely be let out to relieve herself, it is unkind to keep her a prisoner indoors all the time she is in season, or shut up in a shed or garage. Far better to put her in good boarding-kennels. Once house-trained any dog will suffer by being imprisoned in its own home, but will accept the different routine and restriction of kennels.

If you live in an urban area where the local dogs roam free, or in a modern development area where the houses all have low fences and open-plan gardens, or in premises such as a block of flats or a house divided into separate apartments, where the main entrance from the street is shared with other residents, then again it is easier to put your bitch in a good boarding-kennel while she is in season. She will be looked after and treated well, and you will be spared the embarrassment of dogs hanging around your door, and the consequent complaints from neighbours.

While the breeding cycle can vary slightly, a bitch comes into season for the first time at about nine months of age, and thereafter every six months throughout her life, the duration of each season being about twenty-one days. First indications are a slight blood-stained discharge and swelling of the vulva. During the first week or ten days, the discharge increases and becomes bright red, and the vulva and surrounding parts become steadily more swollen. As the period of true oestrus, or 'heat', approaches, the lips of the vulva soften and open slightly, and the discharge is less and generally clearer or lighter in colour. At this stage the bitch will usually be ready for mating. After some days, generally from about the sixteenth day onwards, the vulva gradually returns to normal size and becomes firm again, and the discharge dries up. After the first season most bitches are conscious of the blood-stained discharge and lick themselves clean, so you should check yours each day about the time she is due in season, so that no accidental mis-mating can occur if you have missed the onset of the discharge, and are unaware when the period of true oestrus is reached and she is ready to accept a male suitor. Before coming into season a bitch may seem more excitable than usual. She may bark more often and more noisily, and when out for her daily exercise she will urinate more frequently, and so give advance warning of her condition to the dogs in the neighbourhood. Once in season, her instinct will be to urinate often, and so leave a trail that will be eagerly followed right back to your home. For this reason, when you take her out (on the lead of course) walk very quickly and don't allow her to pause or relieve herself until you are at least a hundred yards or more away from your door. Similarly, on returning from your walk together, walk briskly and don't let her 'leave her mark' within the last hundred yards of home. To mask the odour of your bitch's season, before you take her out wipe over her hindquarters with TCP (the antiseptic that has been the stand-by of dog owners for many years, and which is pungent but harmless if licked or swallowed), or with one of the preparations sold for the purpose.

If at any time it is absolutely essential to prevent your bitch coming into season, an injection administered on the advice of a veterinary surgeon, just before her season is due, will suppress it for six months. Such an injection should be given only after very careful consideration. Although the drug companies concerned stress that there is no danger in their use, these preparations inevitably interfere with the delicate hormone balance of the breeding cycle, and the makers do admit there may be side-effects. If it causes great inconvenience to you, the family and the neighbours whenever your bitch is in season, then as I've said it is better to put her in a boarding-kennel, at least from the sixth to the twentieth day, and when she is about two years old, and fully grown and mature, have her spayed. This operation is carried out expertly these days. Modern sutures and anaesthetics, and anti-infection and pain-killing drugs, minimise risk and ease discomfort. The owner may well suffer greater stress than the patient! Spaying of pet bitches is recommended more and more by veterinary surgeons. Besides avoiding the problems of unwanted puppies, or of having to abort a litter after a mis-mating, spaying prevents trouble later, when in middle age a bitch can develop a pyometra, ovarian cysts or mammary tumours. Once fully developed physically, and happily settled in her rôle as companion and family pet, after spaying a bitch will not change in character or behaviour. She need not put on extra weight either! Give her the care, regular exercise and correct diet that every Dobermann should have, and keep your bitch fit and not fat, whether she is spayed or not. The only change after spaying is that she will never again come into season nor suffer a false pregnancy.

Perhaps when you bought your Dobermann you chose a bitch and not a dog because you felt you would like to breed from her. The best advice for a novice owner is: 'Don't'. Or don't at least until you have considered most carefully all that is involved, and what is your responsibility. In the 1950s and 1960s, when the breed was becoming established in the UK, demand for puppies grew steadily, and anyone with a reasonably well-bred bitch was encouraged to breed at least one litter from her. Then as Dobermanns became more generally available, and the breed rose in popularity, there was much indiscriminate breeding and the market became overloaded. Sadly this is still the case. There is a surplus of puppies in all parts of the country. There are also far too many unwanted adolescent and adult Dobermanns being rejected within a few months of purchase. Not all of these are the result of 'backyard breeding', or a quick cash sale by a dealer who has bought in puppies. Many come from good stock, and have been bred by well-meaning owners who give no after-sale service by keeping in touch and giving advice if needed, and who have no further interest in a dog they have bred when the new home proves unsuitable, or the purchaser cannot cope. Sometimes a Dobermann needs re-homing when circumstances within the family suddenly change, and there is genuine reason why the dog can no longer be kept. More often a Dobermann is discarded because the owner just doesn't want it any more. Dober-mann Rescue, the breed's official registered charity, collects and re-homes several hundred unwanted Dober-manns every year, but its resources are now stretched to the limit, and the interim accommodation generously provided by voluntary helpers of the Rescue service cannot take in all the Dobermanns that urgently need help. The condition of many of these unfortunate dogs and bitches is dreadful. Many have been abandoned by their owners, left shut up in empty premises, sometimes thrown out of a moving car, or tied up and left to die. Some are badly injured as well as undernourished, and need veterinary treatment and weeks of special care and nursing before they can be re-homed. Rescued Dober-manns have been found so weak from starvation as to be past recovery. Many have been beaten, kicked and bat-tered; some have been stabbed, cut; burned, or blinded – the catalogue of cruelty is horrifying, and yet such cases come into Rescue month after month. The fate of so many unwanted dogs and bitches should be a warning, and deter anyone from breeding without very good reason.

Planning and preparation

Fully realising the need to ensure that every puppy ultimately finds a good home and the right owner, you may be resolved nevertheless to breed from your bitch, and to rear the litter well. On becoming a member of one of the breed clubs you will have agreed to observe their code of ethics where it is stated firstly that a Dobermann bitch should not be mated before she is two years old, and that she should be in good health and free from communicable diseases and obvious faults. The latter of course includes faults of temperament, which are as undesirable as faults in construction. A bitch that is nervous, snappy, aggressive or unreliable should never be bred from. A litter will not 'settle' her, nor stabilise her behaviour; instead, her puppies too will be nervous, snappy, aggressive and unreliable. The temperament of the dam has the greatest influence on her puppies, and good temperament is the first essential quality in a Dobermann. Assuming however that your bitch is the right age, and is sound, healthy and well-made, with a delightful character, you need to find the best mate for her.

Great care is needed in the selection of a suitable stud dog. Ideally he should be a dog that has already produced first-class puppies from bitches of similar breeding to your own; that is, puppies of good temperament and character as well as those that look good. Studying sires and their progeny may mean going to several shows, watching carefully and assessing them yourself, but if you make a wise choice the results will be well worth the time and effort involved. The right dog for your particular bitch may not necessarily be the latest champion or the current leader in the award lists. The owner of a single bitch that is the family pet too often thinks only of 'the dog round the corner', or one owned by a friend who is eager to put him at stud. While either may be a nice Dobermann, and conveniently at hand when your bitch is due to be mated, the puppies that result will prove difficult to sell. Litters from parents of unknown quality, and no record of achievement in either the show-ring or in training, are advertised week after week in local papers and *Exchange & Mart*, and too often end up in the wrong hands. As has already been pointed out, that is the danger resulting from over-production of a popular breed. For the kind of buyer you are looking for, only a really good Dobermann puppy will do.

When you have decided which dog you would like as the sire of your future litter, you should discuss it with his owner, who before agreeing to the mating will want to know full details of your bitch's background and pedigree. If approved, the owner of the stud dog will state what fee is payable for his service, and also need to know approximately when your bitch is next due in season so that the dog will be available.

While waiting for her to come into season, get in touch with your veterinary surgeon and let him know you intend breeding from your bitch. Get his advice on worming and obtain the necessary tablets, to be given as instructed before she is in season. Check her vaccination certificate, and if soon due for renewal have her inoculations brought up-to-date. Extra booster injections are not necessary, but protection against the main killer diseases should be maintained. Obtain from the Kennel Club the green Form 1 that will be needed in due course for registering the puppies. As this form also requires the signature of the owner of the stud dog it is as well to take it with you when the bitch goes for mating. Plan ahead, so that everything is done at the proper time. Finally, if you have no kennel accommodation, or have never reared a litter before, take one last hard look at what is involved and consider if you can really cope with a litter of puppies. Are your domestic circumstances suitable? Do your plans for breeding have the full backing of others in the household? Can you provide a quiet, warm place for the bitch to whelp and care for her pups until they are on their feet? Have you an area suitable for the puppies when they are running about? It is tempting to visualise a group of attractive little Dobermanns playing together, but easy to forget that they can quickly become cold, wet, dirty and smelly without supervision, constant cleaning and mopping-up of their play-area, and regular changes of bedding. Are you prepared to spend almost five months caring for your bitch from the first day of her season and throughout the development of her puppies, until the last one goes to its new home? Will you check the suitability of any potential buyer of your puppies, so that each one finds a home where it will be treated properly, and given the care and training and companionship that every Dobermann should have?

Have you worked out the cost of rearing a good litter properly? A considerable sum will be needed. Besides the stud fee and the cost of taking the bitch for mating, there will be veterinary fees for checking the bitch before and after whelping, for tail-docking and dew-claw removal, for worming doses for bitch and puppies, and perhaps for the first inoculation before the puppies are sold. These are the basic costs, but veterinary treatment may also be needed if anything goes wrong at any time with either bitch or puppies. The extra food required – meat, milk, cereal and supplements – is not cheap, and the quantity consumed by a nursing bitch, and later her growing puppies, will surprise you. Registering the litter at the Kennel Club, advertising the puppies in one or more papers, communicating with buyers and later with the new owners are added costs. Good puppies are never cheap to rear, but having given much serious thought to what is involved you are prepared and doubtless still keen to go ahead.

Watch carefully for your bitch coming into season, and directly she first shows colour, and the vulva begins to swell, inform the stud dog's owner and discuss the best day for a visit. Bitches vary considerably, but most of them are willing to accept the dog on the eleventh, twelfth or thirteenth day after the season begins. You will probably have noticed during her previous seasons the day on which your bitch has turned her tail smartly to one side when you pass your hand along her back. Even in a docked breed this reaction is clearly seen. Tail-turning usually indicates when a bitch is ready for mating. When you notice it, advise the owner of the stud dog, and take your bitch for service within the next two days.

From the time of arrival of a visiting bitch, it is the owner of the dog who is in charge of procedure. Your bitch will need to relieve herself before she is introduced to the stud dog. He should have no other distraction apart from the bitch herself. While most breeders today prefer dog and bitch to meet and have a little flirtation before mating, natural behaviour which should lead to the bitch's willing acceptance of her mate, his owner may prefer your bitch to be given no chance of teasing or snapping at the dog. A little initial coy playfulness by a bitch may be expected if she has never been mated before, but total rejection and really aggressive behaviour towards the stud may indicate either that she is not ready, or that there is some unsuspected physical reason why she should not be bred. While it is the owners who like to make all the decisions for their dog or bitch, nature still shows when she knows best! However when it is clear they are ready for mating you will probably be asked to hold your bitch steady, while the owner directs the dog once he has mounted his mate. It has been shown that the first ejaculation of semen contains little or no sperm, almost 100 per cent being delivered within one minute of intromission. For this reason, when ejaculation has taken place an experienced breeder will hold the dog in position for about two minutes before carefully turning him. Dog and bitch will remain tied for anything from 10 to 25 minutes, during which time a considerable amount of fluid is extruded. This is fluid mainly from the prostate gland, which serves to carry the sperm further through the uterus and into the Fallopian tubes. It may be encouraged on its way by intermittent contractions by the bitch during the tie. The sperm will remain in the Fallopian tubes and fertilise the ova as they are shed. When the tie is ended and the animals part, a little fluid may escape from the bitch, but this has no significance and it is *not* necessary to raise the bitch's hindquarters to prevent loss of what is only a surplus. It is not absolutely essential that a tie takes place after copulation, the sperm having been delivered once the dog has fully penetrated the bitch and before he is turned. Many thousands of spermatozoa enter the uterus, of which only a few will be needed to connect with the ova.

The mating successfully accomplished, the dog will be put back in the house or his kennel, and the bitch allowed to rest quietly for a little while. The stud fee is now due and should be paid in full on the spot, the amount having been agreed by both parties beforehand, when the stud was booked. Now too is the most appropriate time to complete the green Form 1 which will be needed in due course for registering the puppies at the Kennel Club. Ask the owner to fill in that part which requires particulars of the stud dog, and to certify that the mating has taken place.

Opinion among the top breeders today is almost equally divided between those who advise a second mating, either 24 or 48 hours later, and those who hold the view that a single mating is all that is necessary. Again, it is the owner of the stud dog who makes the decision, according to his or her particular belief. Sometimes it is arranged for the bitch to be left and kennelled at the stud's premises for two or three days, either for a repeat mating, or to try her again with the dog if she is clearly not yet ready for service. Alternatively she may be taken home, and brought again if required the next day, or the day after. Whatever is agreed depends on the circumstances at the time and on the convenience of both owners.

A reputable breeder will as an act of courtesy usually offer a repeat mating free of charge at her next season if the bitch does not conceive this time. There is no definite obligation on the stud dog owner to offer the repeat service, the fee paid not being dependent on the production of a litter, but it is nevertheless the usual custom today.

Once back at home with your bitch successfully mated, remember that she is still in season, and will continue to be very attractive to any male dog in the vicinity for several days more. For the first four weeks after mating the bitch should be allowed to lead her normal life, with the usual amount of food and exercise. She may show no sign of being pregnant, and should not be prodded or poked to see if any puppies can be felt. Exercise a little patience and wait until there are obvious signs that she is in whelp. Do not expose her unnecessarily to any source of infection. Any virus infection, particularly canine parvovirus, can damage the embryos, so keep the bitch away from shows, or from any large gathering of dogs. Harmful chemicals in the environment, such as weed-killer and insecticides, can also cause damage in early pregnancy.

Four to five weeks after mating, at which stage the unborn puppies start to take shape, they will begin to absorb sustenance from the dam. About this time there-fore her food intake should be increased, perhaps gradu-ally changing her diet to one that is less bulky. A bitch's stomach does not enlarge as the puppies develop, so it is advisable to divide her food between two meals a day. Fresh meat or tripe and some wholemeal biscuit, with the prescribed amount of a vitamin/mineral supplement, will provide the required nourishment for her and the developing puppies without causing her discomfort. If in a couple of weeks' time it looks as if the litter may be a large one, feed her three or four times a day, with more meat than usual, but do not give her too much at one time, and do not overdo the supplements. The desire for strong puppies prompts one to give extra calcium to the bitch during pregnancy. It should again be emphasised that the addition to her diet of too much calcium and vitamin D can cause more trouble than giving none at all. As indicated in the previous chapter, the supplements most often used by breeders are SA 37 or Canovel, with Stress or VetHealth 100 as alternatives. *Give no more than the amount recommended on the packet.* A little Dunlop's Bone-meal can be added from the fifth week if liked.

While bitches are routinely wormed before they come into season, it has not hitherto been considered advisable to administer any worming medicine once they are in whelp. The larvae of *toxocara canis* (roundworms), left over from when she was a puppy, remain encysted and dormant within a bitch's body tissues; they become activated by the hormones present during pregnancy, migrate to the uterus and pass through the placenta into the foetus. That is why most puppies are born infested with worms. A preparation, Panacur, has now been developed which it is safe to give to an in-whelp bitch, and which is effective against the migrating worms and does not harm the puppies in any way. Panacur is obtainable only from veterinary surgeons, so you should consult yours once you know your bitch is pregnant, and ask him to advise on the use and dosage of this preparation.

This may also be an opportune moment to find out his views on tail-docking. It is too late to wait until the puppies are born and then discover that he is strongly against the procedure and is not prepared to remove their tails, although willing to take off the dew-claws. So long as it remains legal to shorten a puppy's tail, an owner with a newly born litter of Dobermanns can ask a veterinary surgeon to do the job, but he in turn has the right to refuse to carry out what he may consider an unnecessary procedure performed for aesthetic reasons only. Tail-docking is a contentious subject! During their training veterinary students are given no instruction in shortening puppies' tails; the whims of owners and their customs relating to pedigree dogs are considered irrelevant to the practice of veterinary medicine. Once in practice, a veterinary surgeon will usually oblige his clients by undertaking to deal with their puppies' tails, and as their professional adviser he should correctly be the one to do the job. He may however be uncertain how to estimate the ultimate length of tail desired when the puppy is fully grown, and just sever and stitch with more hope than experience. The result may be quite satisfactory, but is often disastrous. In the case of the popular guarding breeds such as the Rottweiler, Boxer or Dobermann, where the tail is customarily docked at the first or second joint, the result of a botched job by an inexperienced operator is not only unsightly but causes suffering and shock to the puppies, and distress to the bitch as well. Remedial treatment later on, to repair a stump that has become infected or that doesn't heal, or a tail that is too long and prevents the dog from sitting comfortably, involves surgery under anaesthetic by a veterinary surgeon with a better understanding of the requirements of the breed. A wise veterinary consultant with experience in the treatment of pedigree dogs will take the trouble to find out not only what different lengths of tail are left on in different breeds, but how best to shorten the tail so as to cause minimum pain to the whelp itself, and consequently no distress to the dam. This can be by skilful and accurate cutting, or by the application of a ligature of the proper texture, thickness and strength. The latter process is usually referred to as 'the rubber band method' of docking, but it does *not* mean winding a rubber band round the tail, a barbarous act which can cause gangrene. So, well before your litter is born, discuss frankly with your veterinary surgeon the procedure to be followed when the tails require to be docked. If he is unwilling to perform the task, or admits to being unaccustomed to doing the job, then find an experienced breeder who will undertake to come and do it properly. Four out of five of the breeders who so generously gave advice and help in bringing this book up-to-date dock the tails of their puppies themselves, having first learned carefully from senior experienced breeders the proper way to do it. Perhaps the stud dog owner offered to come and see your puppies and dock their tails, or the secretary of your breed club can put you in touch with a breeder living nearby who is known to do the job well. Whoever is to dock the tails, make arrangements well in advance.

The next decision to be made when planning the whelping of your bitch is whether she will have the litter outdoors in a kennel, or in the house. In either case you will need to provide a whelping-box, as her usual bed will probably not be suitable. A kennel of the type recommended in the previous chapter, which is properly constructed, well insulated and draught-proof, will need some form of lighting as well as heating, and for reasons of safety all electric fixtures must be properly installed. If your bitch is a family pet and will whelp indoors, she will need privacy and a quiet place where she can be away from bustle and noise and disturbance by members of the family coming in and out. Whether indoors or outdoors you should provide her with a whelping-box raised some 3 inches off the floor and measuring approximately 4 ft × 4 ft and 8 to 12 inches deep. Line the box with layers of newspaper and her usual blanket, and accustom your bitch to sleeping in it several days before the litter is due. Have ready two, or preferably three, squares of Vetbed to fit the box. This polyester fur material is ideal for puppies and bitches to lie on. It is warm, and being porous keeps dry, as any moisture passes through to the papers below, and it can be washed again and again. Whether indoors or in a kennel, the whelping-box must be near a source of heat. An infra-red lamp of the dull emitter type has been the standard equipment used by breeders for many years, suspended approximately 3 feet above the box, to help dry out the puppies after birth, and to provide a gentle comforting warmth when later on the bitch is resting elsewhere. Some breeders consider that this type of lamp tends to dry out the skin of bitch and puppies and prefer some other form of heating, but most still find an overhead lamp is best for keeping puppies warm. In a house with central heating, the whelping-box can be placed beside a radiator or storage heater, or in a room that can be kept very warm, as puppies can quickly become chilled.

The normal period of gestation is sixty-three days. During the second half of this period the bitch's teats and mammary glands become enlarged, there may be a slight discharge of white mucus from the vulva, and, if the litter is a large one, an increasing enlargement of the abdomen. She will need to relieve herself more often, as the puppies take up more and more room inside, and they may be seen moving when she is lying relaxed on her side. When obviously in whelp, your bitch should not be allowed to jump, or be chased or played with roughly by other dogs, and she should be exercised on the lead. In the last week she may not want to walk far, but should still have a daily outing.

During the final week of the bitch's pregnancy, your veterinary surgeon should be reminded of the date when she is due to whelp. Should this be at a weekend, when surgery hours are restricted, find out where you can ring in case of emergency and obtain help if something is wrong.

It is not always certain that a bitch will conceive and produce a litter sixty-three days after mating. She may have a false or phantom pregnancy, going through all the usual stages, even to the extent of swelling at the belly and producing milk. A bitch in this condition will then deflate on the sixty-third day, leaving an empty nest and a very disappointed owner.

Whelping

It is quite usual for a litter to arrive two or three days early. There are times however when the dam, obviously in whelp, goes two or three days beyond the date on which her puppies should be born. This could be caused by a dead puppy blocking the passage, or one incorrectly placed, or by a condition known as uterine inertia, when after a period of restlessness the bitch does not go into labour at all. Veterinary advice must be sought. Sometimes an injection is given which may lead to a puppy being born, or the veterinary surgeon may advise a caesarian operation in order to extract as many live puppies as possible and save the mother's life.

Let us assume that, as in the majority of cases, all is going well. As the time for whelping approaches, the bitch should be kept either in the kennel or indoors where the whelping-box is ready. Remove her blanket (if she has been sleeping in the box for the last few nights), and put in plenty of newspapers. When whelping is imminent the bitch's temperature will drop two or three degrees from the normal 101.5°F, the vulva enlarges and softens, she will probably refuse food, and will become more and more restless, starting to rake up the papers in the box, tearing them, and pushing them round to make a bed or nest. This first stage of whelping may last only a couple of hours, or go on all day (or all night).

As the first puppy enters the pelvis the dam will begin to strain; she may pant, and probably tremble a little. Sometimes a puppy will follow within the next few minutes, but rhythmic abdominal contractions may continue for about an hour until the water bag appears, which may rupture early, or be broken by the bitch, who will clean up the fluid. The puppy should quickly follow. As each puppy is born it is natural for the bitch to break open the membrane or bag in which the puppy is encased, and release it from her body by biting through the umbilical cord. Occasionally, especially if it is her first litter, she may not know what to do when the first puppy arrives. It is a simple matter for you to help by breaking the bag with finger and thumb, so that the protective liquid can escape and the puppy is able to breathe. If necessary, clean any mucus or fluid from the puppy's mouth and nose, or hold it out to the bitch for her to lick and clean up. Her vigorous licking will dry the puppy and stimulate it to breathe. If the umbilical cord is still intact you may have to deal with this too. Many breeders advise cutting the cord about 2 inches from the puppy's body, using sterilised scissors. Some veterinary surgeons however advise the owner to hold the puppy round its body, close middle finger and thumb firmly on the cord and pull it apart with the fingers of the other hand. This crushing of the cord, rather than cutting it, approximates more nearly to the action of the bitch, who normally crushes and bites off the cord with her teeth.

Should the puppy be inert and obviously not breathing, it almost certainly means there is mucus or some obstruction in the throat or nose. In such cases hold the puppy firmly by the hindquarters, with the head hanging down, and shake vigorously three or four times. This should remove the mucus and allow the puppy to breathe. If still reluctant to breathe, open the mouth gently with the tip of a finger and clean out any remaining mucus, wipe the nostrils, rub the puppy quickly with a warm towel, and gently rub the chest with the towel to expel fluid and stimulate the lungs to expand. You may if necessary toss the puppy from hand to hand, the hands being held about six inches apart. Do not attempt mouth-to-mouth resuscitation, and do not continue to try to revive an inert puppy for more than three or four minutes, by which time it may have brain damage through lack of oxygen.

If the bitch can manage on her own it is best to leave her to deal with each puppy, even if she may appear to be treating it roughly. A cry or loud squeak from the puppy indicates that it has taken its first breath, and then her licking to clean and dry it, and biting of the cord, encourages it to continue to breathe and to move, and later to suckle.

Following the birth of each puppy the bitch will extrude the placenta, or afterbirth. It is quite normal for her to eat this, and she should be allowed to do so as, although it acts as a laxative, this unsightly mess is very nourishing.

Occasionally, especially after a prolonged period of straining, the bitch will stand up just at the moment of giving birth. Should this occur, quickly move the puppies to one side of the whelping-box so that they do not get wet again, or are trampled or trodden on. Also be prepared to take hold of the puppy just as it is born, because it may already be out of the enclosing membrane and the umbilical cord already severed. In these comparatively rare cases the newborn puppy could hit the floor of the box if not caught in time.

Normally a puppy is presented head first, the easiest shape for its journey through to the outside world. Sometimes the hindquarters come first, with a little more difficulty, but if there is trouble, and the puppy is left half in and half out, you must grasp it gently and firmly, and slowly draw it out as the bitch strains to expel it, but do not pull when she is between contractions. A 'breech' presentation is when the puppy comes rump first, with the hindlegs folded forwards.

Puppies do not arrive at regular intervals. Two or three may be born in fairly quick succession, followed by an interval before the next one is ready to emerge and the bitch rests, content to lick or nuzzle those already born. Once the bitch has resumed straining do not let her continue for too long without producing a puppy. Continual straining for more than an hour may indicate there is something wrong, and you should seek veterinary assistance.

Although a bitch should be interfered with as little as possible once labour starts and when the puppies arrive, she may like to have her owner there for reassurance, but one or at most two persons only should be present at the whelping. Members of the family and all other pets should be kept away.

The newspapers which were originally provided for the bitch to tear up and make into a nest become very wet and stained once the puppies start arriving, and they make a chilly damp bed for the newborn. It may be difficult to remove all the soiled paper while the bitch herself is occupied with giving birth, so have a supply of fresh newspapers beside the box – or, better still, one of the pieces of Vetbed polyester fur that fits the box – and try to cover the soiled, wet and torn papers with a clean and dry layer. Polyester fur allows moisture to pass through to the papers underneath, and although it too will become very soiled it can be washed later. This material provides the best surface for puppies and their dam to lie on. Even clean newspaper is chilly to lie on, and puppies must be kept as warm as possible if they are to survive.

If whelping is prolonged the bitch will become very thirsty. Offer her a drink of water with a little glucose or honey in it, holding the bowl so that she can drink without moving from the box.

Once breathing, and dried and warm, a puppy will soon find a teat and begin to suckle; some may need a short rest before they too start to move towards the milk bar. Should any puppy seem unwilling to suckle, press one of the dam's nipples until milk appears, and with the other hand, using forefinger and thumb, gently squeeze the sides of the puppy's muzzle until the mouth opens, and then present it to the teat. Hold the puppy on the teat until it realises that drink is at hand, when it should begin to suckle. The first milk, called colostrum, is very rich and thick, and contains antibodies against infection. These are vital if the puppy is to have the best chance of survival, so make sure that they all have their share. It may be necessary to place the smaller puppies on the easier teats at the back which otherwise tend to be monopolised by the stronger pups. Any puppy that lies away from the rest and does not feed soon becomes cold and dehydrated; it will be neglected by the bitch and will probably die within a few days.

When it looks as if there are no more puppies to come, the bitch must be taken out to relieve herself. You may have to put on her collar and lead and insist that she goes out, for she will be most unwilling to do so. While she is outside, and being watched by some other member of the family to make sure she does fully relieve herself, the puppies should be lifted gently from the whelping-box on to a warm blanket, while all the soiled papers are removed and replaced with a few layers of clean dry papers, and a fresh piece of Vetbed laid on top. Put back the puppies before the bitch returns, as the sight of anyone handling them can cause her distress, and watch to see that she does not trample on any of them in her haste to get back. Make sure she is happily settled, with all the puppies tucked in close beside her, and offer her a meal. After hours of strenuous effort she will need something that is nourishing but easily digested. While some breeders still give their bitches only milky feeds for a day or two after whelping, it has been shown that it is meat, and not milk, that best helps a bitch to produce her own milk. Cooked fish, or chicken, or rabbit (with all bones carefully removed of course) are suitable for her first meal and are both welcome and easily digested. The bitch's bowel movements will be very loose for a couple of days after whelping, and giving her only milky feeds will tend to aggravate this condition.

With the bitch happily settled with her litter on clean dry bedding, you should inform your veterinary surgeon, and arrange for him to come and check that all is well. Even the most experienced breeders insist on a post-natal examination of their bitch. At this time too it is a courtesy to inform the owner of the stud dog of the puppies' safe arrival. Arrangements should also be made with whoever is to dock the puppies' tails. This, and the removal of dew-claws on the front legs, is usually carried out on the third day, but at least three breeders insist that the minimum shock is caused if the tails are docked (by the so-called 'rubber band method' and not by cutting) when the puppies are 24 hours old. Again it should be emphasised that tail-docking by either method *must* be performed correctly and by an expert, or unnecessary shock and distress will be caused to the puppies and their dam.

The bitch is the best provider of all the puppies' needs for the first three weeks of their life. She will feed them day and night, her milk supply becoming more plentiful as demand increases. She keeps them warm and clean, and stimulates the elimination of their urine and faeces. Proper care of the bitch at this time is very important, and is the owner's responsibility. The milk supply will dry up if the bitch becomes ill, or is under stress. If at any time after the litter is born she is restless or unhappy, behaves strangely, or seems to walk stiffly, or if the puppies cry and are not thriving, get in touch at once with your veterinary surgeon. After whelping a bitch needs privacy and warmth, and a clean bed or box large enough for her to lie stretched out on her side while the puppies are feeding or sleeping. After three or four days put a blanket nearby where she can lie away from the litter if she wants a rest, and give her a short daily walk on the lead. For the sake of the bitch visitors should not be allowed even to peep round the door until the puppies are at least a week old, and no one other than the owner or veterinary surgeon, or whoever comes to dock the tails, should handle the puppies until they are on their feet and starting to take solid food.

To maintain a good supply of milk, the bitch must have fresh water always available, and she must be fed an increasing amount of nourishing, top-quality food. She will soon need at least four meals a day, five if the litter is a large one. Two can be milky feeds – fresh or powdered milk (such as Welpi, Litterlac or Lactol), egg custard, milk with ReadyBrek or Weetabix, rice or semolina pudding – plus at least two meals a day of meat, with some biscuit and the recommended amount of a vitamin/mineral supplement. Quality is important at this time, not bulk. If her normal diet is based on a complete food, this must now be one with a higher protein content, and with some meat or tripe added. Cooked rabbit (all bones removed), grated cheese, scrambled or hard-boiled eggs, or boiled fish can sometimes be added to meals as a change. A lactating bitch may require perhaps four times her normal amount of food to meet the demand of rapidly growing pups. Weigh them at birth, and at least every week after that, and you will understand just how much the bitch has given of herself to maintain their rapid growth.

Clip the tips of the puppies' nails every week, and keep

them blunted, to prevent the bitch's mammary glands becoming scratched and sore, when she may understandably become unwilling to let them suckle.

The importance of keeping bitch and puppies free from worms has already been emphasised. Very young puppies sometimes fail to thrive, and indeed they may die, because of lungs congested with worm larvae, and at any age the presence of worms in the gut prevents a puppy's absorption of nourishment. All breeders recommend that puppies are wormed every two weeks from either three or four weeks of age until they are three months old, and at least every six months after that. Panacur has already been mentioned as being suitable for worming bitches during pregnancy. It can also safely be given to puppies at two weeks old. This preparation can be obtained only from a veterinary surgeon, who will specify the amount to be given to each puppy. Other types of worming medicine can be given at three or four weeks of age, and thereafter at fortnightly intervals. The basis for many such preparations is piperazine citrate, marketed under several different brand names and obtainable over the counter as well as from the veterinary surgeon. It is very important to read the instructions carefully, and to give exactly the right dosage. Another excellent worming preparation is Lopatol; this like Panacur is available only from a veterinary surgeon.

The puppies' eyes open around two weeks of age, but do not focus properly for another week or so. At three weeks their hearing has developed, the first teeth can be felt, and the puppies are on their feet. Before this stage is reached, bitch and puppies should either be moved from the whelping area, or be given more floor space there. The area must be enclosed so they cannot come to harm or, in the early days of their mobility, get lost. Failing a proper metal puppy-pen of hinged sections, a 'barricade' of cartons or boxes laid on their side will serve to keep puppies within the area, and the bitch can easily jump these when she leaves or returns to her litter.

Once on their feet, all the puppies will try to move away from their sleeping area to relieve themselves, and soon the bitch will cease to clean up after them. Keeping the puppies clean then becomes your responsibility. Indoors this can mean constant work; sheets of newspaper on the floor can be picked up as they become soiled and replaced with clean ones, but with a large litter the floor can quickly become wet and dirty. Puppies living outside in a warm kennel, with access to a concrete run, will need thorough cleaning less constantly than when they are indoors, but wherever they are kept puppies must have a clean and hygienic environment. If you are not prepared to keep them properly, you should not have bred the litter in the first place. When on their feet, and able to see and hear, puppies should be kept where they can see people and gradually become familiar with the sights and sounds of everyday life. The most important time for learning is the period between four and sixteen weeks of age.

With a normal size litter it is best to start feeding meat at three weeks of age, but if the litter is a large one then begin a few days earlier. All but one of the breeders who have given advice on puppy-rearing start weaning with raw meat, either scraped with the back of a spoon until it is pulpy, or liquidised in an electric mixer. However the meat is prepared, the first feed should consist of one teaspoonful, given in the fingers to each puppy in turn. Having once tasted red meat they will soon become eager to take it. The quantity should be increased each day, again feeding each puppy in turn. On the third day two meat feeds should be given, and the quantity increased daily until the puppies are four weeks old, when a third feed is added between the two meat meals.

For many years this consisted of fresh milk, perhaps with a raw egg and some glucose, with Farex added a week later to make a thicker mixture. Today there is a wide choice of products available for weaning puppies, and breeders are fairly evenly divided in their opinions as to which type of food they find best. Some still give fresh milk (goats' milk when obtainable sometimes being preferred), but Weetabix, ReadyBrek or Robinson's Groats or Baby Rice are the cereals usually added when the puppies have learned to lap. Many breeders use a powdered milk,

such as Welpi, Litterlac, Laughing Dog Milk Food or
Lactol, or a milk powder for lambs, and thicken it a few
days later with Laughing Dog Puppy Meal or Pedigree
Chum Small Bite Mixer or Omega Tasty, all of which must
be previously soaked to soften. Other breeders prefer
using tinned or pelleted foods instead of basing the
puppies' additional meals on milk or a milk product.
Pedigree Chum Small Bite Mixer, also moistened with
milk, added two weeks later. From the range of complete
foods, Beta Puppy and Febo Professional Puppy Food
Pedigree Chum Small Bite Mixer, also moistened with
milk, added two weeks later. From the range of complete
foods, Beta Puppy and Febo Professional Puppy Food
both contain powdered milk and need only the addition
of warm water to make a balanced meal. Again, Wafcol
Puppy Meal and Omega Tasty can be used on their own
as directed, or with some meat or tripe added when
puppies are five weeks old. Finally, the strong preference
of a few breeders is for no milk or milk products at all to
be given to puppies, other than what they get from the
bitch. These breeders give raw meat as usual at three
weeks or earlier, and at four weeks this is finely minced
and mixed with a breakfast cereal. At five weeks minced
raw meat or tripe with Laughing Dog Puppy Meal or
Omega Tasty is given four times a day, and scrambled egg,
hard-boiled eggs or semolina pudding given sometimes as
a change. Whatever the routine, and the type of food used
for weaning puppies, a sufficient quantity must be given
to maintain their rapid growth without causing diarrhoea
or tummy upsets. All breeders emphasise that if the
puppies are doing well the chosen diet must be adhered
to. Don't keep changing.

A vitamin/mineral supplement may or may not be
necessary, depending on the type of food being given. A
little Dunlop's Bonemeal may be added at five weeks of
age, but too much calcium and vitamin D is dangerous. In
the past, over-use of halibut liver oil and a calcium/
phosphorus additive often did considerable damage. If
either Canovel or SA 37 is given, the amount prescribed
on the packet must not be exceeded; indeed, the prepared

milk powders and all the complete foods, dry or tinned, are already fortified with vitamins so that only half the prescribed amount of any supplement will be needed.

At five weeks the puppies should have four meals a day, customarily two meat meals and two milky feeds, although a few breeders prefer to give one milky feed and three meat meals at this age. By now the dam should be feeding the litter only at midday, last thing at night and first thing in the morning, and by the time the puppies are six weeks old she should have finished with them entirely. She should however still be able to go to them whenever she wants, although not inclined to stay for very long. Even when no longer getting milk from her, puppies still look to their dam for leadership, following her about, trying to lick her mouth and showing pleasure when she is there. The dam's influence is very important; it is from her that puppies first learn to accept discipline, and correction for any unsuitable behaviour, and daily contact with her should be maintained until they are seven weeks old. Given this experience they will later on more readily accept the authority of their owner, and be easier to train.

Puppies start to play at about four weeks and become steadily more active. It is fascinating to watch them at this stage; their individual characters begin to show, and you can see which is the bossy one, which has the most initiative, and which are the quieter ones, prepared to look on or take their lead from another. In playing, a puppy learns it is a member of the pack and finds its level within the little group. This is another very important stage in every puppy's development. In their play area puppies can be given a few things to play with that are not harmful, but which can be investigated and sucked or chewed. An empty cereal carton, piece of knotted cloth, short length of washing-line (not plastic), an old leather glove (not a coloured one), all these provide a passing interest and in time will be carried round triumphantly. Never give a puppy plastic or rubber or soft toys. As their teeth grow and they learn to chew, give your puppies one or two small hard biscuits, such as babies' low-sugar rusks, or half a Bonio, or a piece of Laughing Dog Milkwheat Biscuit. At first these will be ignored, or played with, but by six weeks puppies need something to chew, and pieces of wholemeal dog biscuit are ideal for them to start on. What they don't finish up, their dam will welcome!

Puppies continue to have four meals a day, usually two meat and two milky, the quantities being gradually increased each week. At six weeks about 6 oz meat or tripe should be fed daily to each puppy, but the exact amount may vary according to the individual requirement of each one. When the litter is a large one, the total amount of food required is considerable, as also is the expense involved. As has already been pointed out, properly reared puppies are never cheap. As her milk supply decreases, the bitch will need a similar reduction in her own food, and she can gradually be brought back to her normal diet. She will require regular exercise now to tone up muscles and restore her to her former physical condition.

If provisional bookings for some of the puppies have already been made, the prospective owners can come and see them when they are at the playing stage and nearly ready for sale. If able there and then to choose which puppy they would like, arrangements can be made for them to take the puppy when it is old enough. As stated elsewhere, twenty or thirty years ago puppies were kept by the breeder in their kennels and not sold until they were three or four months old. Research has now shown that the best time for a puppy to go to its new home is between seven and eight weeks of age, when transfer is least traumatic. A puppy that has been well socialised at its breeder's home will at that age adapt most easily to new surroundings, and quickly become attached to its owner. Between four and sixteen weeks of age is a vital period, both for learning and for character formation. While every puppy should have the company of its litter-mates until it is seven weeks old, it will be less capable of developing its full potential if left among them, whether in a home or a kennel environment, until three or four months old. No doubt any breeder who 'runs on' a puppy with possible show potential, and who decides later to sell it, will dispute this view, claiming that an older puppy will adapt to being the sole pet in another home more easily than one only seven weeks old. It is true that some people prefer to take a puppy that is already fully inoculated, house-trained, lead-trained, accustomed to meeting people and perhaps used to travelling in a car. Certainly if the breeder has taken the trouble to bring on the youngster and socialise it to this extent, an older puppy will transfer to a new home and settle down quite quickly. Too often however an unsold puppy is kept in a kennel environment until a buyer turns up, by which time its capacity for learning is reduced and its temperament and character may have suffered. A puppy bred from good stock and properly reared deserves to go to the right kind of home, and form its lifelong attachment to an understanding owner, when it is the right age. Our knowledge of how a puppy develops, and just what are the critical stages for mental awareness and character formation, has come from research in America with litters of puppies bred to become guide dogs for blind people.

Puppies not already booked will need to be advertised for sale. Study of recent advertisements in the local paper will show you if other Dobermann litters have recently been available in your area, and if it is worth advertising your puppies in the same way. The secretary of a breed club will take particulars of your litter and pass on your name to anyone enquiring about puppies, provided you have been a member of that club for a specified number of years. An advertisement in either of the weekly dog papers, *Dog World* or *Our Dogs*, may bring results, particularly if your puppies are bred from good show stock. If the date of a breed club show, or a nearby all-breed open show, coincides with the arrival of your litter, a half-page advertisement in the show catalogue could be worthwhile. Whatever enquiries you get, and whoever may come to see your puppies with a view to buying one, make quite sure they are suitable people to own a Dobermann, and that they understand just what is involved. Never sell a puppy to a family where everyone is out all day, nor to a couple both of whom go out to work.

Remember the questions you were asked before you were able to buy your Dobermann. Having decided to breed a litter, it is your responsibility to see all the puppies find the right homes.

As the time approaches when your puppies will go to their new homes it is important to have all the necessary documents ready for each one. The form for registering the puppies, already signed by the owner of the stud dog, should be completed once the litter is born and doing well. Details of the total number of puppies, their sex and coat colour, can now be filled in, as well as the name suggested for each puppy. Under the current system of registration it is the breeder, and not the purchaser, who must register and name all puppies in a litter. The form (with appropriate fee) should be sent to the Kennel Club. It is advisable to do this in good time, so that when the puppies are sold the Registration Certificate for each one is ready to be handed to the new owner.

Consult your veterinary surgeon about giving any inoculations before the puppies leave your premises. At the time of writing a large number of breeders do have their puppies inoculated at or before seven weeks. An equal number of breeders however prefer the new owner to ask their own vet for his advice, and to follow the vaccination programme that he suggests. Canine parvovirus is still the greatest threat to puppies once the level of maternal antibodies has dropped (their early resistance to infection being derived from the bitch's first milk); puppies are highly susceptible to this dreaded disease. The timing of vaccinations against canine parvovirus may vary as methods of controlling the virus improve. The former killer diseases, distemper, hepatitis and leptospirosis, are now well controlled by vaccines given in a single injection (and repeated a fortnight later). The age at which a puppy is inoculated against these diseases can also vary slightly according to the degree of risk in the locality. Once again it is the veterinary surgeon who will advise when to administer the vaccine. If before it is sold a puppy has been given any kind of inoculation, a certificate of vaccination must be handed to the new owner, with a written reminder too about worming the puppy, noting what particular type of medication it has already been given, and when the next dose is due.

A pedigree form should be made out for each puppy, showing three or four generations. Instructions about feeding should also be given to every owner, so prepare a diet sheet. Most breeders send a puppy off with three days' food as well, so that it is not upset by any change in its meals while it settles down. It is recommended that insurance cover is arranged for all the puppies, at least for a period of six weeks after they are sold. Pet Plan's Puppy Cover includes veterinary fees and the cost of any treatment that may be necessary should the puppy become ill, or lost, or suffer an accident once it has left the breeder. Such insurance is very worthwhile, and the new owner would be well advised to continue with similar cover.

Finally, note down for every new owner some of the important points that may be helpful. Advise patience over house-training. Point out that a puppy needs undisturbed rest and plenty of sleep, besides regular meals and the right kind of food. Stress the need for lead- and car-training, and the avoidance of too much exercise until half-grown. Emphasise the need to socialise and not isolate the puppy, while avoiding over-exposure to infection until the inoculation programme is completed. Insist that when old enough the youngster is taken to a training-class, and becomes properly controlled. Warn about the possible problems that may arise as the puppy grows to adolescence, when he may become more active and potentially destructive unless given interest and the companionship of his owner. A strong and intelligent young dog if neglected will become wilful and rebellious, or bewildered and snappy. It is vital that the purchaser of any Dobermann puppy fully understands what ownership can involve. Above all, tell every new owner to keep in touch with you, and never hesitate to seek advice or help when it may be needed. Your interest should be maintained in any puppy it has been your privilege and your responsibility to breed.

6

Everyday Care and Common Ailments

Common ailments in the dog do not change much from year to year, but since Fred Curnow originally wrote a chapter under this heading new drugs and vaccines have been developed, and methods of treating some everyday problems have altered. It has therefore become necessary to revise this chapter, while basing the contents on the material previously published. Revision has been possible only with the help of our consultant veterinary surgeon, Mr David S. Wilson, B.V.M.S., M.R.C.V.S. It was he who suggested the slightly amended format, advised on present-day treatment, and kindly checked the final draft. I am very grateful indeed for his help and counsel.

A puppy from good stock that is reared by a caring breeder has a good start in life and should grow up fit and well. Properly housed and fed, and well cared for, Dobermanns are basically strong and healthy, but of course they are as liable as any other breed to meet infection or suffer an unexpected mishap at some stage in their life. That is where the veterinary surgeon comes in; he is an expert and should be considered your ally. He has had years of training and practical experience, he knows the prevalence of any particular illness in the locality at any time, and he can recognise the beginnings of more serious trouble when you may think your dog is only mildly out of sorts. There is no need to rush to the vet every time your dog coughs or is sick or has a single loose motion, but if he shows one or several of the general symptoms mentioned later *and is obviously unwell* then consult your vet without delay. Veterinary fees are not cheap (although there are forms of insurance which can help reduce your bill). Having paid a good price for your Dobermann however it is obviously foolish to grudge the fee for a consultation. One injection or a small packet of pills can often suffice to clear up the trouble before it develops into something serious or becomes chronic, requiring a long and costly course of treatment. This chapter is not a do-it-yourself veterinary manual, but aims at helping the owner of a family dog to keep it in good health.

The Everyday Care of your Dobermann

Coat

Daily grooming is most easily done by giving your dog a quick rub all over with a soft cloth or duster, or a hound-glove sold for the purpose. Once a week use a rubber grooming-glove, or a rubber dandy-brush used for ponies, to remove any scurf and dead hair. Always brush or wipe over in the direction the hair is lying. In hot weather, or if the coat is dry, apply Vaseline hair tonic or rub in coconut oil. In winter, or during cold, wet weather, the underbelly and the skin inside the thigh and the armpit can become chapped and red. Always dry your dog carefully after being out in the wet, and if the bare skin underneath shows any sign of soreness gently rub in a little Johnson's Baby Oil.

A Dobermann rarely needs to be bathed. If he is muddy, wipe with a warm, damp cloth. If he is smelly after being at kennels or among other dogs, or if he has rolled in something unpleasant, add a teaspoonful of Dettol and two or three drops of washing-up liquid to a basin of lukewarm water, wet a soft cloth in it, wring out and wipe the dog all over until the dirt is removed and the smell has gone.

Ears

Check once or twice a week that the ears are clean inside. Wipe carefully with a piece of dry cottonwool to remove any dust, grass seeds, etc., but do not poke deeply into the ear or use a cleaning bud or anything hard (even if it is wrapped in cottonwool). Any dark, smelly secretion (popularly called 'canker') should be carefully wiped away using cottonwool and an oil-based cleaner supplied for the purpose. Such veterinary ear-drops are formulated to clear infection and mites, and should be used as directed. Used regularly they prevent mite infestation and smelly discharge.

Eyes

A Dobermann's eyes are deep-set and mucus gathers in the corner. Remove this carefully with a small piece of cottonwool. If the mucus is yellow rather than grey in colour, moisten a piece of cottonwool with eye lotion such as Optrex and wipe the outer lids and the corner of the eye very carefully. If the eye is red, swollen, itching or painful, consult your vet. (See *Conjunctivitis*.)

Feet

Examine these regularly for cracked pads, small cuts, splinters or small thorns between the toes, and rough or split nails. Being so active, a Dobermann as he dashes about enjoying his daily exercise can easily bruise, chip or slightly damage his feet and nails, and will feel discomfort afterwards. For minor soreness, rub in zinc and castor oil cream, or paint superficial cracks with Friars Balsam. Persistent or deep cracks and cuts that are bleeding should be treated as advised by the vet. New applications in powder, cream or aerosol form are continually being brought out and your vet will know best which to apply in each case.

A Dobermann that lives outside, with a kennel and paved run, and has exercise running freely on a hard or gravelled surface, will not suffer from overgrown toenails. A Dobermann that lives in the house, runs about in a garden or is exercised in a park or grassy area, will need regular attention to its nails. When you buy your puppy it has already been used to having its nails attended to regularly, and this practice should be continued. Some owners like to use a strong nail-clipper to trim the claw and keep it blunt. Inexpertly used, this can be painful and make the nail bleed, which will make the dog difficult to handle next time. Personally I prefer to use a strong file, holding the foot firmly and filing each nail downwards, as when sharpening a pencil. This enables the nail to be kept blunt and smooth and obviates any pain or bleeding. Once a toenail has been allowed to grow too long it should be filed back to the required shape gradually, a little at a time over a week or two.

Teeth

Clean with a damp rag dipped in the type of tooth powder (such as Eucryl) that is sold for smokers. If tartar becomes excessive as the dog grows old, ask your vet to scale the teeth. Bleeding gums in an old dog may indicate periodontal disease or some other condition that requires veterinary attention.

Preventive medicine

As outlined above, the owner's part in preventive treatment is with the dog's external features and appearance; keeping him resistant to serious illness and free from worm infestation is the job of the veterinary surgeon. He knows the importance of immunising a puppy against the main killer diseases and may later recommend that your dog be given a newly developed vaccine against kennel cough.

Multiple vaccines in use today in one injection (repeated a fortnight later) give a puppy protection against the most dangerous infectious diseases: distemper, hepatitis, leptospirosis and parvovirus. Until immunity has been built up (generally considered to be two weeks after the second injection), your puppy should be kept away from all likely sources of infection, and allowed to play and run about only in his own home and garden. Public parks, city streets, car parks at dog shows, anywhere that is frequented by other dogs, are dangerous for puppies until the vaccination programme is complete. (But see also advice on pages 137–8.)

The veterinary surgeon will make out a Certificate of Vaccination for you to keep. This records the date of the injections and the type of vaccine used. Whenever further vaccination, or the annual 'booster' dose, is administered, the date and type are again recorded. If ever you need to put your dog in a boarding-kennel, the kennel owners will require to see the certificate of vaccination. No well-run establishment will accept a dog for boarding unless it has been fully inoculated and the programme of immunisation kept up-to-date. For anyone unfamiliar with the diseases mentioned, the following notes may be helpful.

Distemper

It is seldom that a fully inoculated dog gets distemper but the virus is still active, and responsible for serious illness and high mortality among dogs that are unprotected. Usual symptoms, any or all of which may be present, are a runny nose and discharge from the eyes, a dry cough with some retching and diarrhoea. The temperature rises to 104°–105°F, the dog has no appetite and is obviously very ill indeed. He must be isolated, kept warm and have veterinary treatment as quickly as possible. Prompt attention and careful nursing can save his life, but distemper often leaves after-effects such as chorea, paralysis, hardened pads, brown marks on the teeth and impaired general health.

Hardpad

Formerly considered a separate disease, this condition is a symptom or the result of distemper.

Hepatitis

This is a serious disease that attacks the liver and can cause sudden death. The dog looks very ill and miserable, with diarrhoea and vomiting and a high temperature as well. Only prompt veterinary attention can improve the chances of survival. In advanced cases the eye may become blue and opaque. A bitch can become a carrier of hepatitis and it is thought this may be one cause of 'fading' puppies.

Leptospirosis

There are two forms of this disease. Leptospirosis ictero-haemorrhagia is rare but deadly and is carried in rats' urine. The virus attacks the liver and kidneys, causing yellow jaundice and an insatiable thirst. The whites of the eyes and the gums have a yellowish tinge, the dog develops a high temperature, and vomits and passes blood. Immediate attention by the vet is essential.

Leptospirosis canicola is the more common form of the disease and is often referred to as 'lamp-post disease', since a dog can become infected by sniffing the urine of another dog with this condition. The virus affects the kidneys, where it does permanent damage. Symptoms are lassitude and increased thirst. After a long drink the dog will often bring it all up. Veterinary treatment, careful nursing and a restricted diet help recovery, but it is a very serious disease indeed.

Parvovirus

This disease appeared in 1978/79 and spread rapidly among the dog population all over the world, assuming epidemic proportions in some areas. Canine parvovirus is closely related to the virus which causes enteritis in cats. Symptoms are acute diarrhoea and sickness, the dog is depressed and obviously very ill. Rapid dehydration can cause collapse and death, particularly in puppies and in old dogs. Urgent veterinary treatment is essential, and if severely affected the dog is often kept at the surgery for several days on an intravenous drip. Any small puppy that becomes infected can die within a few hours as at that age the virus attacks the heart muscle. In 1981/82 a specific canine parvovirus vaccine was developed and became available for dogs of all ages. Today's adults therefore have better resistance to the disease, and bitches can pass on some immunity to their puppies, but this fades as the puppies are weaned. Vaccination is therefore essential, and anyone with a new Dobermann puppy should contact their vet at once and be advised by him as to the best age for it to be inoculated. Canine parvovirus is still widespread and highly infectious.

Kennel cough

This tiresome complaint can be transmitted from an infected dog in the vicinity. Dog shows, training-classes, matches, boarding-kennels, exercising areas, public parks, even the vet's waiting room, are therefore all likely places for the spread of kennel cough. The virus is airborne in droplets from the breath or sputum of a coughing dog and is inhaled by the next sufferer. He may cough occasionally, sounding a bit husky, or suffer frequent bouts of coughing and become very exhausted. Kennel cough at any age is debilitating but puppies and old dogs are particularly at risk. Benylin expectorant (a cough mixture for children) is soothing, or your vet may prescribe some more specific treatment. In 1981/82 a vaccine became available as an injection or as nose drops, and a single dose gives protection for up to six months. Anyone who regularly attends dog shows, or has to put their dog in a boarding-kennel during holidays, is advised to have him inoculated. Indeed kennel owners may in future insist on seeing the certificate of inoculation against kennel cough before accepting a dog for boarding.

Worms

Worm infestation has always been a problem for puppies. Many and strange have been the potions administered to them by breeders in the past. Puppies and adult dogs still get worms, but eradication is now simple and thorough. Modern drugs are supplied by the veterinary surgeon in precise doses according to the weight and the age of the dog. The old days of fasting and strong purgatives are past. (See *Roundworms* and *Tapeworms*.)

Common Ailments

Anal glands

Their secretion serves as a 'marker scent' which identifies the individual. The glands are situated on either side and just inside the anus and can become blocked. Impacted glands can become inflamed and suppurate if left untreated. The signs are when the dog drags himself along the ground in a sitting position, and continually turns to lick the anus and is obviously uncomfortable. While it is a comparatively simple matter to empty the glands by squeezing out the yellowish secretion, pain and damage can be inflicted by clumsy or inexpert handling, and it is advisable to seek help from your veterinary surgeon. He may give you a special ointment to apply, to prevent infection and clear up the soreness inside.

Bare patches (Hormonal Alopaecia)

Dobermanns and other short-coated breeds often develop bare patches on one or both sides of the back, in the region of the loin, and at the base of the tail. Both sexes are affected, bitches usually more often than dogs, the loss of hair varying according to their seasonal cycle. The condition is hereditary, and caused by an imbalance in the animal's hormone secretions. There is no skin eruption or soreness, spots or inflammation, simply a lack of hair. The area affected can vary both in size and in the sparseness of the hair. Such a patchy coat is unsightly, but has no bad effect whatever on the health or well-being of the dog or bitch concerned.

Conjunctivitis

One or both eyes may become inflamed and red. The dog will rub the eye with his paw, or rub his head along the ground to relieve the pain or itching. Inflammation may be due to grit in the eye, grass seeds lodged in the corner, by the dog lying in a draught or having been allowed to travel in a car with his head out of the window. Bathe the eye gently with a lukewarm saline solution (one teaspoonful salt to a pint of water) or with Optrex eye lotion. A tube of ophthalmic ointment prepared for veterinary use and containing a suitable antibiotic is handy for first-aid. If the inflammation persists and the dog keeps rubbing his eye, seek veterinary advice, as discharge from the eyes can indicate the onset of one of several serious diseases.

Cough

Coughing should never be ignored. It may indicate a number of serious conditions, such as distemper, heart trouble, bronchitis, hepatitis, or be due to a throat infection such as kennel cough, or to the inhalation of dust or sawdust from the kennel. Ask your veterinary surgeon to examine the dog and ascertain the cause of his cough. In the meantime for temporary relief give Benylin or a similar preparation suitable for children, and keep the dog warm and quiet. (See *Kennel cough.*)

Cuts

The smooth coat of a Dobermann gives little protection against cuts and abrasions. Treat a small slit or superficial wound by wiping carefully with cottonwool moistened in a little diluted antiseptic, dab dry, and apply some antiseptic ointment or a little veterinary powder containing an antibiotic. If the skin is torn or badly ripped it is best to have it stitched as soon as possible by your vet. His skill and modern sutures make a neat job of nasty-looking tears that would otherwise take longer to heal and leave a permanent scar.

Small cuts should dry and clot very quickly but bleeding from a deep wound needs to be stopped as soon as possible. Make a pad of some clean tissue or soft material and press it over the wound, holding it firmly in place with a bandage or whatever material may be handy in emergency. A pressure dressing is the correct treatment for both venous and arterial bleeding. Never use a tourniquet as described in old first-aid manuals, as it can make a serious situation much worse. Once the wound is under pressure and covered, get veterinary help at once. (See *Severe bleeding*.)

Cystitis

Inflammation of the bladder can be due to infection or indicate the presence of stones. It is both painful and serious. If the discomfort and the increased frequency in passing urine is due to an infection, your veterinary surgeon will prescribe the necessary medication. A stone or stones in the bladder needs removal by surgery, and is a major operation. Unfortunately the condition can recur.

Diarrhoea

A worrying symptom which should always be treated seriously. It can indeed be a temporary upset, caused by something unpleasant your dog has picked up, by a change of diet, such as giving cooked or tinned meat instead of raw, or by using a different brand of dog biscuit. The motions are frequent, very loose or nearly liquid. Having got rid of whatever caused the internal upset your dog becomes his usual bright self, and is soon looking for his next meal. In this case, feed him lightly and sparingly for a day or two, and watch the result to make sure his motions are back to normal.

Diarrhoea is however a symptom of distemper or parvovirus, or of an intestinal infection. If it continues for more than 12 hours, or if you see blood or blobs of mucus in the motions, or if your dog looks ill and depressed, get in touch at once with your vet. Do not let your dog drink water as this will make things worse. Offer a little cold *boiled* water from time to time to prevent dehydration, and give a teaspoonful of Kaolin-gel or similar veterinary preparation pending precise instructions from the vet.

Dog bites

If your dog is involved in a fight, or suffers attack from another dog, examine him very carefully for any bites. Having no protective long hair, Dobermanns are easily torn. Any bite on the ear will bleed profusely and it is best to have this stitched by your vet at once. Bites on the body, neck or throat are generally puncture wounds, and while they may hardly bleed at all, and sometimes be difficult to find even in a short-coated dog, they can be deep and cause bruising and swelling. Dog bites rapidly become septic so seek veterinary advice as soon as possible.

Eclampsia

Often called milk fever, this condition is caused by a severe lack of calcium in the bloodstream of a lactating bitch. It can happen at any time after the puppies are born, often during the first three days, and even more often after two or three weeks' nursing. The bitch becomes nervous, restless and irritable, she shivers and shakes and may be unsteady on her legs. Call the vet at once, as the bitch can collapse and die without prompt attention and immediate injections of calcium. The condition can recur so any brood bitch that has shown signs of eclampsia must be carefully watched when nursing another litter.

Eczema

An acute skin irritation indicating an allergy. It may be caused by bad feeding: too much biscuit or starch, or tinned or greasy meat, or food that is too rich. Eczema is often caused by parasites, especially fleas and lice. It can also be an allergic reaction to the dog's bedding, or to man-made fibres, such as a new nylon carpet in the home, or to being bathed in some strong detergent.

Eczema can be wet or dry. Patches usually appear on the neck, flank or belly, or on the legs. The skin becomes red and inflamed, the fur is wet from the dog licking the place continually, and then the hair is scratched away and the area grows larger, with a yellow crust. Cut away the hair round the sore place, clean carefully with cottonwool and apply something soothing, such as calamine lotion, or a paste of olive oil and flowers of sulphur, or a preparation prescribed by your vet. Try to ease the itching and prevent your dog from scratching and making the condition worse. Ascertain the cause of the allergy by changing the diet, giving less starch and more raw meat, or feeding tripe or boiled fish, and give some chopped greens such as parsley. Watch for parasites and treat accordingly. If necessary, change the dog's bedding material.

Fleas

Infestation by fleas is not very common in a Dobermann, with its short hair and lack of undercoat. Occasionally however fleas are picked up from another animal or from a dirty environment. Fleas live in the dog's coat and feed on his blood, but drop off to breed in warm, sheltered, dusty corners of the kennel or the dog's bed, or beneath a radiator or at the edge of a carpet. Their bite causes intense irritation and, if neglected, dry sores that resemble eczema. Fleas may be carriers of tapeworm eggs, a further urgent reason for getting rid of them at once. Treatment by a specific pesticide, such as Nuvan Top in an aerosol spray, kills fleas on the dog and gives protection for two weeks. A similar brand of aerosol can be used on the dog's bedding, his favourite armchair, or in any warm protected corner where the fleas may be breeding.

Gastritis

Irritation or inflammation of the stomach, which may be the result of swallowing a foreign body, or of eating filth or part of a carcass, or be a symptom of distemper, hepatitis or parvovirus infection. Whatever the cause, the condition should be treated as serious. The symptoms are continual vomiting, even after the stomach has been emptied of its contents; the dog brings up frothy, sometimes bloodstained, fluid and becomes very thirsty. Do not let him drink, for any liquid will be vomited back at once. Seek veterinary assistance before the condition worsens and the dog becomes dehydrated. Your vet will check the cause and prescribe the necessary treatment.

Lice

Lice breed on the dog itself, their eggs or 'nits' being attached to the hair with a substance resistant to pesticides which kill the adult louse. Lice feed on blood and their bite causes great irritation. Bathing the dog with a suitable insecticide shampoo will kill the lice, and this must be repeated a week later to kill the eggs that have hatched out. A third bath a week or ten days afterwards using the same insecticidal shampoo should eliminate all the parasites. Change the dog's bedding as it will probably harbour lice too.

Mange

There are two types of mange: sarcoptic and demodectic. Both are caused by mites. Sarcoptic mange is highly contagious and can be passed easily from dog to dog, and even from dog to human. It is caused by a tiny spider-like mite that burrows into the skin and causes intense itching. Small red pimples appear on the skin, usually around the neck and ears and on the head. The dog scratches the affected parts, which become crusty, bare and sore.

Demodectic or follicular mange is caused by a wormlike mite that lives in the hair follicles and the sebaceous glands of the skin. The hair falls out and pustules may develop. It is often caught from the nursing bitch, whose puppies some time later develop small bald patches, with slight irritation and a thickening of the skin. Scrapings taken by your vet and examined under a microscope will confirm the presence of mange-mites and indicate the type of treatment required to get rid of a very unpleasant and persistent condition. Modern lotions and special washes are effective but it still takes time to clear every trace of these parasites.

Metritis

An inflammation of the uterus which usually appears three or four days after whelping. It can be caused by a retained afterbirth or a remaining dead puppy, or by bacterial infection. The bitch's temperature rises, and her milk may dry up, and there is an unpleasant smell to the discharge from the vulva. Get in touch with your vet at once.

Nephritis

Inflammation of the kidneys promotes extreme thirst. It is usually the result of damage by the leptospirosis canicola virus. Modern drugs can help to improve the dog's kidney function, while a special low-protein diet can reduce the work the kidneys have to do, but the condition is incurable and is often the cause of death in older dogs.

Phantom pregnancy

A condition that occurs in many Dobermann bitches, either when they have been mated but have failed to conceive, or when no mating has taken place. The bitch goes through all the stages of an apparent pregnancy, starting about six weeks after being in season. Her abdomen swells as if she is carrying puppies; a couple of weeks later the mammary glands enlarge, the nipples grow bigger and milk can be extracted. The bitch may rake around, making a bed for her imagined puppies, and she becomes moody and withdrawn. On the date when the puppies would have been due, the pattern of pregnancy being complete, the bitch deflates, her milk starts to dry up and her mood gradually returns to normal. The belief that letting a bitch have a litter will prevent her having false pregnancies after subsequent seasons is a fallacy. The tendency to false or phantom pregnancy is part of the individual bitch's physiological make-up, whether she is a maiden or has been bred from.

Pyometra

An acute inflammation and infection of the uterus that occurs approximately two months after the bitch started her season, and usually in bitches of seven years and upwards. The bitch goes off her food, drinks a lot and may discharge a pink pus. If there is no discharge (the pus being retained within the uterus) the other symptoms could be more acute and the bitch may die from toxaemia within a few days. If the pink discharge is copious the other symptoms will be less acute. Either way, the bitch is seriously ill and requires immediate veterinary attention. Treated early, the infection may be cleared by antibiotics, but pyometra in middle age usually requires a total hysterectomy, that is, surgical removal of the ovaries and uterus.

Because of the risk of pyometra and its seriousness, many veterinary surgeons nowadays are advising owners to have bitches spayed once their breeding programme is completed, or if they are kept as family pets or working dogs and not bred from at all.

Roundworms

These are white and threadlike, round in cross-section and of varying length. Few puppies are free from them. Signs of worm infestation are a dull, harsh coat and some distension of the stomach, depraved appetite and often vomiting and diarrhoea. Puppies can now be dosed for roundworms at the age of ten days, although three weeks is more usual for the initial dose. The dose should always be repeated ten days later, and again ten days after that. The safest and most efficacious preparations for eliminating roundworms are available only from veterinary surgeons, who will advise on the type and amount to be given. Roundworms also infest adult dogs; eggs passed in the faeces are picked up by another dog and hatch in the intestines. Nowadays it is recommended that all dogs are dosed regularly with a vermifuge as a routine precaution, whether or not worms are seen or suspected.

Stings

Midges, flying ants, sand-flies, bees, wasps, etc. can annoy and sting your Dobermann on the underbelly, face, ears or mouth. Apply antihistamine cream to relieve the local inflammation, and keep a supply of antihistamine capsules in the first-aid box to reduce pain and swelling if the dog has been stung inside the mouth or throat.

Tapeworms

These intestinal parasites are white in colour and made up of flat segments joined together rather like a string of beads. They are most often found in adult dogs, who may become thin and emaciated, with a 'tucked up' belly and smelly breath. Segments of tapeworm can be seen in the dog's faeces and sometimes protrude from the anus, Elimination of a tapeworm used to be difficult, and old-fashioned preparations that were strong enough to kill the tapeworm could nearly kill the dog as well. Modern drugs are safe, quick and effective.

A tapeworm needs an intermediate host for its development, such as a flea or a rabbit, depending on the type of worm. Though nowadays easy to get rid of, tapeworm infestation is likely and will recur if the dog has fleas or has access to rabbit carcasses.

Ticks

These parasites are easily seen in the short hair of a Dobermann and are picked up in many parts of the country, particularly on heath and moorland, and in areas where sheep graze. They attach themselves firmly, burying their head beneath the skin, and their body becomes bloated and purplish-grey in colour as it fills with blood. To remove ticks without further damaging the skin, soak a piece of cottonwool in ether, surgical spirit or paraffin and hold it over the place for a few minutes, until the tick dies and releases its hold. Wipe the area of punctured skin carefully with a little dilute antiseptic, and apply some antibiotic cream or powder.

Tonsillitis

This can be caused by bacterial or virus infection. The throat is sore, red and inflamed, the dog is unwilling to eat and may retch or cough as if trying to dislodge something from his throat. Your vet will advise on suitable treatment to clear up the infection.

A halibut liver oil capsule given daily during the winter months often proves effective in building up the dog's resistance to this type of infection.

Emergencies

A few conditions which are often listed under common ailments are in fact acute enough to require emergency action, and immediate attention by a veterinary surgeon. This chapter therefore concludes by listing these briefly, so that owners may be informed and forewarned.

Fits

So-called teething fits, when a puppy goes into convulsions and may become unconscious, are usually due either to serious infestation with roundworms or to distemper. A puppy in a fit should be wrapped in a blanket and taken to the vet at once.

Fractures

In the case of severe injury or accident, or with any suspected fracture, wrap the dog in a blanket, support the injured part and get him to the vet as soon as possible.

Gastric torsion (Bloat)

This condition occurs in many large breeds of dog, including the Dobermann. An hour or two after a large meal, the stomach twists right round, so that both ends are blocked. Gas from fermentation of the food is unable to escape, so the stomach swells, causing agonising pain and increasing pressure on the heart and lungs. The dog is unable to vomit, his abdomen becomes distended, he is obviously in acute pain and has increasing difficulty in breathing. Without immediate veterinary attention (by surgery, to release the gas) the dog will collapse and die.

Gastric torsion can be caused by strenuous exercise after eating, by too much cereal in the diet, by allowing the dog to drink a lot of water just after his main meal, or it can happen to a dog that gulps his food down too quickly. Whatever the cause, and if ever it happens, the condition is fatal unless treated immediately.

Obstruction by foreign body

If your dog is seen to swallow something quite unsuitable (such as sharp bones, a tainted carcass, a toy, any small object made of metal, plastic or lead, a sock, nylon stocking, length of bandage, etc.) make him bring it up at once. The best emetic is washing soda. A few lumps forced down his throat will make him vomit immediately and the article will be safely recovered.

Any foreign body that is swallowed unknown to the owner can lodge inside the dog and cause an obstruction. Signs are discomfort and pain, the dog may vomit, or try to vomit; he may strain as if constipated and become disinclined to eat. Veterinary examination is required as soon as possible, to locate and then remove the obstruction.

Poisoning

Today there are chemicals and drugs in liquid, powder, crystal, pellet, paste or tablet form which are dangerous and can be deadly if picked up and eaten by a dog. If there is the slightest reason for suspecting yours has swallowed any such poisonous substance, notify your veterinary surgeon immediately. He will advise you if an emetic should be given, and will prepare a suitable antidote to be administered as soon as possible. Veterinary surgeons are kept informed by drug companies, and by the manufacturers of weedkillers, bleaches, agricultural chemicals and pesticides, of the constituents of their products and the best way to counter their effect if accidentally swallowed. If possible take with you to the surgery the packet or container of the substance swallowed by your dog.

Retention of urine

A very serious condition that often goes unnoticed by the owner and should be mentioned here because of the distress it causes the dog.

Frequent squatting (by a bitch) or lifting the leg (by a dog) indicates the marking of territory and is a sign to other dogs (and bitches) taking the same route. It may happen however that an obstruction is preventing the passing of any urine at all, and the unfortunate dog or bitch is frantically trying to relieve itself. Urine retention is painful, damaging and dangerous, and immediate veterinary assistance is required.

Severe bleeding

Whether from a severed vein or artery, blood loss must be checked at once by applying pressure to the wound. Hold your thumb over the place to staunch the flow and encourage clotting, while a pad is prepared. Apply this to the wound and bandage firmly. Do *not* apply a tourniquet. Keep a severe wound under direct pressure while getting the dog to the vet as quickly as possible. (See *Cuts*.)

7

Showing

'What a lovely dog! Why don't you show him?' Someone, some day, will probably say this, as your Dobermann grows to adult size. A well-bred, well-cared-for Dobermann can develop into a very handsome animal, worthy of competing against his fellows in the show-ring. You may see him simply as a family pet and companion, and may never have considered he has potential as a show dog, or you may have chosen him as a puppy with the intention of showing him later on. In either case, showing can be a pleasant hobby that brings many new friends, the tension and thrill of competition, and a day out with your own special dog.

If you are already a seasoned exhibitor, you will know about the different types of show, and how to present and handle your dog in the ring. If however you are new to showing, some advice, and explanation of shows and show procedure, may be helpful.

No dog can compete at a show unless it is registered with the Kennel Club. The first step therefore is to check that you hold the correct document. Here once again the importance of buying from a reputable breeder becomes apparent. Soon after the puppies were born the breeder will have registered the litter at the Kennel Club and named the puppies, and, when you bought your puppy, will have handed over to you the green and white Certificate of Registration bearing its KC-registered name and number. On the reverse of this registration certificate is a form for transfer of ownership. The breeder should sign this and you can complete the form and send it to the Kennel Club with the appropriate fee. The KC will record the transfer, and send back a fresh Certificate of Registration showing that you are now the owner of this dog. You can now go ahead and enter for a show.

If your puppy came from a 'backyard breeder', through an advertisement in a local paper or in a publication such as *Exchange & Mart*, it is unlikely that you will have any written proof that your puppy has been registered, or indeed that either or both of his parents were themselves KC-registered. Remember that your puppy's pedigree by itself is not an official document. It is written out by the breeder to show from which dogs and bitches the puppy is descended. It should have the KC registration number noted beside the name of sire and dam, but this is often omitted and is not compulsory. An attractive pedigree form carrying three or four generations of imposing names may impress a novice purchaser, but by itself it carries no weight at all with the Kennel Club. A dog cannot be registered at the Kennel Club unless both the sire and dam are KC-registered, and without proof of this you cannot obtain a KC registration for your dog, no matter how well-bred he is claimed to be.

Assuming however that all is in order, and your Dobermann is registered at the Kennel Club and transferred in your name, you are now able to show him when he is ready. As recommended earlier, you should join one of the breed clubs (listed in Appendix B). Their newsletters will tell you about any shows or matches they are running, and where classes are held for ringcraft training and practice. You can spoil his chances if you enter your Dobermann for a show and are unfamiliar with ring procedure, and do not know how to handle him to advantage. All over the country too there are all-breed canine societies, which are registered with the Kennel Club, with a membership drawn from their particular area. These societies also hold ringcraft classes and organise matches and shows. At these events your Dobermann will meet dogs of other breeds and become used to being among them. At a ringcraft training-class you will be given advice on the way you should stand and move and handle your dog, and he will become accustomed to being examined by different people acting as the judge. Practice is important, both at home and in class; it must be a pleasant activity that the dog enjoys, so that later in the actual show-ring he is relaxed and confident, and without apprehension.

When practised, and of course when your puppy is more than six months old and so eligible for competition under Kennel Club rules, enter him for a match. If this is confined to members of your local society, enter and have a go. If the match is to be held against a team from another society or breed club, express your willingness to take part, and if the organisers feel your puppy is ready for competition they will invite you to join the team. Matches can be 'home' or 'away' events; they are good experience for young dogs, and very good practice for novice handlers! As you both gain experience, enter your Dobermann at local shows. Buy one of the weekly dog papers, *Dog World* or *Our Dogs*, in which forthcoming shows are advertised. Classes for Dobermanns are included in most shows today, open as well as championship. The advertisement will give the name and address of the show secretary, so write and ask for a schedule and entry form. Your breed club show, whether open or championship, deserves your full support. Being confined to the one breed, and with separate classes for dogs and bitches, you can assess how your youngster compares with others of the same age, and of similar experience. Enthusiastic after some earlier success at local shows, you may enter him in the Maiden and Novice classes as well as Puppy or Junior, but don't tire a young dog, and don't rush a slow maturer. At all shows, eligibility for Puppy, Junior and Special Yearling classes is by reason of age, not the number of prizes won. Maiden, Novice, Graduate, etc. are classes limited to dogs that have previously won no more than a stated number of prizes.

Shows and matches have been mentioned but without explaining just how they differ. They should now be defined more clearly.

Exemption shows

As the name implies, these are exempt from Kennel Club regulations. They are usually run in aid of a charity, or in conjunction with a local fête or similar event, and are not organised by breed clubs or registered canine societies. No more than four classes for pedigree dogs may be scheduled, and the dogs entered need not be KC-registered. Entries are taken at the show. Besides the four for pedigree dogs, the remaining classes are fun events, such as 'the Dog with the Waggiest Tail', 'the Dog in Best Condition', 'the Dog most like its Owner', and so on. The noise and bustle and laughter, the crowd of people taking part or looking on, and all the different dogs that may be there, make an exemption show fun for the owner and excellent experience for a puppy.

Matches

Like all types of competition other than exemption shows, these are organised by canine societies and by breed clubs. All dogs taking part must be registered at the Kennel Club. The maximum number at a match is sixty-four, but thirty-two is the number usually invited to take part. A match is a knockout competition; each dog is drawn against one other; both are examined and judged in the usual way, the winner goes on into the next round and the losing dog is eliminated. There are only two prizes, which are awarded to the two finalists.

Primary shows

A maximum of eight classes may be scheduled, the highest being Maiden, so this is a small show event, held on weekend afternoons or weekday evenings. Only members of the organising society or club may compete, and entries are taken at the show. A primary show makes a good starting-point for a young puppy.

WT Ch. Chaanrose Night Queen T.D.ex, W.D.ex, U.D.ex, C.D.ex

Ch. Ashdobe's Brown Berry T.D.ex, W.D.ex, U.D.ex, C.D.ex

Koriston Pewter Strike of Doberean T.D.ex, W.D.ex, U.D.ex, C.D.ex, in action

Sally Anne Thompson

Training for manwork: (Bob Ling with Gin v. Forell)

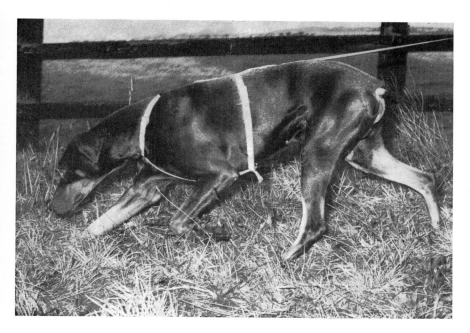

Ch. Tavey's Stormy Acacia in tracking harness

Training with dumb-bells: (Ch. Tavey's Stormy Willow, Achenburg Heida, Katina of Trevellis, Ch. Tavey's Stormy Master)

Ch. Borain's Raging Calm, winner of seventeen Challenge Certificates

Ch. Findjans Poseidon

Sanction and Limited shows

Limited to exhibitors living within a specified area, or to members of the organising society or club. Restricted to a maximum of twenty-five variety classes, the highest being Post-Graduate. A dog is not eligible if it has won a challenge certificate. Entries must be made beforehand, by a date specified in the schedule.

Open shows

As the title implies, these are open to all dogs, including champions. In the past, open shows were required to provide benching for all exhibits, but today the organisers may apply to the Kennel Club for exemption from this regulation, and open shows are advertised as being unbenched. Classification has steadily expanded to cater for more and more breeds, and there are many variety classes as well. To cope with the numbers of dogs being shown, several rings and several different judges are required, and consequently the larger all-breed open shows are sometimes held over two days. Well-established societies have a wide range of trophies and special prizes on offer. This type of show is very popular with exhibitors because a first prize won in a breed class at an open show counts as one point towards a junior warrant. This is a special award given by the Kennel Club to dogs (and bitches) that have won twenty-five points prior to the age of eighteen months. Originally points were gained by a win in puppy classes. From 1990 only points won by a dog between the ages of 12 and 18 months count. Each of the Dobermann breed clubs holds an open show every year, with separate classes for dogs and bitches, and trophies, rosettes and special prizes to be won.

Championship shows

These are the events at which Kennel Club challenge certificates are awarded, one for the best dog in the breed and another for best bitch. Challenge certificates for Dobermanns can be won at most of the general championship shows, at group championship shows (those confined to the working breeds) and at breed championship shows (those run by the various Dobermann clubs). Three challenge certificates (commonly referred to as 'c.c.s') awarded by three different judges entitle a dog to the title of champion.

A first prize won in a breed class at a championship show counts as three points towards a junior warrant. Entry to all but one of the general championship shows is open to all dogs, the exception being Cruft's Dog Show. To qualify for entry at this prestigious show, a dog must already be a champion, or be entered in the Kennel Club Stud Book, or must have won a prize (generally a first prize) at a championship show in the previous twelve months in one of several classes specified in the Cruft's schedule.

Entries must be received by the show management by a date specified in the schedule. The general championship shows are held over at least two days. Not all are weekend events; some are held mid-week. Dobermanns are included in the working group, so make sure when you have entered that you turn up on the right day! At all championship shows benching must be provided for each exhibit. A dog must be kept on its allotted bench (and securely fastened) for the duration of the show, unless it is at the ringside waiting to go in for a class, or is in the ring being judged, or unless it is being exercised (on the lead) in the official exercise area, when it may be off the bench for a maximum of fifteen minutes.

Now for the preparation of your Dobermann as a show dog. Training for show, as for every other part of his life with you, begins from the day you take your puppy home. He must become used to noises both familiar and unexpected, to having contact with strange people, and accustomed to the sounds and sights of everyday life, both in the home and beyond it. That is part of the essential education for a family dog, so to him a dog show is just another social happening or a day away with his owner. He will need training only to stand for examination and to move across and around the ring.

If you have followed the advice on everyday care given in earlier chapters, your dog will be accustomed to being handled as you groom him regularly. From the time you bring him into your home, whether or not he is ever entered for a show, take every opportunity to handle your puppy. Stroke him gently when he comes to you or stands at your side asking for attention; sometimes stroke him when you put down his dish at mealtimes; always stroke him when you put on his collar and lead before going out, and on return from a walk when you take off his collar. Ask any friends that come to visit you, and who are interested in and used to dogs, to speak to your puppy or growing youngster and stroke him when he goes to them. He must have confidence in the friends who come to see you as well as when handled later on by the judge at a show.

Next you must teach your puppy or youngster to stand still while being shown. Place him on a low table some twelve inches from the ground, or on the top step of some stairs, or on a sturdy bench in the garden. Any firm flat surface will do, provided it is not wobbly or slippery. Start by placing the dog's front legs in the desired position, and without losing contact slide your hands along his back and sides to the hindquarters and firmly place the hindlegs in the correct position. A show dog must stand foursquare, with his weight evenly distributed on all four feet. The illustrations of famous champions included in this book demonstrate the required show stance. A young dog at first may resent being placed in position, and you must persevere, encouraging him quietly, moving your hands over him gently but with firmness, and giving him a pat on the shoulder when he has remained still for a few moments, and deserves praise. Once the dog will hold this position, standing proudly and alert, you can practise placing him in show stance at ground level beside you indoors and outdoors, once or twice every day if there is a show in prospect. As he becomes accustomed to this routine, and pleased at the praise you give him (and probably a titbit as well), you can decide where you yourself will stand when actually showing him. Depending on the size of the ring, the number of dogs in the class, the noise from an adjoining ring, the temperament of your own dog and his behaviour on that day, you can either stand in front of him, so that he is looking at you, or at his side, perhaps with a hand under his chin for reassurance and to keep him in position. This is where practice in a ringcraft training-class can be helpful.

In the show-ring itself, when it comes to your turn in the class the judge will first look at your dog in profile, then from the front and from behind, will examine the head and check the mouth and teeth and the correctness of the 'scissor bite', and then run his hands over the dog to reveal the shoulder placement, depth of ribcage, firmness of topline, strength of loin, muscle tone, rear angulation, and so on. Your dog will need to know you are near while a stranger's hands are thus going over him, but you must not impede the judge's examination nor his clear view of your Dobermann. Having examined and assessed your dog standing, the judge will ask you to move him. At indoor shows long rubber mats are usually laid diagonally right across the ring and along the sides. You move your dog on these, either away and straight back again, or away and across the far end of the ring and back towards the judge, so that he can check on soundness of movement. This is where a handler can get the most out of his dog. Study yours at home and in training, and you will find he moves better at certain speeds than others. Few young Dobermanns move correctly at both slow and fast speeds, so find out which best suits your own dog and practise that particular action.

Sometimes, having seen your dog move away and directly back, the judge will ask you to do it again, and will place himself at one side, so that he can study in profile the steady movement and driving action of the dog as it crosses in front of him and back again. As a handler must at no time obstruct the judge's view of the dog, you must practise moving yours on your right as well as on your left side, changing the lead from one hand to the other at the end of the ring, so that when you bring him back and across in front of the judge again the dog is still between you and the judge. It is the dog's movement a judge wishes to see, not the handler's legs!

Because in the show-ring the dog moves freely and rhythmically and must remain standing when halted, some owners refuse to take their dog to an obedience training-class, where close heelwork is required and the dog must sit when the handler halts. This is a great mistake, and quite unnecessary. Whether show dogs or not, Dobermanns should always have training in basic obedience. The exercises in heelwork, recall, sit-stay and down-stay should be taught and practised both in class and at home, so that the dog is under control and learns to give full attention and a quick response to his owner. For this reason, far from being a drawback, if he has already learned the basic obedience exercises a dog will more readily and easily accept training in show procedure. Certainly the command 'heel' in an obedience class means the dog must concentrate and walk closely at his owner's side and at his owner's pace, with a smart sit when they halt, but movement in the show-ring, or during ringcraft training, is to the dog another and quite separate exercise. By using a different word of command when you are showing him, such as 'move' instead of 'heel', holding the lead loosely with your hand away from your body and encouraging him to gait freely, looking ahead and not at you, a dog that is carefully practised will never confuse showing procedure with heelwork. The use of a different collar and a lighter lead for show, when training as well as in the ring, will make it even more clear to your dog what is required of him. Not one of the Dobermanns mentioned in later chapters as being successful in obedience and in working trials ever tried to sit and not stand when coming to a halt in the show-ring.

Besides being well trained and skilfully handled, a Dobermann should be shown in good condition, well muscled and fit and neither too fat nor too thin. As a family pet this is only what he deserves anyway. Final preparations for a show are best made the day before. If your Dobermann lives in the house it should not be necessary to bath him before a show. Having removed any dead hair by normal grooming, a good rub-down with witch hazel, going the way of the hair, will remove all dust from his coat, and this will dry out in a minute or so. Either smear a small quantity of Vaseline hair tonic or coconut oil on the palms of your hands and rub in well, again going the way of the coat, or spray some Royal Coatalin on to a brush and apply this to the coat; give particular attention to the feet and toenails. Polish off extra grease with a piece of Turkish towelling. Check that his eyes and ears and teeth are clean, and his feet undamaged and clean, with nails neither jagged nor too long. To give your dog a neat appearance use either trimming scissors, or a pair of good scissors with blunt ends and not sharp points, and carefully trim off all whiskers and those odd long hairs above the eyes, on the cheeks and beneath the chin. Long and often straggly hairs also grow under the belly, at the rear of the rump and down the back legs, and these may need to be trimmed away carefully. Whiskers and long hairs tend to spoil the look of a good skull and well-filled foreface, which is after all what the judge is looking for. The removal of any straggly hairs on the body, particularly those on the rump and hindlegs, gives a clean look to the outline.

Preparation for next day's show should also include packing a bag with the grooming equipment just used, as well as any extras you will need for the finishing touches. Take a leather collar, benching-chain and blanket if your dog is to be benched at the show. Put in the show collar and show lead, a supply of dried liver (or whatever titbit is used as his reward for standing well), the clip for holding the card with your ring number (which will be handed to you as you go into the ring), and show pass or car park sticker required for entry to a championship show. Take a bottle of water and bowl for giving him a drink at the show, and, if the day is to be a long one, take his feeding-dish and his usual meal ready prepared, and feed him before you set off for home.

On the day of the show allow time to give your dog either his usual morning run, or a walk on the way to the showground, so that he may relieve himself. Do not wait until you are at the show itself and risk him making a mess either just outside or inside the venue. If he does so, have a plastic bag in your pocket and pick up any faeces at once, fold over the bag, knot it and drop it in the nearest litter-bin. Help to keep the show venue clean, whether it be an indoor or an outdoor event.

Once inside the show the final touch-up to your dog's coat can be given about half an hour before he is due in the ring. Use the piece of towelling that yesterday wiped away any excess oil on the coat and go over the dog to give the coat a final polish. If necessary apply a little more of the Royal Coatalin to the brush and use that for an extra sheen. To bring up the highlights, smear a little Vitapointe on to your hands and rub them lightly over muzzle, head and ears; wipe over the toes and nails with the towel or oily brush to give them a shine. Just before you leave the benches to go into the ring, finally polish your Dobermann all over with a piece of velvet or, better still, a silk scarf. KC regulations require that there must be no trace of grease on the coat when a dog is being shown.

When the class is called, be ready to go into the ring, where your dog will feel just as nervous or as confident as you are yourself. Do not fuss him unduly. Do not make him stand for a long time in any one position. Give him a pat or two, talk to him to keep his interest alive while waiting your turn to go into the centre of the ring for the judge's examination and assessment. If your dog should win his class, keep yourself available to go back when the last class has been judged, and the steward calls all winners or unbeaten dogs into the ring for the judge to award the card or rosette to the exhibit he considers is the best on that day. At an open show all Best of Breed winners compete for the Best in Show award, either in their groups or all together in the main ring. At a championship show it is usual nowadays for two judges to be appointed for Dobermanns, one for dogs and one for bitches. From those unbeaten in his classes each judge considers which is the best, and if in his opinion it is 'worthy of the title of champion' he awards it the challenge certificate. Then the winners of the dog and bitch challenge certificates are called into the ring and both judges together decide which shall be Best of Breed and which the Best Opposite Sex. At a club show that is the final award, the Best of Breed being automatically the Best in Show.

At a group championship show, where if Dobermanns are scheduled all the other breeds present will also be from the working group, the Best of Breed winners compete under a new judge for the Best in Show award. At a general championship show the Best of Breed winners similarly compete under a new judge against all those in the same group, and then on the last day of the show the six group winners (Working, Utility, Gundog, Hound, Terrier and Toy) are called to the main ring, where they are judged for the final award of Best in Show.

Early successes in the show-ring with your youngster may encourage you to continue showing, with the hope of one day making him a breed champion. Competition in the breed today is keen, presentation generally excellent, and to campaign a dog to the top costs money; you need skill, dedication, time and patience, and a little luck too, but ultimate success is worth the effort for those that achieve it. For the far greater number that are good well-made Dobermanns, but that will never quite make the top, local shows, championship shows that are within reach, and club events can bring considerable success and make showing worthwhile. A win anywhere is exciting, and at any level showing should always be an enjoyable day out among friends who share the same interest. You will learn to take the disappointments as well as the successes. Judges interpret breed standards in slightly different ways, your dog may have an off-day, you may not handle him to his best advantage, so he may win at one show and be unplaced at the next. The uncertainty is part of the fun, and whenever it comes, success is always sweet. Whether successful or otherwise, never forget that your Dobermann is a show dog only for the time he is in the ring, but he is your friend for the whole of his life, and there lies his true value.

8

The Dobermann in Obedience

The Dobermann breed clubs in the United Kingdom have from the start given support to those members who enjoy training as well as showing their dogs. Indeed the clubs have, where possible, organised training-classes, provided a suitable trainer and a good nucleus of members could be found. Most of the Dobermanns trained by their owners have, however, attended those classes open to all breeds, which are run by societies formed in all parts of the country in response to increasing general interest in dog-training. With a capable and sympathetic instructor to give advice on problems as well as guidance in the basic principles of control, a well-run class can be enjoyable and worthwhile. A Dobermann particularly enjoys sharing in any activity with its owner, and successful training leads to a closer and more understanding relationship between them.

Once the basic exercises of obedience and control have been learned most training societies encourage their members to go on and take part in competitions at shows. Success in obedience has always required a dog of balanced temperament, and an owner with patience and determination. To succeed with a Dobermann, noted for its initiative and quick reactions, means real dedication to the task and love of the breed. It is much easier to win competitions with the more submissive breeds of dog.

All classes of obedience tests at shows are run under KC rules. A leaflet may be obtained from the Kennel Club (1–5 Clarges Street, Piccadilly, London W1Y 8AB) which gives the rules and definitions for obedience classes and full details of the exercises, their markings, etc. There are five separate classes of obedience tests, graduated upwards from beginners through novice, Class 'A' and Class 'B' to the open class, Class 'C'. All classes include a stay exercise (where the dogs remain in sit, down or stand position for a given length of time until rejoined by the handler), a retrieve (progressing from an article of the handler's choice to a dumb-bell and then to an article supplied by the judge), a recall (to sit in front or follow at heel) and heelwork (walking closely at handler's side on and off the lead). The higher grades of test include additional exercises: send away and drop on command, scent discrimination, etc. In the two lowest classes handlers may give extra commands or encouragement to their dogs; in Class 'C' only one command or a signal may be given, and all the exercises are carried out with the dog off the lead. A Kennel Club Obedience Certificate may be won by the best dog and the best bitch in Class 'C' at championship shows, provided a minimum of 290 out of 300 marks is obtained. A dog or bitch winning three obedience certificates under three different judges becomes an obedience champion.

In the early days when still a rare and relatively unknown breed, Dobermanns in obedience classes attracted considerable attention, and their success in competition was good publicity and brought credit to the breed. Although it may now seem to have happened a long time ago, their individual contribution to the breed's history still deserves to be recorded. In their day these Dobermanns equalled the best in obedience. The trainability of the breed was evident and proven.

A few Dobermanns in the early days were professionally trained and handled. From the first litter bred by the Surrey Constabulary the Chief Constable, the late Sir Joseph Simpson, K.B.E., K.P.M., presented a brown dog, Mountbrowne Joe, to the Dobermann Club for stud purposes. As the Kennel Club will not allow a dog registered in the name of a club to be shown either in breed or obedience classes or working trials Joe was transferred to Mrs Mary Porterfield, who trained and handled him at all times. Following release from quarantine, Mrs Julia Curnow's Prinses Anja v't Scheepjeskerk was trained by Audrey Montgomery and handled by her with great success during the summer of 1950. The Dobermann Club's Obedience Cup is awarded annually on points for each class won during the previous calendar year. The first holder was Prinses Anja, and Mountbrowne Joe won it in the following year. A son, daughter and grand-daughter of Prinses Anja have also won this trophy in later years.

Prinses Anja v't Scheepjeskerk was the dam of Jupiter and Juno of Tavey. Jupiter became a breed champion at the age of fifteen months and then went to Bob Montgomery for training in obedience. At the same time Dennis and Philippa Thorne-Dunn sent Juno to Audrey Montgomery, with whom she stayed for almost four months. During that time the wins of brother and sister were roughly parallel: at one show Jupiter was 1st and Juno 2nd in the novice class; a week later Juno was 2nd and Jupiter 3rd (and Juno won two breed classes at the same show). The following week at a championship obedience show, with the classes divided, Jupiter won novice dog and Juno won novice bitch. It is fascinating to speculate what might have happened had Juno been able to remain with Audrey Montgomery, but she returned to her owners and became a breed champion the following year.

At this point Bob Montgomery became the joint owner of Jupiter with Julia Curnow and handled him through all the grades of obedience tests. At his very first attempt in Class 'C' Jupiter won the class and the obedience certificate. For more than a year Jupiter was in Class 'C' at championship shows and was 2nd twice (and awarded reserve for the obedience certificate) and 3rd twice. In May 1955 he again won an obedience certificate and a month later added his third. So Jupiter of Tavey became an obedience champion as well as a breed champion, an achievement unmatched in the breed anywhere for more than ten years.

Now three more Dobermanns have gained this same dual title but in competition overseas. In New Zealand a bitch, Alert Enchantress, became a breed champion in

1967, qualified in working trials and then became an obedience champion in 1971, all under New Zealand Kennel Club rules. In 1985 it was reported in the dog press that a Dobermann in Scandinavia had acquired what is surely a record number of titles: Doberhill Black Lorang is a Norwegian, Swedish, Finnish, Nordic and International show champion as well as a Norwegian, Swedish, Finnish and Nordic obedience champion, and he has qualified in working trials. In the UK, Sheila Mitchell's Ashdobes Brown Berry became a breed champion in 1978. She also successfully graduated in working trials and qualified as 'Tracking Dog Excellent' the following year. In 1986 Sheila Mitchell and her dogs went to live in Denmark, where within four months the English breed champion Ashdobes Brown Berry, T.D.ex., graduated with honours through the lower classes of obedience tests and, with top marks three times in the premier grade, became a Danish obedience champion. A remarkable achievement, particularly as she is the first Dobermann in Denmark ever to hold this title, and as she won it at the age of eleven.

For thirty-five years Jupiter of Tavey remained the breed's only British obedience champion. Then a black Dobermann bitch came to the top in national competition. Paul Gavin's Lady Gessler of Bryan graduated through to championship Class 'C' and in 1988 won an obedience certificate, the first Dobermann bitch to do so under KC rules. In 1989 she won two more, and so became an obedience champion. The winner of an obedience certificate qualifies for entry in the prestigious obedience championships at Cruft's the following year, so Lady Gessler and Paul were there both in 1989 and 1990. Though not in the prize-list on their first appearance, at Cruft's 1990 Lady Gessler was outright winner of the bitch obedience championship, a triumph for dog and handler, and for the breed.

Hitherto the nearest to the title of obedience champion had been Derek Tretheway's brown dog, Lionel of Rancliffe. A winner in every grade of tests, Lionel reached the top and was campaigned steadily in the hottest championship competition during 1967 and 1968, winning four reserve and two obedience certificates. Another brown dog, Ian Inskip's Heiner Rustic, also won his way up to championship Class 'C' at this time and he won an obedience certificate in 1968.

The only other Dobermann to win an obedience certificate has been Terry Hadley's Yuba Adonis, a son of Ch. and Ob. Ch. Jupiter. His opportunities for competition were infrequent, but having reached Class 'C' in 1963 Yuba Adonis took a reserve certificate and a year later won his first obedience certificate. His owner did not continue in this type of competition, having greater interest in practical work. Yuba Adonis once searched for and found a car key dropped in a ten-acre field, and was frequently called in to help look for lost property. His owner had his own security business and says of his dog: 'I have earned my living with him over the past few years. He has a perfect temperament; can be handled by anyone when I am with him but would not back down for a lion. He has been put to the test many times with rough blokes who meant business. As a guard he is supreme.'

The breed champions Juno of Tavey and Tavey's Stormy Acacia worked in obedience competition before their top show successes. Both were trained and handled by Audrey Montgomery. Others who became champions were trained from the start both to work and show, and were handled by their owners in breed and obedience rings alike. After gaining their title they continued in obedience competition at local and club shows. The breed champions most successful in obedience, however, were Mrs Margaret Bastable's Ch. Xel of Tavey and Harry Inskip's Ch. Tavey's Stormy Master, both of which graduated steadily through obedience and breed classes, and as breed champions both won in Class 'C' at big obedience shows.

Ch. Tumlow Whinlands Flurry was first owned by Mrs Elizabeth Harris and in her hands became a breed champion in three successive shows. Transferred later to Mrs Sheila Mitchell, Flurry became a family pet and for the first time lived in the house; she started training only on her fourth birthday. After so long in kennels Flurry had no idea of picking up any thrown article and it took nine months of patient work before she would retrieve, after which her progress was steady.

At club shows some notable family successes have been scored. In 1958, when competing in the same class, David Kingsberry's Brumbies Bandit was 1st, Brumbies Black Butterfly was 2nd, and their dam, Brumbies Black Baroness, was 4th. At the Midland Branch show in 1966 the litter-sisters Czarina and Edrika of Rhodesdobe, handled respectively by Lillian and Dudley Wontner-Smith, between them won four 1sts and three 2nds in four obedience classes.

At all-breed obedience shows, too, Dobermanns in the past sometimes took the majority of prizes: at a show in the Midlands Jim Bramley's Delmordene Aster won beginners and novice and was 2nd in Class 'A', while Bryan Pole's Annastock Moonraker (Aster's sire) was 2nd in Class 'B' and 1st in Class 'C'. Some years earlier at a show in Scotland, where these were the only Dobermanns in the obedience classes, Miss Betty Booker's Hussar of Skipwith won beginners and novice with full marks, and my own dogs Lorelei of Tavey won Class 'A' and Vyking Drum Major won Class 'B' and was 2nd in Class 'C'.

Of course there were other Dobermanns besides those named above that had success in obedience competition. All were trained and handled by their owners. Some competed for only one season, others were successful over a period of time and were regular supporters of the obedience classes which were scheduled at the breed club shows. It has not been possible to list them nor the prizes they won.

Thus far the record of Dobermanns that kept the breed flag flying in obedience competition until approximately the late 1960s. Now the account can be brought up-to-date. Enthusiasts still enjoy the challenge of competition, most of them at club shows or rallies, a few at all-breed obedience shows, which have steadily increased in number. The entries for every class at these shows have multiplied beyond belief, and the standard of performance required to win is of an almost unnatural perfection. Competitive obedience has now become a way of life for many people. The way to the top with a potential obedience champion requires complete dedication, meticulous training and daily practice to perfect every movement of both dog and handler, and, for the real enthusiast, the right kind of dog. Border Collies and Working Sheepdogs predominate among the prizewinners in the top classes, being dogs that accept endless repetition and the restriction of carrying out a learned routine time after time within a small area. All credit to the handlers who compete against them with a dog such as a Dobermann.

Breeders who care about the welfare of their puppies now urge the purchasers to take them to a training-class, not to make them obedience champions, but simply to make them *obedient*. At present, with too many Dobermanns easily available, there are frequent stories of cruelty and neglect, and reports of dogs in trouble. Being spirited and active, and a physically powerful dog when fully grown, it is essential that a Dobermann is well-behaved and under control. Once again it bears repetition – 'Teach your dog a good habit before he learns a bad one' is the recipe for success with any dog. It is vital for a Dobermann.

People buy a puppy without knowing what they are taking on; families who have never had a dog before, and whose home and circumstances may be quite unsuitable for any dog, get a Dobermann through an advertisement in their local paper, instead of seeking out a reputable breeder who may give advice and guidance. Some people want a 'guard dog', but do not realise their responsibility to keep it under control; others are prepared to give their Dobermann a good home, but without much idea of how to do it. The need for proper training under supervision is greater than ever.

The secretaries of the breed clubs (see Appendix B) can provide a list of the training-classes in their area. Some are run especially for Dobermanns, and of these, three deserve special mention. The Birmingham & District Dobermann Club (registered as a breed club in 1986) was formed in 1977 as a Dobermann Training Club and was registered as such with the Kennel Club in the following year. From a dozen or so handlers and dogs in the early days, about forty now attend regularly every week. The aim of this club is education and training, leading to a better understanding of their dogs by owners in this urban area. The basic obedience exercises of heelwork (walking on the lead without pulling or flying out at other dogs), stay (remaining quietly when left in the sit or down position) and the recall (coming when called), are the essentials for good behaviour by a dog in everyday life. Ringcraft is also practised in class. To stand for examination, or stand-stay in a show position, is just another exercise in the dog-training curriculum and does not conflict with obedience, when the dogs must sit at heel when their handler halts. The Birmingham & District Dobermann Club encourages a competitive spirit among its members. Obedience diplomas are awarded once basic control is achieved, there are ringcraft-handling competitions, a summer rally, exemption shows for Dobermann Rescue and an agility competition. In addition this go-ahead club has initiated Dobermann character tests, which require no training but are designed to show a dog's reaction to situations encountered in everyday life. A Dobermann of good character and temperament should show self-assurance, courage, loyalty and alertness. The tests are simple and straightforward, the dog is kept on the lead throughout the tests, the atmosphere is friendly and informal, but the underlying purpose is a serious one, and the club's diploma well worth having.

The Pennine Dobermann Training Club was formed in April 1984. Its original purpose was to provide ringcraft training for Dobermanns in the Manchester area, but it soon became apparent there was a far greater need to promote interest in welfare and general training, and to help owners to have a Dobermann that was sociable, well-behaved and under control. As well as instruction in the basic obedience exercises and ringcraft, a prolonged tea-interval allows owners (who are encouraged to bring the family) to talk freely about their dogs, and discuss problems and any particular difficulty. The weekly session is as much a Dobermann advisory centre as a class for formal obedience. The club encourages anyone who has a problem with their dog to come along on a training night, and no Dobermann is ever turned away.

The Dobermann Club always led the way in support of those of its members interested in obedience and training, and this has been acknowledged earlier in this chapter. The hard-working Obedience and Training Sub-Committee of this club is always ready to help with classes around London, of which the best known, and the longest running, is the Dobermann Training Class at Broxbourne, Hertfordshire. About forty Dobermanns and their owners attend every Sunday and during a ten-week course learn basic obedience and receive advice on particular problems. Members support obedience and fun classes at the Club rallies and the spring show, and often go on to do well in all-breed obedience competition, in working trials and in the Dobermann Club Working Tests.

It was the success of the latter that prompted the Sub-Committee to draw up Dobermann Obedience Tests, designed to provide incentive to owners firstly to give their Dobermann a basic grounding in social discipline, then to go on to proficiency in the obedience exercises at beginners and novice level, and eventually to enter open obedience competition. There are five different grades of test, of which the first two are of an easily attained standard and must be passed on three separate occasions before a diploma is awarded and the dog can graduate into the next higher test.

The scheme was worked out in detail and submitted to the main Committee, who gave their official permission for the Dobermann Club Obedience Tests to go ahead. The first tests took place at the club rally in 1985, with fifty-five entries. Tests were held on two more occasions later that year, with well over sixty and with fifty-five entries respectively. It is hoped that these specialised obedience tests for Dobermanns will become as well established as have the same Club's working tests. They are straightforward, well thought out, and worth working for.

So the original title of this chapter – the Dobermann in Obedience – continues valid to the present day. Circumstances may be greatly changed, but intelligence and trainability are still evident, and must always be maintained in the Dobermann breed.

9

Working Trials

In the Kennel Club Stud Book of 1953 are the names of
the first Dobermanns to gain entry by reason of wins in
breed classes at shows. The working potential of the breed
had, however, already hit the headlines and attracted
interest. For three years Dobermanns had won recognition
and Stud Book entry through their achievements in
championship working trials.

These events are run under Kennel Club rules, the
various stakes scheduled covering either one or two days
of tests. The stakes are competitive in that prizes are given
to the first three dogs in each grade, but the chief
attraction for competitors is that at championship trials a
certificate of qualification is awarded to every dog that
obtains the requisite percentage of total marks allotted to
the stake. The top working qualifications of 'Police Dog'
(P.D.) and 'Tracking Dog' (T.D.) are officially added to the
registered name of the dog by the Kennel Club in its
records and registers. It is, however, customary for the
owners of dogs that have qualified in any working trials
stake to add the grade of qualification obtained when
quoting the dog's name on a pedigree or entry form. This
unofficial practice has not been censured. Qualification
has never been easy, and graduation through the different
stakes is recognised in the dog world as proof of the ability
desirable in any working breed.

The schedule of working trials stakes remained almost
unchanged from their post-war resumption in 1947 until
the end of 1960. The Junior Stakes carried no qualification but served as an introduction to trials for those dogs
already trained for obedience competition. The other one-
day stake, officially called 'Senior B' was better known as

the 'Companion Dog Stake' since this was the qualification awarded to dogs passing the required tests of general obedience and agility. The first of the two-day trials stakes was called 'Senior A', more generally known as the 'Utility Dog Stake'. The tracking and seek-back took place in open country one day, and the general obedience and agility on the second day. From 1955 a dog had to qualify 'U.D.ex.' before being allowed to enter the Open Stakes. There have always been two separate and different Open Stakes: one Police Dog, the other Tracking Dog Stake. In both, the tracking took place on the first day and the general obedience and agility on the second. The Defence Work section of the Police Dog Stake followed the general obedience on the second day. Under Kennel Club Working Trials Rules the winner in the Open Stake at a championship trial was awarded a working trials certificate provided at least 80 per cent of maximum points had been secured. Two such working trials certificates under two different judges entitled a dog to become a working trials champion.

During the 1950s interest in dog-training increased steadily throughout the country, the standard of general obedience became higher, and more civilian handlers came into working trials competition. When the police had their own regional and national trials fewer were entered in working trials under Kennel Club rules. To meet this changing situation three members of the KC Working Trials Council – Mr R. Matchell and Mr R.M. Montgomery with the late Sir Joseph Simpson in the chair – were appointed to consider revision of the schedule. They combined the widest possible experience of training and handling dogs of different breeds, and of organising and judging working trials. Their recommendations were in due course approved and passed through all stages at the Kennel Club. The revised working trials schedule, which became operative on 1st January 1961, has continued in the same general form until now.

The Junior Stakes were abolished. The Companion Dog Stake was still a one-day event with tests of general obedience and agility, some in a modified form. In the renamed Utility Dog Qualifying Stake the jumps in the agility section were now compulsorily of maximum size and a dog was still required to qualify 'U.D.ex.' before being allowed to enter the Open Stakes. A new stake of equivalent category was introduced, called the All Breeds Working Dog Stake. In this stake the size of the jumps varied according to the size of the dog. This enabled smaller dogs to qualify in a two-day stake, but 'W.D.ex.' did not allow them to enter the Open Stakes. The Utility Dog was the Qualifying Stake until the end of 1966. The exercises of general obedience in the Open Stakes were reduced in number and greater emphasis was placed on the specialised tests relevant to either a police dog or a tracking dog. The conditions for gaining a Working Trials certificate remained the same.

The most important change was in the grouping of exercises in each stake according to their type: Heelwork (separate in C.D. only), Control, Agility, Tracking, Search, Patrol (P.D. only). The marks for each exercise were greatly reduced and the group total marks now became the vital factor in the final reckoning for a qualification. No dog could qualify unless it obtained 70 per cent or more marks in each group. The added qualification of 'Excellent' still required at least 80 per cent of the possible total marks for the stake. By these requirements the overall standard of performance at working trials was immediately raised. From 1961 on qualification in any stake became more difficult and was a real test of all-round ability, for the new system of marking allowed only a small margin of error and an otherwise brilliant dog could forfeit qualification by failure in just one exercise.

In this revised and challenging form the schedule still operates today, with one important amendment which came into force on 1st January 1967. With ever-greater interest in trials there had by then been a steady build-up of entries in the Open Stakes by dogs qualified 'U.D.ex.' but not yet up to the standard required for a P.D. or a T.D. qualification. The Open Stakes were increasingly overcrowded with a considerable proportion of the dogs still too inexperienced to have any chance of qualifying.

The Working Dog Stake was therefore upgraded by raising the tracking requirements and making the jumps in the agility group compulsorily of maximum height. The Utility Dog Stake became the first in a two-stage graduation. A dog was now required to qualify 'U.D.ex.' and then 'W.D.ex.' before being allowed to enter the Open Stake, and the position is the same today.

A leaflet may be obtained from the Kennel Club (1-5 Clarges Street, Piccadilly, London W1Y 8AB) which gives the rules and regulations currently in force for working trials, together with full details of the stakes, conduct of each exercise, their marking, etc.

In the USA and in Canada apparently similar qualification (CD, CDX, UD, TD, TDX) may be gained by purebred dogs trained for 'obedience trials' and 'tracking tests' held under the rules of the American and Canadian Kennel Clubs. The titles 'Tracking Dog' (TD) and 'Tracking Dog Excellent' (TDX) are awarded to dogs that have successfully worked a Leash Track of approximately the same standard of those of the British Utility Dog and Tracking Dog Stakes respectively. They certainly prove aptitude and ability in tracking, but the tracking tests in both North American countries are organised as a separate activity and are confined to a leash track only. The qualifications CD, CDX and UD may be gained by purebred dogs trained for obedience trials; the exercises in each of these grades more closely resemble those of the obedience classes at shows in the United Kingdom than the British working trials. Obedience trials take place at both indoor and outdoor shows, a high average pass-mark is required, and a dog must pass three times under three different judges before being granted a certificate and permitted to use the appropriate letters after its name, but the exercises of obedience and control in America and Canada are fewer in number and appear to be more limited in scope than in the British working trials. The maximum size of the jumps in the higher grades is considerably less than in our schedule, and the nosework is confined to tests of scent discrimination (and in Canada a seek-back as well), very much as in our obedience classes.

The American and Canadian CD, CDX and UD titles resulting from their obedience trials are not comparable to the C.D., C.D.ex. or U.D. qualifications gained by the Dobermanns mentioned in this account of working trials in the UK. Their TD and TDX titles are proof of a standard of proficiency in tracking equivalent to British U.D. and T.D. qualified dogs, but are considered a specialist activity and are not gained in association with any other kind of tests.

In the United Kingdom the number of working trials certificates available each year is controlled by the Kennel Club, allocation being dependent upon the support given to working trials in the previous years and upon the status of the organising body. Up to the end of 1954 the only society running championship working trials was the Associated Sheep, Police and Army Dog Society, known as 'A.S.P.A.D.S.'. Originally a German Shepherd Dog breed club putting on a championship breed show each year, membership had been opened to owners of all breeds of dog. It was the Society's policy to run working trials with the local organisation based upon the nearest A.S.P.A.D.S. branch, of which between ten and twenty existed in all parts of the country up to the middle of the 1950s. Each branch held a weekly obedience-training class for dogs of all breeds. In time the A.S.P.A.D.S. branch organisations formed the nucleus of many of the best independent training societies in existence today. From a single working trials meeting in 1947, records show two A.S.P.A.D.S. trials held in 1948 (one with Police Dog, the other with Tracking Dog Open Stakes), three in 1949 and four annually from 1950 to 1954, with the Open Stakes alternately Police Dog and Tracking Dog.

Before Dobermanns were imported or trained in the UK, Harry Darbyshire was competing in working trials with his own German Shepherd Dogs, which won and qualified in the various stakes. Sir Joseph Simpson and his wife also supported working trials with their Labradors. It was therefore not surprising that this mutual interest should be continued after Sir Joseph had become Chief Constable of Surrey and Harry Darbyshire was appointed by him sergeant in charge of the dog section. Police dog-handlers trained at constabulary headquarters at Mount-browne, Guildford, were encouraged to enter and qualify their dogs in working trials.

The first Dobermann to do so was the Surrey Constabu-lary's Ulf v. Margarethenhof. At trials in June 1949 he was entered in three stakes. At that time entry in any of the lower stakes was restricted only by reason of previous wins in higher grades and the Open Stakes were open to all. In two days of tests Ulf v. Margarethenhof won a place in each stake. He qualified C.D.ex., U.D.ex., P.D.ex., and was the winner of the Open Stake and of his first working trials certificate, a spectacular début for the breed. Entered in the Open Stakes at subsequent trials during the next fourteen months Ulf was either 2nd or 3rd on each occasion and added T.D.ex. to his other qualifications. In July 1950 he again won the Police Dog Stake and his 2nd working trials certificate and became the breed's first working trials champion.

Having gained his title Ulf v. Margarethenhof was not entered again in working trials. His ability was, however, inherited by successive generations of Dobermanns in police service. His influence on the working side was equalled only by Donathe v. Begertal, foundation bitch of the Mountbrowne line. In the classified list of qualifiers in Appendix G it can be seen that every one of the Dobermanns bred by the police traces back to Donathe v. Begertal; all but two have Ulf v. Margarethenhof as their sire or grandsire. The two dogs and three bitches from their first litter all qualified U.D.ex. (and four qualified C.D.ex. as well) before they were two years old. Of these Mountbrowne Juno and Mountbrowne Justice were not entered in trials again. The others were prizewinners in every stake in which they qualified and all of them won a working trials certificate. Mountbrowne Jenny won the Tracking Dog Stake and a certificate in 1952. Tipped to become the breed's next working trials champion this brilliant little bitch contracted distemper and died before she was three years old. Mountbrowne Joe in civilian hands won a Police Dog Stake and a certificate in 1953.

Mountbrowne Julie won the Open Stakes three times and became a working trials champion in 1955. From Donathe v. Begertal's second litter Mountbrowne Karen was retained for duty with the Surrey Constabulary, and in 1955 she, too, became a working trials champion.

The three brown Dobermanns bred by the Durham Constabulary from Mountbrowne Julie were also prize-winners in the Open Stakes where they excelled in manwork. Indeed it was their keenness – and consequent failure to recall from the running criminal without a bite – that cost them the top award time after time. One of them, Joseph of Aycliffe, did become a working trials champion like his dam and grandsire. It is believed that a comparable standard of achievement in three successive generations has not been equalled in a working breed.

Joseph's sister, Jenny of Ayclifden, was mated to her famous grandsire, W.T. Ch. Ulf v. Margarethenhof. The resulting litter of eight puppies when they were fully grown passed out successfully from their basic and advanced courses of training as police dogs, and all were retained for service in the county. It is rare to achieve 100 per cent success in temperament and ability with every member of a litter of this size. In championship working trials two of them – Arno of Aycliffe and Anna of Aycliffe – won a working trials certificate, and Alouette and Asta of Aycliffe both qualified in lower stakes.

Members of later litters of police-bred Dobermanns had fewer opportunities for competition in working trials. When entered they qualified well. Mountbrowne Yukon and Mountbrowne Astor excelled in tracking ability. Mountbrowne Amber, fresh from a course of advanced training, won both trials stakes in which she was entered in 1957 and, later, she qualified in both Open Stakes.

Such successes in trials were not cheaply won. Although there were fewer entries then than now, there were more exercises to be carried out in each stake and twelve months could elapse before there was an opportunity to enter a dog again. Police dogs, whether Dobermanns or German Shepherd Dogs, were in public competition against civilian German Shepherd Dogs and Labradors handled by men and women with many years' experience of training. The standard of the day was high.

Dobermanns in police service were, of course, selected and bred for working ability. Civilian stock was assessed primarily for conformation and show potential but did not thereby necessarily lack ability. Selection was made from original stock with intelligence and good temperament. Dobermanns bred from dogs and bitches imported by private owners made the grade when trained for working trials, although in number they were relatively few.

The first civilian Dobermanns entered in working trials were trained by professional handlers. Mountbrowne Joe has already been mentioned; his owner Mary Porterfield ranked as a professional handler because of her other work with dogs. Bob and Audrey Montgomery were professional trainers of all types of dogs. In their hands, and after only a limited time for training, Vyking Don of Tavey was a prizewinner in Junior Stakes in 1950 and Prinses Anja v't Scheepjeskerk qualified C.D.ex. and U.D. in 1951. Bob Montgomery became joint-owner with the breeder of Ch. and Ob. Ch. Jupiter of Tavey. With him Jupiter qualified C.D.ex. and won the Junior Stakes at trials in 1953.

No training courses were available then for civilian handlers wanting to train their own dogs. The exercises of basic obedience and control were learned at local all-breed training classes; a scale jump was either improvised or practised occasionally when visiting a friend with such equipment. Sound advice on the mysteries of tracking could rarely be obtained and then, generally, only from a handler with an understanding of other breeds. Experience was gained from watching trials and talking to the police handlers, and then by having a go and learning through failure and success.

Other than Mountbrowne Joe the first owner-handled Dobermann to qualify was my own Vyking Drum Major, a son of Vyking Don of Tavey. Entered in trials during our annual holiday he qualified C.D.ex. in 1951, won the stake when qualifying U.D.ex. in 1953, was 2nd in the Tracking Dog Open Stakes when Mountbrowne Karen was the winner in 1954, and qualified P.D. in 1956.

David Kingsberry first came into working trials in 1955 with his bitch Brumbies Black Baroness. She qualified U.D.ex. and was twice a prizewinner in the C.D. stakes when she qualified 'excellent'. Her son Brumbies Bandit was also twice a prizewinner when qualifying in the C.D. stakes.

Lorelei of Tavey, a daughter of Prinses Anja v't Scheepjeskerk, was chosen for me by Fred Curnow as a puppy with show and working potential. At our annual outing to a general championship show she took three reserve best bitch awards and one challenge certificate; she won first prizes in breed and obedience classes and working trials alike over a period of three years. She was 2nd in both the C.D. and the U.D. Stakes, then won the U.D. Stake four times and was the first civilian Dobermann bitch to qualify T.D.ex.

No list of names such as appears in the Appendix can convey the tension and excitement that often accompanied wins and qualifications in working trials. In 1951, when Donathe v. Begertal won both stakes in which she was entered, two of her daughters were in 2nd and 3rd place. Later that year Mountbrowne Joe, Mountbrowne Jenny and Prinses Anja v't Scheepjeskerk were in 2nd, 3rd and 4th places when qualifying in the same stake. Study of marked catalogues shows that sometimes the Dobermanns that took top placings were the only representatives of their breed in the stake.

Such, however, was not the case in 1956. A well-known manufacturer of dog foods had presented to the A.S.P.A.D.S. the Carta Carna Challenge Cup for the best working police dog in the country. The annual contest for this trophy was the P.D. Open Stake at the summer meeting. In 1956 it was on offer at A.S.P.A.D.S. trials held in the Darlington area, with local organisation in the hands of the Durham Constabulary. In the Open Stake four out of ten police dogs that were entered were Dobermanns. The U.D. and C.D. Stakes had the largest entry to date, with thirty-three and thirty-four respectively. Ten out of nineteen police dogs that were entered in the U.D. Stake were Dobermanns. The results were as spectacular as was the entry. The winner of the Open Stake was Joseph of Aycliffe, who qualified and won his first working trials certificate and the Carta Carna Cup for the 'Police Dog of the Year'. In 2nd and 3rd place behind him came W.T. Ch. Mountbrowne Karen and Jenny of Ayclifden. These three Dobermanns were the only dogs in the stake to qualify 'excellent'. Competition in the Utility Dog Stake was neck-and-neck until the final exercise, when my Lorelei of Tavey won, with Mountbrowne Olaf 2nd and Mountbrowne Pluto in 4th place. Brumbies Black Baroness was 2nd in the Companion Dog Stake. Neither before nor since have so many Dobermanns taken part in one event.

The officers in some police forces considered that participation in trials under Kennel Club rules had no value for a police dog. They therefore welcomed the introduction in 1958 of annual trials for police dogs organised on the authority of the Home Office. These were open to handlers representing every force with a dog section. The national entry at first was judged within a week. After a few years the increase in numbers led to trials being held first in different regions, the two leading dogs from each regional trial competing later in the National Police Dog Trials. The availability of their own special trials tended to diminish police support for working trials under Kennel Club rules.

At the same time a steadily increasing demand for working trials events was coming from the civilian handlers of German Shepherd Dogs, Border Collies, Boxers and Labradors. Licence to hold trials was therefore gradually extended by the Kennel Club to other societies with an interest in training. In 1955, the A.S.P.A.D.S.' allotment was raised to five championship meetings and their annual share has been maintained at this figure to the present day. The total number of working trials championships was increased to six in 1955, seven in 1957, nine in 1958, and ten in 1960. Increased support for working trials was not, however, given by many owners of Dobermanns at this time. Besides David Kingsberry and myself with dogs already mentioned, the only civilian handlers to come into trials were Derek Lee, whose Eclipse of Tavey qualified C.D.ex. in 1959, and Betty Booker, whose Hussar of Skipwith was successful in the Junior Stakes a year or two earlier. Otherwise, interest in the breed at this time was concentrated on the show possibilities and not on the working side.

When the revised schedule of working trials became operative in 1961 there were few Dobermanns left in police service. Replacements were bred by the Durham Constabulary from later imported stock, but none of them has ever been entered in civilian trials. For a year or two police dogs that added to the qualifications they had already gained under the old schedule included Arno of Aycliffe, Mountbrowne Amber, Mountbrowne Yukon and Bowesmoor Gina. Police dogs new to trials that qualified under the 1961 schedule were Faust of Cartergate, Flame and Fangio of Aycliffe, Bowesmoor Herma, Goliath of Dissington and Mountbrowne Barry. Flame of Aycliffe and Faust of Cartergate were both winners of the stake when they qualified U.D.ex.

With the phasing out of the Dobermann as a police dog a compensating interest in the working side of the breed developed among civilian owners in the 1960s, and has continued until the present day. Maverick the Brave was the first of the breed to qualify P.D.ex. under the new schedule, and Barnard of Caedan the first to qualify T.D.ex. They were soon followed by Yuba Adonis, P.D.ex., who came into trials after winning an obedience certificate, and by Dandy of Dovecote, T.D.ex. and 2nd in the stake. Also qualifying in the Tracking Dog Stake at this time (and prizewinners too, though not in first place) were Dollar Premium, Gurnard Gloomy Sunday and my Tavey's Stormy Jael, who all combined show success with working ability. The sire of each was a breed champion.

Three breed champions that have been successfully trained after gaining their title were Ch. Wyndenhelms AWOL, Ch. Hillmora the Explorer and Ch. Chevington Royal Black Magic; all qualified U.D.ex. Sheila Mitchell's Ch. Ashdobes Brown Berry combined simultaneously a show, obedience and trials career, and is to date the only breed champion to hold a T.D.ex. qualification. Working ability has been inherited in later generations too: Doberean Patience (Lorelei's daughter) won the Utility Dog Stake within a few weeks of an award of reserve best bitch at a championship show; Wyndenhelms Escort (son of Ch. AWOL) qualified U.D.ex.; Ashdobes Vaguely Great (daughter of Ch. Brown Berry) is W.D.ex. and her litter-brother Ashdobes Vaguely Noble U.D.ex. My Koriston Pewter Strike of Doberean (grand-daughter of Tavey's Stormy Jael) had considerable show success and came 3rd in a stake of fifty-one entries when she qualified T.D.ex.

From the Trevellis line of show Dobermanns, Bernard and Dorothy Horton bred Hawk of Trevellis as a working dog. Bernard trained and handled him year by year through into the Tracking Dog Stake, where Hawk was 4th but failed to qualify on that occasion. After Bernard's death Hawk passed into the ownership of Harry Appleby, an experienced handler and a friend of Bernard's. With him Hawk won the Tracking Dog Stake in 1966, qualifying T.D.ex. and gaining a working trials certificate, the first civilian-bred Dobermann ever to achieve this success. A year later Hawk qualified P.D.ex., but he did not compete in trials again.

Fifteen years passed before a Dobermann again won the top working award. Then two bitches of widely different breeding appeared in working trials, graduated into the Open Stakes and stayed at the top, surpassing every previous individual success.

John Fleet's Chaanrose Night Queen was bred from show-winning stock (her grandsires were Ch. Flexor Flugelman and Phileen's Duty Free of Tavey, and her dam had already produced three breed champions). She was bought as a family pet but showed tracking ability and enthusiasm for work, so was trained for trials. During a year of graduation through the lower stakes, Night Queen was a prizewinner every time she qualified. In 1981 at her first attempt in a Tracking Dog Stake she qualified T.D.ex., won the stake and her first working trial certificate. Campaigned later that year and into the next, Night

Queen had several near misses (but still qualified T.D.ex.
a further six times) before again winning the stake, and
with her second certificate became a working trials
champion. Just to show her title was worthily earned, she
won the T.D. Stake again two months later.

Earlier that year, 1982, John Middleweek and his brown
bitch Linrio Domingo, having previously graduated
through the lower stakes, was ready for the Tracking Dog
Stake. By contrast with Chaanrose Night Queen, Linrio
Domingo's breeding was largely German, her grandsires
being the imported German Ch. Greif von Hagenstern
and Linhoff the Pagan (a son of Wilm von Forell). At her
first attempt she qualified T.D.ex. and came 2nd in the
stake. Three months later, Linrio Domingo came first in
an entry of seventy-one, winning both the T.D. Stake and
the working trial certificate.

By these wins both bitches were eligible to take part in
the 1982 Kennel Club Working Trial Championships.
Started in 1975, this annual event is sponsored by the
Kennel Club and comprises just the two Open Stakes:
Police Dog and Tracking Dog. Entry is by invitation, and
open only to the winners of either championship stake
during the calendar year. Chaanrose Night Queen put the
seal on her year of trials success by winning the T.D. Stake
in the KC Championships, so with four wins had by then
proved herself a working trials champion twice over.

The 1983 trials season brought further success to these
two outstanding bitches. In March Linrio Domingo won
the T.D. Stake and her second certificate, and so she, too,
became a working trials champion. (In 2nd place on that
occasion was W.T.Ch. Chaanrose Night Queen.) Linrio
Domingo qualified T.D.ex. again soon afterwards; Night
Queen qualified three times more that year, being placed
2nd twice and then winning one more working trial
certificate (her fifth). Again both bitches were invited to
compete in the Kennel Club Championships, but neither
qualified on that occasion. However, W.T.Ch. Linrio
Domingo was the winner of the T.D. Stake at the Kennel
Club Championships the following year, and the only
qualifier too.

Feeding time
Sally Anne Thompson

Anne Cumbers

Puppies, aged four weeks, in the nest

Phileen's Duty Free of Tavey

Ch. Olderhill Sheboygan

Ch. Iceberg of Tavey, winner of twenty-nine Challenge Certificates

Sally Anne Thompson

Sonata of Tavey

Ch. Challenger of Sonhende

Bremenville Miss Sonya

Trudi of Ely demonstrates
a soft mouth

His bitch being a working trial champion by her wins of the Tracking Dog Stake, John Middleweek hoped she might also win the Police Dog Stake. Whereas Night Queen remained a tracking specialist, Linrio Domingo was trained in manwork as well. She did qualify P.D.ex. twice, coming 2nd each time, but a win of that stake eluded her. Her record nevertheless remains a proud one, and not easily equalled.

In 1984 Night Queen qualified T.D.ex. at five different trials, was placed, but no higher than 3rd. The following year she not only qualified three times more, but won the Tracking Dog Stake for the sixth time. In spite of nearly a year's absence owing to her handler's illness, W.T. Ch. Chaanrose Night Queen took part in the KC Working Trial Championships for the fourth time in 1985. No other Dobermann has ever achieved such a record of wins and consistent success. In all, from June 1981 to May 1986, Chaanrose Night Queen has qualified T.D.ex. no less than 24 times. It is hard enough to reach the top in trials today. To stay there in constant challenge over five years shows quite exceptional ability, dedication and teamwork by dog and handler.

The overall standard of performance required to qualify in any stake is far higher today than when the early Dobermanns qualified, but no proper comparison can be made because conditions for training and the opportunities for competition are now so different. The earliest amateur civilian handlers (of whom I was one) worked very much on their own, learning mainly by trial and error: failure in competition showed up weaknesses and faults, success confirmed that training was on the right lines. After the introduction of the new schedule in 1961, and the subsequent increasing support for working trials, regular practice in nosework and jumps, group training sessions, competitive rallies and inter-club matches were organised by enthusiasts in all parts of the country. More recently, coaching is available by professional trainers who are experts in tracking, agility and manwork as well as the exercises of general obedience. In the early days, opportunity for entering trials might come only once a year, or twice if one was lucky. The present annual total of championship trials is twenty, with twelve societies licensed to run them.

With increased opportunities however has come a longer programme of graduation: no dog may now enter either the Utility, Working or Tracking Dog Stakes at championship trials until it has previously obtained a certificate of merit in the same stake (and with the same 80 per cent of total marks) at an open trial. This certificate of merit carries only the right to enter a championship event; it does not bestow qualification in the stake concerned, which as before can be obtained only at championship trials. Organising societies must hold each year at least one open trial for every championship. This ruling was introduced in 1969. Ever-increasing entries in trials during the 1980s led to still further amendment to the rules. By the end of the decade, to qualify for entry into either the Tracking Dog or the Police Dog (now re-named Patrol Dog) Stake at a championship trial, a dog must have further proved its ability and experience by *twice* qualifying W.D.ex., and by *twice* gaining a certificate of merit in T.D. or P.D. at an open trial.

Appendix G records the name and details of every Dobermann that since 1949 has qualified U.D.ex. and above. It is clear that except for the Mountbrowne line, bred and reared exclusively for police work, no particular bloodline has proved more successful than any other in breeding dogs of working ability. Good show stock consistently produces good working trial prospects. Of course not every qualifier is a show dog, but with a Dobermann, beauty and brains can still go together.

10

Dobermann Club Working Tests

In Germany a working qualification is not required before a Dobermann can gain the title of Sieger or Siegerin; the Dobermann Verein does, however, encourage its members to qualify their show stock in the working field. In West Germany there are well-equipped clubs with fields and woodland adjoining an ample training-ground, jumps and all the usual equipment, a clubhouse with meeting-room, bar and restaurant, and outside kennels for the dogs. Membership can be confined to the owners of a particular breed, or open to all the working breeds. Instruction is given in every aspect of training for the Schutzhund qualifications (Sch.I, II, III, etc.), with discipline as strict for the handlers as for their dogs. Most of the dogs and bitches imported into the UK from Germany have been bred from stock carrying some working qualification. The first Dobermanns bred in this country were all descended from German or Dutch imports, and their successes in obedience and working trials have been recorded in previous chapters. After a decade of breeding, and the consequent expansion in numbers, some people felt it would be a good thing if owners could have the opportunity of proving their dog was still capable of working in the traditional way. The Committee of the Dobermann Club has always included those who admire the breed for its ability as well as its appearance, and they supported the idea. A copy of the German club's tests for Dobermanns was obtained and translated. A sub-Committee of members with experience of training and handling was appointed to draw up tests suitable for

Dobermanns in the UK; the members co-opted to this sub-committee were Mrs Margaret Bastable, David Kingsberry, M.R.C.V.S., Bob Ling and myself. Two meetings took place under the chairmanship of Fred Curnow in the winter of 1960–61.

At that time, 'Schutzhund' had little meaning for handlers outside Germany; it was realised later that the German tests on which the Dobermann Club based its working tests were in fact those set for the various grades of Schutzhund qualification. It is now more widely known, and respected by the handlers of working dogs in the UK, that a Schutzhund dog carries official confirmation both of working ability and the desired German character for its breed. The owners of qualified dogs would like to think that the Dobermann Club Working Tests have a corresponding worth in the UK.

While adhering to the basic pattern of the German tests it was agreed to consider amendment where any exercise might cause confusion to a dog already trained for obedience or working trials, or where they seemed inappropriate to the rôle of the civilian Dobermann in Britain. In Germany, Dobermanns are kept primarily as working dogs and are considered guards but with aptitude for nosework. They are required to show courage and be resolute in manwork and to prove they are obedient and under control. In the show-ring they are tested for temperament (reacting to a threat while being restrained on the leash), and conformation is assessed by the judge walking round and making visual examination. In Britain, Dobermanns in the show-ring must allow themselves to be handled. In their home life as family dogs they are required to be alert and courageous, but the training of civilian dogs for manwork is considered undesirable except in the hands of an expert. The inclusion of guarding, defence and attack in each grade of the Schutzhund tests did not therefore seem suitable for Dobermanns in Britain.

The German working tests consisted of 'Dobermann Tests I, II and III' and a 'Dobermann Tracking Test'. Tests I, II and III were all of similar pattern and were divided into sections: 'Scent Performance', 'General Obedience', and 'Guarding and Defence'. A few of the individual exercises were described in very great detail, others were given in terms so general that they were open to wide variations of interpretation. The working tests for British Dobermanns are the same in number but have been drawn up with a different emphasis at each stage.

Test I originally had three sections, of which two remain unchanged. The first, nosework, consists of a leash-track, laid by the handler twenty minutes previously, with two turns and two articles. The larger section, general obedience, is covered by eight exercises: heel on lead (passing through and standing among a small group of people as well as the usual turns, halts and changes of pace), heel free, drop on command and recall, retrieve (of dumb-bell or article of handler's choice), stand for examination (the dog allowing itself to be handled as if at a show), steadiness to gun-shots, the down exercise (staying down five minutes with the handler in sight), and a clear jump over a 3 ft hurdle. The third section in the original tests was headed 'Guarding and Defence', renamed later in the UK as 'Test of Courage'. The German version specified a sudden threat by a mock attacker as the handler walked by with his dog on a lead. A Dobermann should react in defence of his owner, either by standing his ground, or by going forward to challenge the stranger, or by barking to deter him. Courage must be shown; the instinct to defend his owner should be inherent in the breed. The inclusion of a test in this form was strongly criticised subsequently, on the grounds that it was an incitement to owners to teach their dogs to bite and become aggressive. When the tests were drawn up it was the opinion of the sub-committee that no biting or manwork was required. In order to avoid controversy and prevent misinterpretation, however, in 1981 this section was removed from Test I. A pass-mark in both nosework and general obedience sections is compulsory before attempting the next higher grade of test.

Test II covers more advanced nosework and general obedience and is aimed at encouraging handlers to train their dogs to a standard beyond that of the basic Test I. Nosework includes a controlled search for four articles (the dog working within an area approximately twenty-five yards each way) and the leash-track is one hour old, with four articles and four turns. Under general obedience the exercises of heel on lead, heel free, drop on command and retrieve are repeated from the earlier test except that the retrieve article is provided by the judge. Additional exercises in this section are the send away, speak on command, retrieve over a 3 ft hurdle and the standard tests of agility: 6 ft scale jump and 9 ft long jump. It requires a well-trained dog with steadiness and ability to pass this test with the required minimum of 70 per cent of total marks (at least 50 per cent in each section), but it is still within the scope of a civilian handler with an interest in working trials.

Increasing support for the working tests in the 1970s showed there was a need for an intermediate grade between Tests I and II. In September 1978 a Test IA was introduced. Entry is open to dogs holding the Club Diploma for Test I.

Test IA has three sections. In nosework the track is thirty minutes old with two turns, laid by a stranger while handler and dog are out of sight. Three articles, provided by the organising committee and approved by the judge, are laid on the track, one on each leg with the last at the end of the track. There is a search within a marked area of twenty-five yards each way for four articles provided by the judge, and a minimum of two must be found to qualify. General obedience includes heel on lead, heel free, recall, retrieve a dumb-bell, send away, clear jump over 3 ft hurdle, 6 ft long jump, sit-stay (handler in sight) and down-stay (two minutes, handler out of sight). The third section is a temperament test, roughly based on the original test of courage in Test I. A stranger (without a weapon) hides in undergrowth and makes suspicious movements and noises as the handler walks by with his dog on a loose lead. The handler halts and the stranger emerges and walks briskly to within 15 ft of him. The dog must stand his ground and remain between his handler and the stranger; he may bark or stand silent, watchful and alert. Any show of cowardice results in disqualification. A pass-mark in all three sections of Test IA must now be obtained before a dog may attempt Test II.

Having successfully passed Tests I, IA and II either of the two remaining tests may be attempted; one is suitable for a fully trained police dog, the other is a tracking test of a high standard. In Test III the leash-track is half a mile long, thirty minutes old with three turns and three articles. Instead of repeating the full range of exercises in general obedience there is heel free, a send away of at least fifty yards with a redirection to another designated spot, the down exercise (the handler being out of sight for ten minutes), and controlled jumping. This last exercise is included in trials for police dogs, when the handler walks past a line of jumps – four hurdles, a 9 ft long jump, and a 6 ft scale jump – and the dog at his command clears each obstacle in turn. Criminal work, the third section of this test, corresponds to the standard required of a British police dog on completion of a training course. It consists of four separate exercises: location of criminal by the dog quartering and searching; escort of criminal; escape prevention (by the dog holding fast and leaving automatically when resistance ceases), and a test of courage. In this, the handler having been incapacitated, the dog must of his own accord give chase to the escaping running criminal and when threatened by him detain the man by circling or biting him. A pass-mark in each section and 70 per cent of total marks is required for a diploma in this test.

The final test has been renamed the Advanced Tracking Test. It may be attempted once Test II has been passed. A leash-track is the sole exercise in this test, laid if possible over varying terrain, with four articles and a minimum of five turns. The German version of this test had three cross-tracks introduced at precise places but these have been omitted as, with a time lapse of three hours before the track is run, some interference inevitably occurs at one point or another. A pass in this tracking test can be achieved only by a dog of considerable experience and tracking ability.

The working tests as agreed by the original sub-committee were adopted by the full Committee and later by the members of the Dobermann Club at their Annual General Meeting in March 1961. Copies of the tests in their current form may be obtained from the secretary of the Dobermann Club.

The first tests were held in July 1961 and Harry Darbyshire judged. There was a good attendance of members watching the proceedings and learning from his comments and advice. Records show that four bitches and two dogs gained their diploma in Test I that day. In December of that year, with the same judge, three more Dobermanns passed Test I.

In the next three years working tests were included in the programme of the Summer Rally of the Dobermann Club. The tracking took place in the morning on suitable land nearby, and the remaining tests in the afternoon in the grounds of the home of whichever member of the club was host or hostess for the occasion. The Club Rally is principally a social affair to which all members and their Dobermanns are invited, but they are encouraged to be participants as well as spectators of the various activities arranged, the programme being varied each year but always including events for show exhibitors and for those who enjoy working their dogs. The holding of the club working tests in conjunction with the rally was a very good way of bringing together members with different interests in the same breed, and the purpose of the working tests was fulfilled when the same dog or bitch combined good conformation and working ability, and was seen to take part in both types of activity. In those days the owners came from widely separated parts of the country, having worked on their own to train their dogs to track and search and jump, and they enjoyed both the social and the working aspects and the atmosphere of a club occasion.

In 1965 the Dobermann Club appointed a sub-committee of six members to run the working tests, under the chairmanship and supervision of Rex Hodge, who was Club secretary at the time. From now on the tests took place independently of any other club activity, generally twice a year. Good organisation was vital as, with two or three different tests taking place on the same day, more ground was required for tracking, jumps had to be supplied and set up for the general obedience, and more stewards and helpers were needed. Rex kept a detailed record of all dogs that qualified, and was responsible to the main Committee for the proper conduct of the tests.

In 1974 Nan Griffiths succeeded Rex as secretary of the sub-committee and played a very active part in running the tests for the next nine years. The judges at first were either police officers who had themselves handled a Dobermann in police service, or civilians whose dogs had passed at least two of the working tests. Now new judges were brought in, all of them experienced in handling working dogs but not necessarily Dobermanns. Other newer members came forward to serve on the sub-committee in their turn, and they too worked with enthusiasm. For eight years tests were held each spring in Shropshire, at the home of Jim and Marty Burrell, and this enabled a greater number of members than before to take part. Other than in Shropshire (and once in York-shire) the working tests have been held within reach of London. Bob Carter followed Nan as the secretary of the working sub-committee and he in turn has been succeeded by Terry Brace.

Appendix H gives details of those Dobermanns that have successfully passed one or more tests since their inauguration. Some that failed at their first attempt have passed at a later date. It has always been recognised that the diploma for a pass in any test is not easily won. The conduct of the tests has always been strictly controlled by the Dobermann Club, either, as has been shown, at the Summer Rally, or later through the sub-committee appointed for that purpose. Entry is confined to members; there has been no distortion of the purpose of the tests, and no lowering of the standard required for a pass. The record to date has proved the wisdom of this policy.

It was, therefore, with justifiable pride that in 1986 members of the present sub-committee celebrated twenty-five years of the Dobermann Club Working Tests by running the full range of tests over two days, and inviting past and present club members to the presentation of diplomas and a party afterwards. Jim Burrell and I were privileged to share the judging on this very special occasion, and eleven diplomas were awarded. The party afterwards was well supported by Club members from both the show and the working side. Margaret Bastable was present, like me a member of the group that drew up the tests originally. Rex Hodge was there, his years as chief organiser having set the pattern now being followed, while George Thompson and I met again, both of us handlers at tests held in 1961 and 1962. It was an occasion of happy memories and of promise for the future. The schedule of working tests has been proved adequate for assessing working ability, nosework potential, agility, obedience, courage and steadiness of temperament. A Dobermann bred from sound stock can still rightly be classed a working dog.

11

Dobermanns in Police Service

When the late Sir Joseph Simpson, K.B.E., K.P.M., became Chief Constable of Surrey he initiated the formation of a dog section. The breed of dog usually associated with police work was at that time still known as the 'Alsatian'. It is now more correctly called the German Shepherd Dog (or 'GSD'), is registered as such at the Kennel Club, and will be referred to by that name in this chapter. Besides two dogs of that breed already under training with the Surrey Constabulary, two Dobermanns were selected in Germany and imported in September 1948. They entered police service on 1st March 1949. They were a brown dog, Astor v.d. Morgensonne, and a black-and-tan bitch, Donathe v. Begertal. At the same time, a black-and-tan dog, Ulf v. Margarethenhof, was taken over by Harry Darbyshire and joined the dog section at constabulary headquarters at Mountbrowne, Guildford. This dog had been brought over from Germany by an American and after release from quarantine was found to be unmanageable and out of control.

The policy laid down in Surrey at that time has formed the basis of present-day policy and the ever-widening use of police dogs. Although since 1958 the German Shepherd has been the breed officially recommended as being the most suitable for police work, in the early days Dobermann and German Shepherd litters were bred at Mountbrowne in roughly equal numbers. Between January 1950 and November 1955 ten Dobermann litters are recorded. Handlers came from various county forces, took over their particular dog when it was about ten months old and stayed for preliminary training at Mountbrowne. After a few months back in their own area they returned to Surrey for an advanced training course.

Donathe v. Begertal had three litters. Being frequently under pressure to use the Surrey police dogs for breeding with civilian stock, Sir Joseph Simpson presented the brown dog, Mountbrowne Joe, to the Dobermann Club for stud purposes. Joe was kept at the Bowesmoor kennels by Mary Porterfield and was trained and handled by her.

Ulf v. Margarethenhof and Astor v.d. Morgensonne were both used in regular police work in Surrey. Ulf was trained by Harry Darbyshire, who handled him in working trials (where he became the breed's first working trials champion) and in all his most important police work. Anyone who knew Ulf will still remember his tremendous tracking ability, his zest for work and his enthusiasm and speed in manwork. He had a passion for firearms and was so quick to 'go in' at the firing of a shot that his face was often singed by the powder. This led to his being used in cases involving searching for weapons and in following up dangerous men known to be violent or armed, besides normal police-dog duty. The following are the only two cases which still remain in the records at the Mountbrowne Kennels.

In December 1949 a child of eight years old was reported missing. The weather was very cold. Local police were called in and made a thorough search of the area, which was residential with adjacent public ground. No trace of the child was found. Next day Ulf was brought over; after searching for some time he made his way along a hedge and some distance further on came upon the child lying in a deep ditch, unconscious and suffering from exposure. The dog undoubtedly saved the child's life.

In July 1950 a woman was attacked in a wood and sustained a fractured skull. She was found some time later and taken to hospital. Before losing consciousness she was able to say her assailant wore white gloves. Approximately twenty hours after the attack had taken place Ulf v. Margarethenhof was taken to the spot where the woman was found. He led Harry Darbyshire along one of the many small paths in the wood. Some way along he stopped, and after hunting about in some heavy undergrowth he brought out a pair of white gloves, bloodstained. The dog then continued tracking through the wood and out into fields and led his handler across to some wooden bungalows; he stopped beside one which was found to have been broken into. Examination by detectives showed someone had spent the night there, and a search revealed that a gold watch had been stolen. Fingerprints were found and a description of the watch was circulated. The following week the watch was offered in pawn in a neighbouring town. The person offering it was arrested; when his fingerprints were taken they were found to be identical with those in the bungalow. The man concerned was convicted. Without the dog there would have been nothing to connect the break-in and subsequent pawn of a stolen watch with the assault in the wood.

Ulf v. Margarethenhof remained in the dog section at Mountbrowne until he died in November 1956, aged ten years.

Astor v.d. Morgensonne received his initial training from Alan Osment, one of the three original dog-handlers in the Surrey Constabulary. The dog later passed to other handlers. In December 1950 a man of about eighty was reported missing from Farnham. Astor and his handler joined the search party. The dog found a scent and tracked steadily through undergrowth and down the long steep side of a wood. At the bottom was a stream, where the old man was found lying in the mud suffering from exposure. He was taken home, and recovered.

The Dobermanns bred for police service or used by them are listed in Appendix I. Details are given of the dogs' breeding, their handlers' names and the force with which they worked. Except in the private scrapbooks of the handlers and in the memories of those who worked with the dog sections, few records still remain of cases in which Dobermanns assisted the police in other parts of the country. The following reports have been given by officers of the various forces mentioned, with the permission of the Chief Constable. They are quoted to show the variety of the work done by the dogs.

Mountbrowne Remoh joined the Essex County Constabulary and did some excellent work in the early days of the dog section. A thirteen-year-old girl, asleep in bed, was awakened by a man who committed an indecent assault on her. She screamed and the man leapt from the first-floor window and escaped. About one hour later Remoh arrived with his handler and the dog quickly picked up a track at the foot of a ladder leading to the girl's bedroom. The dog followed the track across the garden and adjoining fields into a nearby army camp, where he crossed the parade ground and continued through the motor transport lines up to a barrack-room hut. The door of the hut was open and the dog went over to a bed where a soldier was sleeping. The soldier was questioned by detectives and later identified by fingerprints found at the scene of the crime. At the quarter sessions later he was convicted of indecent assault.

Mountbrowne Tasco was the first Dobermann used in the Hertfordshire Constabulary and he worked as a police dog for nearly six years. During the first three months of his service he found five missing persons. He was involved in numerous arrests for crime and was an excellent operational tracking dog.

Mountbrowne Astor was one of the first two dogs used by the Devon Constabulary. This dog proved exceptionally good, particularly for tracking, and he was on active duty until officially retired at the age of twelve years. During this time he was engaged on numerous incidents, brief details of which have been given by a senior officer of the district concerned. In January 1957 Astor assisted in the search for a missing woman on Dartmoor, who was eventually traced and found to be suffering from exposure. Normal attempts to revive her failed and Astor and another dog were used to lie down on each side of her for a period of an hour and a half until she recovered, the body temperature of the dogs being higher than that of a human being.

Astor was concerned in the arrest of ten escaped prisoners, which included six from H.M. Prison on

Dartmoor. Of particular interest was the case where one of the escaped prisoners from Dartmoor removed his boots and stockings and walked along the tarmacadam road for a mile and a half to avoid being tracked by police dogs. At the point where the boots and socks were removed Astor indicated that the scent was even stronger and the prisoner was soon located and arrested.

Mountbrowne Onyx went into the dog section of the East Sussex police. Although his handler recommends the German Shepherd for general work, he says 'I have yet to find any dog equal to the Dobermann for tracking and nosework; his agility also is exceptional.' During his working life Onyx was responsible for twenty-one arrests and for tracing seven missing persons, and in eleven cases was responsible for finding stolen property. One of the latter cases involved jewellery which had been buried under a railway bridge.

The handler particularly remembers one incident when he and Onyx were called to tearooms where the premises had been broken into and foodstuff stolen. It was two and a half hours before dog and handler arrived. By casting the dog along the verges at each side of the road a track was picked up some 75 to 100 yards from the premises. The dog tracked across country, negotiating thick mud through farmyards, and although harassed by cattle on two occasions he refused to leave the track. He followed it for approximately five miles to a barn, where a tramp was found still sorting out the stolen property.

Mountbrowne Olaf and Mountbrowne Pablo worked with the Cheshire Constabulary. It is said of them: 'Both these dogs gave excellent service as police dogs. . . . It would be true to say that both were good and well up to the standard of the German Shepherd Dogs in use at the time.' Olaf was put to sleep through old age.

One incident concerning Mountbrowne Pablo received considerable press publicity. One night in January 1963 there was an armed robbery of a taxi driver near Macclesfield, where Pablo was on patrol with his handler. Soon afterwards they went with other officers to the home of one of two men suspected of being responsible for the robbery. Both these men were known to be of violent disposition. After knocking, the door was opened by a woman who said that her husband and his companion were not in. As the detective-sergeant entered the house a gushing sound was heard and boiling water splashed down from the darkness of the stairway. The handler went forward and sent Pablo up the stairs. There was a crash and a large quantity of a vile-smelling liquid came splashing down on the dog and on the handler's head and face. Pablo yelped with pain and the handler staggered back, blinded by acid and fumes. Two men rushed downstairs and struggled with the police officers, all of whom suffered severe burns from what was later proved to be concentrated nitric acid. The two men were arrested and all the officers were given hospital treatment to their face and eyes.

Pablo was thoroughly examined and treated to counter the effect of the acid but two days later he began to show signs of extensive and severe burns on head, neck and shoulder. After efforts had been made to heal the dog's wounds the Chief Constable decided to have him destroyed on humanitarian grounds. The report ends: 'As a police dog Pablo was very hard and tough and not given to being fondled or petted. He was a very persistent type of dog who never gave up.' The four police officers concerned in this arrest were awarded the Queen's commendation for outstanding police work.

The two Dobermanns first used by the Northumberland County Constabulary were Mountbrowne Amber and Mountbrowne Bruce. Amber went as a young puppy to be brought up by her intended handler, P.C. Jack Hyslop. When he was promoted shortly before her official training was due to begin, P.C. Tom Yeouart took her over. An official photograph of the advanced course at Mount-browne in March 1957 shows all the dogs were Dober-manns, with Amber at their head. One of her cases was a shopbreaking incident where quantities of cigarettes and chocolates were stolen. Six hours afterwards Amber picked up a scent and tracked for a considerable distance, crossing railway lines and various types of ground. She found small pieces of tobacco on the way and stopped to dig up some packets of cigarettes. She took Tom Yeouart over to one particular tent at a camping-site; he searched it and worked back again, casting the dog free to each side. In two places she found buried quantities of cigarettes and chocolates. In April 1959 Tom Yeouart left the force. Jack Hyslop returned to the dog section as Sergeant in charge and as the handler of Mountbrowne Amber.

In the mid-1950s a Home Office Committee recommended the holding of trials for police dogs, to be organised annually on a national basis and open to handlers representing every city or county force with a dog section. The schedule drawn up at that time has subsequently been changed very little and it covers every aspect of police work in which a dog can be used, the different tests being held over four days. Tests of general obedience and agility are of standard pattern. The criminal work includes an exercise in crowd control as well as the usual tests of courage, chasing, attack and 'stand-off', when after a chase the dog must refrain from biting a stationary figure. Tests of nosework include a long leash-track, a short track on a road or other hard surface, searching a building for a hidden person and searching for articles. In May 1960, when thirty-three dogs took part, Mountbrowne Amber with her handler Sergeant Hyslop became the first Dobermann ever to win these National Police Dog Trials, finishing fifty marks ahead of the next dog.

In routine police work Mountbrowne Amber worked successfully with both her handlers. Equipment stolen from an explosives store was used for a series of safe-blowing offences in Northumberland, the gang responsible remaining undetected for several months. When three men ran off after being disturbed on locked premises by a patrolling policeman, Amber and Sergeant Hyslop were called in. The dog tracked for several miles through the night across difficult country, ignoring the hazards of cattle, sheep and wandering Collie dogs. From a hole in a stone wall she retrieved a lump of gelignite wrapped in a handkerchief and darted back again to bring out a pair of rubber gloves. Using his torch, Jack Hyslop found deep in the hole another pair of gloves, several detonators, wire and a battery. The dog continued to track until daylight when she came out on to a main road, and three men who had been seen to board the early bus at this point were arrested. The equipment found by the dog during the long night's track proved to be identical with that stolen and used in the earlier break-ins.

When the Lancashire Constabulary obtained Mount-browne Juno from Surrey their dog section also included a tough and somewhat anti-social brown dog, Dober v. Oldenfelde. He had been brought over from Germany and when found to be unsuitable as a family pet he was acquired by the police. To meet the increasing demand for dogs, the Lancashire Constabulary kennels became an official breeding and training centre for German Shepherd Dogs, and Dobermanns were discontinued. In Durham, however, Dobermanns were used for several more years. Their kennels too have become an official breeding centre for police dogs, and training still takes place there. Many first-class German Shepherd Dogs have been registered with the Durham Constabulary affix 'Aycliffe'. While he was their Chief Constable, Mr A.A. Muir, C.B.E., D.L. continued to support the training of Dobermanns for police work and he authorised the introduction of new stock from Germany.

The first of these, John v. Waldhorst, began regular work after quarantine and a course of training. The first time he was on patrol in 1961 his handler was on observation in a car park, following a number of reports of larceny from vehicles and theft of cars. Four youths entered and were overheard discussing which vehicle they should take. One sat on a motor-bike and tried to start it. Another noticed the dog-handler, who challenged them and all ran off. Set loose by his handler, John gave chase, rounded up all four youths and circled them until the handler came up. All were apprehended.

Later imports from Germany brought in by the Durham police were a bitch, Gitta v. Frankenland, and a dog, Bandit v.d. Starkenburg, but of their subsequent success either for breeding or as working dogs no details are available.

Argus of Aycliffe, a son of W.T. Ch. Ulf v. Margarethenhof, was only eighteen months old when he was taken by his handler to a builder's yard where a fire during the night had caused extensive damage to timber, stores and lorries. It was thought to be a case of arson. The yard had been the scene of so much activity since the fire was noticed over five hours earlier that there seemed little scope for a dog. Noticing scratches on the gate which might have been made by someone climbing over, the handler worked the dog from there. Argus turned away from the gate and tracked steadily into the town, ignoring early shoppers as he went along the pavement of the main street. Although the handler felt it was impossible, the dog seemed to be genuinely following a scent and he tracked right to the door of a house in the residential part of the town. A man who lived there was found to be a former employee at the yard. When taken to the police station, flakes of rust and of paint from the gate and small metal particles from the yard were found on his shoes and clothing. He was charged and taken into custody within seven hours of the fire being started. The police officers in the case were commended for an efficient and well co-ordinated job. It was established later that the man arrested had taken rags soaked in varnish from his house to start the fire in revenge for his dismissal. The handler believes that the dog tracked on the smell of the varnish from the gate back to the house.

In cities, police dogs can have a useful function. A case has already been quoted where Mountbrowne Pablo assisted in the arrest of two men known to be violent. Dogs had not yet been used by the city police of Newcastle-upon-Tyne when two sergeants of the Durham Constabulary went with their dogs to show how these might be used. The dogs selected were Argus and Arno of Aycliffe. A big warehouse in the city was found to be insecure one night, and required searching for an intruder. On each floor there were great piles of crates, stacked in rows running the whole length of the building. Access to each floor was by a step-ladder without siderails. Argus went in with his handler who sent the dog down and up each row, in turn, to search for anyone who might be concealed between or behind the crates. After each floor was searched Argus went up the ladder to the floor above and worked in the same keen and methodical way. Twenty minutes later the handler reported to the city police that the search was complete and there was no one concealed on the premises. The inspector said that a similarly thorough search using a squad of men normally took half a shift to complete.

One Saturday evening the Durham handlers on patrol with the Newcastle police came upon an inspector, a sergeant and three policemen vainly trying to disperse a noisy crowd emerging from a dance-hall. One handler with his dog went forward and did the job alone, with no delay and no bloodshed. The Newcastle city police now have their own dog patrol.

The Durham Constabulary holds an annual competition for all its police dogs, with tests of obedience, agility, tracking, searching and criminal work. The six dogs with the highest marks then take part in another competition for a trophy and the title of 'Handler of the Year'. In 1960, the total of dogs was eight Dobermanns and eleven German Shepherds. In the final, Dobermanns took the first five places with only three-and-a-half marks between them.

Flame of Aycliffe went to the Bedfordshire Constabulary. An official report states that up to her retirement 'Flame had thirty-two arrests to her credit, and this does not include cases where an arrest was made by another officer as a result of work done by the dog.' The report continues that Flame's tracking ability was well enough known to need no examples and goes on: 'An incident occurred during the early days of the 'mod and rocker' era when a large-scale pitched battle took place in the small town of Leighton Buzzard. The inspector in charge called for reinforcements and among them was Flame. This bitch was rather small in stature and did not at first sight have the deterrent value of a German Shepherd Dog. Using the dog on a long lead, the handler was able to break up the fight in which some 150 youths were concerned and enabled the other officers present to make a total of seventeen arrests.'

Another Dobermann used in Bedfordshire was Goliath of Dissington. On one occasion Goliath was called late in the evening during a violent rainstorm to a wood where a gamekeeper had disturbed two poachers, who had threatened him with a gun and then made off. By the time the dog arrived five hours had elapsed and that, added to the absolutely impossible conditions, led the handler to believe that the dog would be of no use. However, he cast the dog around in the wood and finding a scent Goliath followed it to a railway embankment, tracking along the embankment and then on the ballast by the railway line. He continued for approximately three miles, during which time he recovered on the track a bag containing game and a twelve-bore shotgun. The track led eventually to the back door of a cottage. When interviewed the occupant of the cottage admitted the offence. The report continues: 'This example goes to show that the Dobermann, a much maligned animal and admittedly less suitable than the German Shepherd Dog, can on occasions track in conditions when the average GSD would not even start.'

Concerning the three Dobermanns which worked with the Bedfordshire Constabulary (Mountbrowne Yukon, Flame of Aycliffe and Goliath of Dissington) the report adds that 'the Dobermanns, like the German Shepherd Dogs we use, were patrol dogs working a full eight-hour tour of duty each day, and were in no way regarded as specialists but as valuable members of the Division to which they were attached. The number of occasions when the work of the dog has led to an arrest are many and the type of offences involved varied.'

The Metropolitan Police have used at least six Dobermanns operationally since 1949. Bowesmoor Hero was currently working when this book was originally prepared. Other dogs reported to have proved successful as police dogs were General, Jagga and Duke 9 (a brown dog). The most famous of the Metropolitan police Dobermanns has been Metpol Fritz, who worked with the same handler throughout eight years of service, from 1954 to 1962, when Fritz died. Metpol Fritz is the only Dobermann to have been awarded the 'Black Knight' Trophy, donated by Lady Munnings, which is presented each year to the best all-round Metropolitan police dog. Fritz won the trophy in 1959.

In May 1958, as a result of tracking a 'look-out man' to a suburban railway station at about midnight, two men found there breaking open a safe were surprised by Metpol Fritz and his handler. The men leapt out of the window to the pavement 20 feet below. Dog and handler followed and the officer fell on one man, who was arrested. Fritz was severely winded and his handler broke his ankle. While on sick leave the officer made persistent enquiries and eventually arrested the second man. The officer and his dog were commended.

The last Dobermann reported to have served with the Metropolitan Police was Rajah, who had several arrests to his credit. His handler, P.C. Roy Squire, was a keen supporter of the breed, and took part in the Dobermann Club Working Tests both as a handler and later as a judge.

When an emergency arises and the local police forces have no dogs of their own (a rare occurrence today), civilian dogs are sometimes called in to help. When a child or an old person has been reported missing, obviously the larger the search-party the better, and in the past members of many training clubs have come with their dogs to lend assistance. An unusual call was made to Dobermann Club member Michael Garrod, who with his bitch Dena of Illustria joined in the search for a wolf which had escaped from Whipsnade Zoo.

Before there were any police dogs in Scotland north of the Tay two civilian Dobermanns were on call for emergencies, and besides taking part in several searches for missing persons they were used in the following-up of long-term prisoners who had escaped. My dog Vyking Drum Major was called out for the first time one dark and windy evening after a prisoner had broken away from a working party at dusk. The dog had no previous experience of working at night but he tracked across fields and ploughed land, negotiating walls, ditches and wire fences, with the escort of police and prison officers sometimes treading on the tracking-line in their enthusiasm. After some three miles the track was lost in churned-up ground near a farmhouse. From a telephone call to HQ the search-party learned that the prisoner had just been recaptured as he reached a main road less than half a mile ahead. During the track, whenever the dog had changed direction a police officer with the group left to report their position by telephone, and police cars had thus been ready on the road when their customer arrived.

One cold dry February morning in 1958 a well-known safe-breaker went 'over the wall' of one of Scotland's big prisons and was noticed walking down a main road by a prison officer going on duty. When challenged the prisoner ran off. The alarm was given and, when Lorelei of Tavey and I were brought two hours later to help in the search, the road near the prison was crowded with cars and spectators. A jacket belonging to the prisoner was brought for the dog to identify his scent, and when the tracking-harness was put on she worked slowly along each side of the road. She then tracked steadily and with intense concentration from the grass verge along the road and down a gravel lane towards the local school. Police officers behind called to me to stop the dog as the school building had already been searched. The rest of the day was spent in unsuccessful searches elsewhere. Next morning the prisoner was recaptured a short distance away. He told the police that he had gone up the fire escape and had spent all the previous day on the roof of the school. It would appear the dog had correctly picked out and followed his scent among the lighter footsteps of the children going later to school.

In November 1954 the Association of Chief Constables formed a Working Party on police dogs. One of their many important recommendations was the setting up of the Standing Advisory Committee on Police Dogs under the chairmanship of H.M. Inspector of Constabulary. This committee set up the regional and National Police Dog

Trials, the first of which were held in July 1958.

A recommendation of the Working Party made in June 1957 was that: 'The German Shepherd Dog is considered to be the most suitable breed for police work, although there is no reason why other breeds which are found to be suitable for police work should not be used.' This view was later endorsed by the Standing Advisory Committee and experience since has shown no reason for revision.

Opinions for and against the Dobermann are held equally strongly by those who love and those who heartily dislike the breed, and in any argument on the subject as much prejudice is shown by one side as by the other. However much enthusiastic supporters would like to see the Dobermann used more often by the police, there are a number of reasons why the German Shepherd Dog is preferred. In the eyes of the general public the German Shepherd is more impressive; he is powerful and alert, with pricked ears and an appearance that enforces respect and even fear. On patrol a German Shepherd is ever-watchful and looks the part whatever he is doing. A Dobermann easily gets bored and needs some movement or noise or an incident to arouse its interest, when it becomes instantly equally effective.

As it was the late Sir Joseph Simpson who started Dobermanns working for the police it is perhaps appropriate to end by quoting from an article he wrote for a feature on the breed in *Dog World* of 28th May 1954. Permission to quote from his article on 'Dobermann Pinschers as Police Dogs' was given by his widow, the late Lady Simpson, and by the proprietors of *Dog World*.

'Our aims [i.e. at Mountbrowne] have been to produce the attributes of a good working dog, concentrating on nose, temperament, strength, speed and stamina. . . . The strong point about a Dobermann is that he is a first-class tracker, indeed second to none in this department. Its advantages in tracking are an extremely sensitive nose, with stamina and speed and the ability to continue through extreme heat and over parched ground. . . . When a dog is highly trained it will keep its nose close to the ground and hardly raise it from the track. It then appears to be tracking at a modest walk, but a timed speed of any given distance will surprise those who are watching. The dog has been proved to be resolute and to compare favourably with the finest examples of other breeds in criminal and manwork. The greenest novice must admit that a Dobermann's reactions are the quickest that can be witnessed.

'As the breed has its strong points so too it must admit to weaknesses. The short coat which stands it in such good stead in hot weather is a handicap in cold. The Dobermann must be housed more carefully in winter than other breeds. While he will track under the coldest and most penetrating conditions without apparent ill-effect, the dog displays great discomfort if required to remain still in the open with his handler, as when keeping observation through long hours of winter weather. There is a tendency to moodiness and wilfulness in the Dobermann and unless sympathetically handled he can easily be spoilt. He matures later than most breeds which must be taken into account in training and handling.

'The Dobermann when working is undoubtedly spectacular and to the uninitiated it has a great appeal. It is hard to make people asking for advice on the subject realise, until they learn by bitter experience, that the Dobermann is not really the dog for the novice handler, unless that handler is under continuous expert supervision by someone experienced in the intricacies of the breed.'

KENNEL CLUB REGISTRATION TOTALS

1948	—	Nil	1969	—	1553
1949	—	Nil	1970	—	1645
1950	—	Nil	1971	—	1566
1951	—	94	1972	—	1594
1952	—	112	1973	—	1891
1953	—	138	1974	—	2029
1954	—	135	1975	—	2265
1955	—	205	1976	—	920*
1956	—	189	1977	—	594
1957	—	241	1978	—	2097
1958	—	236	1979	—	3107
1959	—	358	1980	—	4634
1960	—	385	1981	—	4824
1961	—	510	1982	—	6244
1962	—	608	1983	—	8499
1963	—	567	1984	—	8905
1964	—	875	1985	—	9953
1965	—	789	1986	—	8564
1966	—	1017	1987	—	6413
1967	—	1119	1988	—	4508
1968	—	1528	1989	—	4992†

Note: From 1948 to 1950 all puppies were registered under 'Any other variety'.

*A new system of registration, mainly to record dogs intended for competition or export, was adopted in 1976 but proved complicated and caused delays. This accounts for the apparent drop in registration totals for 1976 and 1977, during which years in fact more Dobermanns were bred than before. The backlog of registrations which had built up was reduced after February 1978, when another change was made. A two-tier system enabled puppies to be recorded simply by a litter-number *or* registered by name.

†In April 1989 the Kennel Club reverted to a single-tier system of registration. A direct comparison of the totals for 1988 and 1989 cannot therefore be properly made.

APPENDIX B

BREED CLUBS

THE DOBERMANN CLUB
Secretary
Mrs C. Wright
Woodview, 41 Gill Bank Road, Ilkley, W. Yorks, LS29 0AU

MIDLAND DOBERMANN CLUB
Secretary
Mrs M. Thompson
25 Heather Avenue, Heath, Chesterfield, Derbyshire, S44 5RF

NORTH OF ENGLAND DOBERMANN CLUB
Secretary
Mr D. Brown
48 Park Avenue, Sale, Cheshire, M33 1HE

SCOTTISH DOBERMANN CLUB
Secretary
Mrs Joy Galbraith
27 Graham Avenue, Hamilton, Strathclyde, ML3 8AB

WELSH DOBERMANN CLUB
Secretary
Mrs P. Hart
Bridale, Lower Lamphey Road, Pembroke, Dyfed, SA71 5NJ

NORTHERN IRELAND DOBERMANN CLUB
Secretary
Mr W. Castles
2 Ballygowan Road, Craiganorne, Larne, Co. Antrim,
BT40 3EH

BIRMINGHAM AND DISTRICT DOBERMANN CLUB
Secretary
Mr P.B. Rock
Otherton House, Penkridge, Staffordshire, ST19 5NX

SOUTH WEST DOBERMANN CLUB
Secretary
Mrs G.A. Pascoe
Trevannick House, Wellington Plantation, Feock, Truro,
Cornwall, TR3 6QP

SOUTH EAST OF ENGLAND DOBERMANN CLUB
Secretary
Mrs M. Barton
Mill Cottage, Linfold Bridge, Kirdford, W. Sussex, RH14 0LG

NORTH EAST COUNTIES DOBERMANN SOCIETY
Secretary
Mrs Pat Weeks
Crossing Cottage, West Tanfield, Ripon, N. Yorks, HG4 5JP

AMERICAN KENNEL CLUB STANDARD OF THE DOBERMAN PINSCHER

(Adopted by the Doberman Pinscher Club of America and approved by the Board of Directors of the American Kennel Club, 6 February 1982.)

GENERAL CONFORMATION AND APPEARANCE

The appearance is that of a dog of medium size, with a body that is square; the height, measured vertically from the ground to the highest point of the withers, equalling the length measured horizontally from the forechest to the rear projection of the upper thigh. *Height* at the withers – *Dogs* 26 to 28 inches, ideal about 27½ inches; *Bitches* 24 to 26 inches, ideal about 25½ inches. Length of head, neck and legs in proportion to length and depth of body. Compactly built, muscular and powerful, for great endurance and speed. Elegant in appearance, of proud carriage, reflecting great nobility and temperament. Energetic, watchful, determined, alert, fearless, loyal and obedient.

The judge shall dismiss from the ring any shy or vicious Dobermann.

Shyness A dog shall be judged fundamentally shy if, refusing to stand for examination, it shrinks away from the judge; if it fears an approach from the rear; if it shies at sudden and unusual noises to a marked degree.

Viciousness A dog that attacks or attempts to attack either the judge or its handler, is definitely vicious. An aggressive or belligerent attitude towards other dogs shall not be deemed viciousness.

HEAD

Long and dry, resembling a blunt wedge in both frontal and profile views. When seen from the front, the head widens gradually toward the base of the ears in a practically unbroken line. Top of skull flat, turning with slight stop to bridge of muzzle, with muzzle line extending parallel to top line of skull.

Cheeks flat and muscular. Lips lying close to jaws. Jaws full and powerful, well filled under the eyes.

Eyes Almond shaped, moderately deep set, with vigorous, energetic expression. Iris, of uniform color, ranging from medium to darkest brown in black dogs; in reds, blues, and fawns the color of the iris blends with that of the markings, the darkest shade being preferable in every case.

Teeth Strongly developed and white. Lower incisors upright and touching inside of upper incisors – a true scissors bite. *42 correctly placed teeth*, 22 in the lower, 20 in the upper jaw. Distemper teeth shall not be penalized.

Disqualifying Faults Overshot more than ³/₁₆ of an inch. Undershot more than ⅛ of an inch. Four or more missing teeth.

Ears Normally cropped and carried erect. The upper attachment of the ear, when held erect, is on a level with the top of the skull.

NECK

Proudly carried, well muscled and dry. Well arched, with nape of neck widening gradually toward body. Length of neck proportioned to body and head.

BODY

Back short, firm, of sufficient width, and muscular at the loins, extending in a straight line from withers to the *slightly* rounded croup.

Withers pronounced and forming the highest point of the body.

Brisket reaching deep to the elbow. *Chest* broad with forechest well defined. *Ribs* well sprung from the spine, but flattened in lower end to permit elbow clearance. *Belly* well tucked up, extending in a curved line from the brisket. *Loins* wide and muscled. *Hips* broad and in proportion to body, breadth of hips being approximately equal to breadth of body at rib cage and shoulders. *Tail* docked at approximately second joint, appears to be a continuation of the spine, and is carried only slightly above the horizontal when the dog is alert.

FOREQUARTERS

Shoulder Blade sloping forward and downward at a 45 degree angle to the ground meets the upper arm at an angle of 90 degrees. Length of shoulder blade and upper arm are equal. Height from elbow to withers approximately equals height from ground to elbow. *Legs*, seen from front and side, perfectly straight and parallel to each other from elbow to pastern: muscled and sinewy, with heavy bone. In normal pose and when gaiting, the elbows lie close to the brisket. *Pasterns* firm and almost perpendicular to the ground. *Feet* well arched, compact, and catlike, turning neither in nor out. Dewclaws may be removed.

HINDQUARTERS

The angulation of the hindquarters balances that of the forequarters. *Hip Bone* falls away from spinal column at an angle of about 30 degrees, producing a slightly rounded, well-filled-out croup. *Upper Shanks*, at right angles to the hip bones, are long, wide, and well muscled on both sides of thigh, with clearly defined stifles. Upper and lower shanks are of equal length. While the dog is at rest, hock to heel is perpendicular to the ground. Viewed from the rear, the legs are straight, parallel to each other, and wide enough apart to fit in with a properly built body. *Cat Feet*, as on front legs, turning neither in nor out. Dewclaws, if any, are generally removed.

GAIT

Free, balanced, and vigorous, with good reach in the forequarters and good driving power in the hindquarters. When trotting, there is strong rear-action drive. Each rear leg moves in line with the foreleg on the same side. Rear and front legs are thrown neither in nor out. Back remains strong and firm. When moving at a fast trot, a properly built dog will singletrack.

COAT, COLOR, MARKINGS

Coat smooth-haired, short, hard, thick and close lying. Invisible gray undercoat on neck permissible.
Allowed Colors   Black, red, blue, and fawn (Isabella). *Markings* – Rust, sharply defined, appearing above each eye and on muzzle, throat and forechest, on all legs and feet, and below tail. *Nose* solid black on black dogs, dark brown on red ones, dark gray on blue ones, dark tan on fawns. White patch on chest, not exceeding ½ square inch, permissible.
Disqualifying fault   dogs not of an allowed color.

FAULTS — THE FOREGOING DESCRIPTION IS THAT OF THE IDEAL DOBERMAN PINSCHER. ANY DEVIATION FROM THE ABOVE DESCRIBED DOG MUST BE PENALIZED TO THE EXTENT OF THE DEVIATION.

DISQUALIFICATIONS

OVERSHOT MORE THAN ³⁄₁₆ OF AN INCH; UNDERSHOT MORE THAN ¹⁄₈ OF AN INCH. FOUR OR MORE MISSING TEETH. DOGS NOT OF AN ALLOWED COLOR.

This Standard is copyrighted by The American Kennel Club and is reprinted by special permission of The American Kennel Club.

APPENDIX D

SOME INFLUENTIAL SIRES AND DAMS

Bruno of Tavey
- Benno v.d. Schwedenhecke
  - Faust v.d. Nievelsburg
  - Kitty v. Friedwald
- Pia v.d. Dobberhof
  - Brando v. Berggreef
  - Alie v.d. Heerhof

Cartergate Alpha of Tavey
- Derb v. Brunoberg
  - Axel v.d. Germania
  - Unruh v. Sandberg
- Beka v. Brunoberg
  - Frido v. Rauhfelsen, Sch.H.I.
  - Unruh v. Sandberg

Prinses Anja v't Scheepjeskerk

Graaf Dagobert v. Neerlands Stam

Waldo v.d. Wachtparade, Dutch Ch.

Roeanka v.d. Rhederveld

Alindia v't Scheepjeskerk

Bucko v.d. Heerhof

Andranette v. Rio de la Plata

Tasso v.d. Eversburg of Tavey

Sieger Alex v. Kleinwaldheim

Ajax v. Simbach

Carola v. Sudharz

Siegerin Christel v.d. Brunoberg

Frido v. Rauhfelsen, Sch.H.I.

Unruh v. Sandberg

Birling Rachel

   Birling Bruno v. Ehrgarten

      Dulo v. Bernau

      Blanka v. Lindenbaum

   Birling Britta v.d. Heerhof

      Waldo v.d. Wachtparade, Dutch Ch.

      Alma v.d. Heerhof

Lola of Cartergate

   Arko v.d. Schäffertrifft

      Burschel v. Dammeritzee

      Anka v. Schulzenhof

   Bärbel v. Edmundsthäll

      Bodo v. Steinfurthohe

      Valle v. Park

Ch. Taveys Stormy
Abundance

Am. Ch. Rancho Dobes Storm

- Am. Ch. Rancho Dobes Primo
- Am. Ch. Maedel v. Randahof

Am. Ch. Rustic Adagio

- Am. & Int. Ch. Kilburn Ideal
- Rustic Radiance

Ch. Taveys Stormy
Achievement

Am. Ch. Rancho Dobes Storm

- Am. Ch. Rancho Dobes Primo
- Am. Ch. Maedel v. Randahof

Am. Ch. Rustic Adagio

- Am. & Int. Ch. Kilburn Ideal
- Rustic Radiance

Taveys Stormy Governess

- Ch. Taveys Stormy Achievement
  - Am. Ch. Rancho Dobes Storm
  - Am. Ch. Rustic Adagio
- Tamara of Tavey
  - Tasso v.d. Eversburg of Tavey
  - Prinses Anja v't Scheepjeskerk

Ch. Acclamation of Tavey

- Am. Ch. Stebs Top Skipper
  - Am. Ch. Dortmund Delly's Colonel Jet
  - Damasyn the Easter Bonnet
- Orebaughs Raven of Tavey
  - Am. Ch. Rancho Dobes Primo
  - Am. Ch. Orebaughs Gentian

Ch. Tumlow Impeccable

Ch. Acclamation of Tavey

Am. Ch. Stebs Top Skipper

Orebaughs Raven of Tavey

Taveys Stormy Governess

Ch. Taveys Stormy Achievement

Tamara of Tavey

Am. Ch. Checkmate Chessman

Am. Ch. Alemaps Checkmate

Am. Ch. Wahlmars Baroness

Vanessa's Little Dictator of Tavey

Am. Ch. Valheims Vanessa

Am. Ch. Alemaps Checkmate

Am. Ch. Campeons Tenta Dora

Ch. Iceberg of Tavey

- Ch. Acclamation of Tavey
  - Am. Ch. Stebs Top Skipper
  - Orebaughs Raven of Tavey
- Juno of Cartergate
  - Ch. Claus of Cartergate
  - Ch. Helena of Cartergate

Wilm von Forell

- Ger. & Int. Ch. Cliff of Fayette Corner
  - Arco of Fayette Corner, Sch.H.III.
  - Bella v. Berg Modela
- Ger. Ch. Cita Germania
  - Cäsar v. Weideneck
  - Reni Germania

Ch. Triogen Tornado

- Ch. Triogen Traffic Cop
  - Ch. Acclamation of Tavey
  - Triogen Teenage Sensation
- Triogen Treble Chance
  - Ch. Taveys Stormy Nugget
  - Triogen Teenage Wonder

Ch. Flexor Flugelman

- Tumlow Green Highlander
  - Edencourts Banker
  - Taveys Stormy Pepita
- Tumlow Radiance
  - Ch. Acclamation of Tavey
  - Tumlow Odile

Phileens Duty Free of Tavey

Am. Ch. Tarrados Corry
- Am. Ch. Felix v. Ahrtal
- Am. Ch. Highbriar Jasmine

Kay Hills Outrigger
- Am. Ch. Dolph v. Tannenwald
- Kay Hills Kat a Maran

Taveys Satellite

Am. Ch. Kay Hills Dealer's Choice
- Am. Ch. Dolph v. Tannenwald
- Kay Hills Kat a Maran

Arawak Perfecta
- Am. Ch. Dolph v. Tannenwald
- Arawak Hi-A-Leah C.D.

Ch. Findjans Poseidon

- Phileens Duty Free of Tavey
  - Am. Ch. Tarrados Corry
  - Kay Hills Outrigger
- Ch. Mitrasandra Gay Lady of Findjans
  - Ch. Tumlow Satan
  - Findjans Fair Allyne

Olderhill Salvador

- Phileens Duty Free of Tavey
  - Am. Ch. Tarrados Corry
  - Kay Hills Outrigger
- Olderhill Dhobi
  - Ch. Iceberg of Tavey
  - Charmer of Trogen

Chornytan Midnite Mark

- Chater Icy Storm
  - Ch. Iceberg of Tavey
  - Heidiland High Society
- Phileens Lady Luck
  - Camerons Snoopy of Tinkazan
  - Ch. Yucca of Tavey

Ch. Perihelias Resolution

- Ch. Findjans Poseidon
  - Phileens Duty Free of Tavey
  - Ch. Mitrasandra Gay Lady of Findjans
- Ch. Perihelias Madame Rochas
  - Ch. Taveys Gridiron
  - Jadans Aravorn the Huntress of Perihelia

BREED CHAMPIONS TO DECEMBER 1989

Name of Champion	Sex	Born	Sire	Dam	Owner	Breeder
Sheumac Storm	D	6.7.51	Wolfox Birling Rogue	Belle of Upend	G. A. Tunnicliffe	Mrs E. A. Sandland
Wolfox Birling Rogue	D	23.2.49	Birling Bruno v. Ehrgarten	Birling Britta v.d. Heerhof	Mrs B. Douglas-Redding	L. Hamilton-Renwick
Empress of Tavey	B	28.8.50	Bruno of Tavey	Prinses Anja v't Scheepjeskerk	Miss J. Skinner	Mrs J. Curnow
Elegant of Tavey	B	28.8.50	Bruno of Tavey	Prinses Anja v't Scheepjeskerk	Mrs J. Curnow	Owner
Alli of Girton	D	14.8.51	Djonja of Upend	Bernadette of Upend	H. Greenhalgh	K. E. Kitteridge
Bridget of Upend	B	21.3.50	Birling Roimond	Frieda v. Casa Mia of Upend	Mrs J. Richardson	Mrs B. Butler
Lustre of Tavey	D	28.9.52	Tasso v.d. Eversburg of Tavey	Prinses Anja v't Scheepjeskerk	Mrs J. Curnow	Owner
Claus of Cartergate	D	30.5.52	Birling Roimond	Cartergate Alpha of Tavey	L. R. Thorne-Dunn	Miss E. M. Would
Caprice of Cartergate	B	30.5.52	Birling Roimond	Cartergate Alpha of Tavey	J. T. Foers	Miss E. M. Would

Name of Champion	Sex	Born	Sire	Dam	Owner	Breeder
Francesca of Fulton	B	13.5.51	Wolfox Birling Rogue	Birling Rachel	Mrs J. Currie	L. Hamilton-Renwick
Juno of Tavey	B	22.3.52	Bruno of Tavey	Prinses Anja v't Scheepjeskerk	L. R. Thorne-Dunn	Miss J. Curnow
Jupiter of Tavey	D	22.3.52	Bruno of Tavey	Prinses Anja v't Scheepjeskerk	Mrs J. Curnow	Owner
Precept of Tavey	D	3.9.53	Tasso v.d. Eversburg of Tavey	Elegant of Tavey	Mrs E. M. Cathcart	Mrs J. Curnow
Mahadeo Brown Berrie	B	19.1.54	Jupiter of Tavey	Empress of Tavey	Mr and Mrs A. Thompson	Miss J. Skinner
Adges Going Places	B	2.7.53	Tasso v.d. Eversburg of Tavey	Helga v. Kleinwald-heim	Misses J. Skinner and M. Menzies	Miss A. Langsdon
Rhythm of Tavey	B	28.6.54	Bruno of Tavey	Gloss of Tavey	Mrs J. Curnow	Owner
Daybreak of Cartergate	D	15.3.54	Tasso v.d. Eversburg of Tavey	Cartergate Alpha of Tavey	S. J. Taylor	Miss E. M. Would
Day of Cartergate	D	15.3.54	Tasso v.d. Eversburg of Tavey	Cartergate Alpha of Tavey	Miss E. M. Would	Owner
Reichert Judy	B	18.5.52	Bill v. Blauenblut	Birling Rachel	Sgt Darbyshire and Mrs M. Porterfield	Mrs J. McHardy
Xel of Tavey	B	15.6.55	Adel of Tavey	Lacrosse Up and Doing	Mrs M. Bastable	Mrs J. Curnow
Challenger of Sonhende	D	24.7.54	Claus of Cartergate	Juno of Tavey	R. H. Jackson	L. R. Thorne-Dunn
Ace of Tavey	D	25.6.50	Bruno of Tavey	Beka v. Brunoberg	Mrs V. Simons	Mrs J. Curnow

Name	Sex	Date	Sire	Dam	Breeder	Owner
Bowesmoor Mona	B	25.5.57	Treu v. Steinfurthohe	Reichert Judy	G. Thompson	Mrs M. Porterfield
Carrickgreen Walda Nagasta	B	20.4.57	Alex v. Rodenaer	Barnelms Bess	P. Clark	M. Migliorini
Satin of Tavey	B	21.8.54	Bruno of Tavey	Elegant of Tavey	Mrs D. Horton	Mrs J. Curnow
Taveys Stormy Abundance	D	7.5.56	Rancho Dobes Storm	Rustic Adagio	Mrs J. Curnow	Owner
Taveys Stormy Adagio	B	7.5.56	Rancho Dobes Storm	Rustic Adagio	Mrs J. Curnow	Owner
Taveys Stormy Acacia	D	7.5.56	Rancho Dobes Storm	Rustic Adagio	Mrs J. Curnow	Owner
Taveys Stormy Daughter	B	20.11.57	Taveys Stormy Achievement	Tamara of Tavey	E. Protheroe	Mrs J. Curnow
Baba Black Pepper	B	7.4.55	Bruno of Tavey	Baba Black Sheep	Miss E. Hoxey	Mrs D. M. Ince
Caliph of Trevellis	D	5.6.58	Taveys Stormy Abundance	Satin of Tavey	E. Plumb	Mrs D. Horton
Talaureen Hurricane	D	25.7.56	Jupiter of Tavey	Quicksilver of Tavey	Mrs E. Barnacle	Miss E. Tatler
Taveys Stormy Achievement	D	7.5.56	Rancho Dobes Storm	Rustic Adagio	Mrs J. Curnow	Owner
Venture of Vreda	B	17.6.58	Taveys Stormy Abundance	Ardent of Trevellis	N. D. Thatcher	Mrs A. Thomas
Auldrigg Corsair	D	15.8.58	Taveys Stormy Achievement	Fascination of Sonhende	W. Gallaher	Mr and Mrs A. Auld
Acclamation of Tavey	D	2.7.59	Stebs Top Skipper	Orebaughs Raven of Tavey	Mrs J. Curnow	Owner
Cordelia of Trevellis	B	5.6.58	Taveys Stormy Abundance	Satin of Tavey	C. Starns	Mrs D. Horton

Name of Champion	Sex	Born	Sire	Dam	Owner	Breeder
Helena of Cartergate	B	27.2.57	Precept of Tavey	Lola of Cartergate	Miss E. M. Would	Owner
Tumlow Storm Caesar	D	27.7.59	Taveys Stormy Achievement	Baba Black Pepper	Mrs F. Platt	Miss E. Hoxey
Taveys Stormy Leprechaun	B	28.10.59	Taveys Stormy Abundance	Utopia of Tavey	E. Protheroe	M. Theobald
Tumlow Fantasy	B	14.6.60	Acclamation of Tavey	Taveys Stormy Governess	Miss E. Hoxey	Mrs J. Curnow and Miss E. Hoxey
Taveys Stormy Objective	D	29.6.60	Taveys Stormy Achievement	Orebaughs Raven of Tavey	Mrs J. Curnow	Owner
Annastock Lance	D	21.7.61	Taveys Stormy Achievement	Annastock Amberlili of Catharden	Mrs J. Parkes	Owner
Caliph of Barrimilne	D	30.4.58	Taveys Stormy Achievement	Xel of Tavey	M. Fagot	Mrs M. Bastable
Jove of Cartergate	D	6.8.59	Claus of Cartergate	Helena of Cartergate	Miss E. M. Would	Owner
Taveys Stormy Wrath	B	25.5.61	Acclamation of Tavey	Taveys Stormy Governess	Mrs J. Curnow	Mrs J. Curnow and Miss E. Hoxey
Taveys Stormy Wonder	D	25.5.61	Acclamation of Tavey	Taveys Stormy Governess	Mrs J. Curnow	Mrs J. Curnow and Miss E. Hoxey
Taveys Stormy Nugget	D	14.6.60	Acclamation of Tavey	Taveys Stormy Governess	F. Williams	Mrs J. Curnow and Miss E. Hoxey
Adoration of Dumbrill	B	25.4.60	Taveys Stormy Abundance	Utopia of Tavey	M. Theobald	Owner
Dolina Naiad	B	16.2.61	Acclamation of Tavey	Gypsy of Sonhende	Mrs F. Auld	Mrs S. Atkinson

Name		Date	Sire	Dam	Breeder	Owner
Taveys Stormy Master	D	25.4.60	Taveys Stormy Abundance	Utopia of Tavey	H. Inskip	M. Theobald
Tumlow Impeccable	D	25.5.61	Acclamation of Tavey	Taveys Stormy Governess	Miss E. Hoxey	Mrs J. Curnow and Miss E. Hoxey
Tumlow Whinlands Flurry	B	16.1.62	Acclamation of Tavey	Tumlow Storm Away	Miss E. Hoxey	Mrs E. Hewan
Wyndenhelms AWOL	B	25.7.60	Caliph of Trevellis	Bowesmoor Mona	G. Thompson	Owner
Ampherlaw Sir Galahad	D	29.3.62	Auldrigg Corsair	Ampherlaw Gretel	H. Hogg	Mrs G. Brandon
Carrickgreen Confederate	D	10.2.59	Taveys Stormy Abundance	Carrickgreen Walda Nagasta	Mrs C. McNee	P. Clark
Dolina Nereid	B	16.2.61	Acclamation of Tavey	Gypsy of Sonhende	Mrs S. Atkinson	Owner
Edencourts Avenger	D	27.4.62	Acclamation of Tavey	Taveys Stormy Daughter	Mrs A. Hewitt	E. Protheroe
Hans of Tickwillow	D	24.4.61	Taveys Stormy Abundance	Trudi of Ely	W. A. Hopkin	Owner
Iceberg of Tavey	D	16.9.63	Acclamation of Tavey	Juno of Cartergate	Mrs J. Curnow	Miss E. Would
Achteloch Heidi	B	21.3.62	Acclamation of Tavey	Tumlow Storm Charmer	L. C. McLeod	Mrs B. Pope
Gurnard Gemma	B	1.11.63	Acclamation of Tavey	Gurnard Hedda	A. Barnard and Mrs D. Billingham	Owners
Taveys Stormy Willow	B	25.5.61	Acclamation of Tavey	Taveys Stormy Governess	C. Starns	Mrs J. Curnow and Miss E. Hoxey
Tumlow Katrina	B	16.6.63	Taveys Stormy Achievement	Tumlow Fantasy	Miss E. Pudney	Miss E. Hoxey

Name of Champion	Sex	Born	Sire	Dam	Owner	Breeder
Cadereyta of Roanoke	B	30.5.64	Tumlow Impeccable	Heidi of Tickwillow	Mrs D. C. and Mr J. Richardson	D. Hodson
Crontham King	D	12.10.63	Annastock Lance	Taveys Stormy Queen	D. Gilfillan	R. Whittle
Empress of Bute	B	23.2.64	Dirksbys Arcadian of Tavey	Maid of Bute	Miss P. Wilson	Owner
Opinion of Tavey	B	19.10.64	Acclamation of Tavey	Juno of Cartergate	Mrs J. Ryan	Mrs J. Curnow
Oberan of Tavey	D	19.10.64	Acclamation of Tavey	Juno of Cartergate	M. Gover	Mrs J. Curnow
Triogen Traffic Cop	D	8.2.63	Acclamation of Tavey	Triogen Teenage Sensation	A. Hogg	Owner
Triogen Tuppenny Feast	B	29.5.64	Acclamation of Tavey	Triogen Teenage Wonder	Mrs D. C. and Mr J. Richardson	A. Hogg
Triogen Tuppenny Treat	B	29.5.64	Acclamation of Tavey	Triogen Teenage Wonder	Mrs J. Scheja	A. Hogg
Clanguard Comanche	D	9.8.64	Carrickgreen Confederate	Fricka of Codmore	Mrs H. Morgan	W. J. Beattie
Rajada Juliet	B	30.5.64	Tumlow Impeccable	Heidi of Tickwillow	R. Hodge	D. Hodson
Carlagon Ravishing	B	29.7.65	Acclamation of Tavey	Triogen Tarragon	L. Lock	Owner
Heidiland Trouble Spot	D	18.4.65	Taveys Stormy Achievement	Triogen Traffic Trouble	R. Selbourne	Miss A. Chaffey
Kassel of Royaltain	B	4.5.64	Acclamation of Tavey	Barrimilne Helga	Miss P. Quinn	Owner

						Owner
Tramerfields Dubonny Princess	B	25.11.65	Tumlow Storm Caesar	Capri of Tramerfield	J. Hall	Owner
Delmordene Buccaneer	D	21.12.65	Crontham King	Achenburg Heida	Mr and Mrs J. Bramley	Owners
Bronvornys Explorer	D	27.4.64	Taveys Stormy Achievement	Triogen Tuff Talk	G. M. Barry	Mrs U. T. Harper
Nayrilla Athene	B	22.4.67	Vanessa's Little Dictator of Tavey	Opinion of Tavey	Mrs P. Mitchell	Mrs J. Ryan
Skybank Tango	B	11.9.66	Edencourts Banker	Skyline Tuta	I. Williams	P. Tompkyns
Triogen Tornado	D	20.3.67	Triogen Traffic Cop	Triogen Treble Chance	A. Hogg	Owner and Mrs A. Kelly
Wismar of Royaltain	B	24.1.66	Tumlow Impeccable	Barrimilne Helga	Mrs S. Chambers	Miss P. Quinn
Clanguard Cadet	D	30.8.65	Carrickgreen Confederate	Fricka of Codmore	D. Montgomery	W. J. Beattie
Baroness of Tavey	B	4.11.66	Vanessa's Little Dictator of Tavey	Taveys Westwinds Quintessence	Mrs V. Killips	Mrs J. Curnow
Dizzy Debutante	B	5.7.65	Iceberg of Tavey	Taveys Stormy Kamella	Mrs D. Hart	Mrs M. J. Gillespie
Nagold of Royaltain	B	25.11.67	Tumlow Impeccable	Barrimilne Helga	Mrs D. Yule	Miss P. Quinn
Nayrilla Adonis	D	22.4.67	Vanessa's Little Dictator of Tavey	Opinion of Tavey	Mrs D. Neale	Mrs J. Ryan
Royaltains Babette of Tavey	B	4.11.66	Vanessa's Little Dictator of Tavey	Taveys Westwinds Quintessence	Miss P. Quinn and Mrs P. Gledhill	Mrs J. Curnow

Name of Champion	Sex	Born	Sire	Dam	Owner	Breeder
Kingroy Karla Kay	B	8.3.68	Stormy Baron	Devis Hurricane	M. Witham and P. O'Connor	C. White
Rioghal Raquel	B	16.4.67	Cubist of Tavey	Clanguard Cantata	L. Galbraith	M. Grierson
Taveys Stormy Medallion	D	26.3.64	Taveys Stormy Achievement	Taveys Stormy Willow	Mrs D. Parker	Mrs C. Starns
Royaltains Reluctant Hero	D	9.6.68	Heidiland Trouble Spot	Kassel of Royaltain	H. Astley	Miss P. Quinn
Achim Zeitgeist	D	19.10.66	Taveys Stormy Nugget	Taveys Stormy Pride	Mrs G. Bradshaw	Mrs J. Parkes and M. Bradshaw
Hensel Midnight Max	D	7.11.67	Taveys Stormy Medallion	Barrimilne Black Diamond	Miss C. Parker	Mr and Mrs G. Henson
Roanoke Bobadilla	B	9.5.68	Roanoke Nayrilla Apollo	Cadereyta of Roanoke	Mrs D. C. and Mr J. Richardson	Owners
Achenburg Delilah	B	18.6.68	Achim Zeitgeist	Katina of Trevellis	Mrs M. Woodward	Owner
Tumlow Bonanza	B	13.5.69	Tumlow Impeccable	Tumlow Odette	O. Powell	Mr and Mrs R. Harris
Tumlow Whiplash	D	18.6.68	Tumlow Peter Royal	Tumlow the Witch	A. Barnard	Mr and Mrs R. Harris
Nordosten Kantata	B	20.3.70	Clanguard Cadet	Xantippe of Sonhende	Mrs J. Crawshaw	Mrs V. Crawshaw
Auldrigg Pinza	D	3.6.70	Tumlow Impeccable	Tumlow Odette	Mrs A. Wilson	Mrs F. Auld
Ecstasy of Tramerfield	B	12.10.68	Edencourts Avenger	Tramerfield Dubonny Princess	Miss R. Anderson	J. Hall
Linhoff Pearl Diver	B	25.10.69	Wilm von Forell	Linhoff Triogen Tessa	K. Frankland	Owner
Tumlow Aerolite	B	28.2.69	Edencourts Banker	Taveys Stormy Pepita	Mrs E. Hewan	Mr and Mrs R. Harris

Name		Date	Sire	Dam	Breeder	Owner
Tumlow Carousel	B	15.6.69	Tumlow Impeccable	Tumlow Blue Charm	Mrs R. McAleese	Mr and Mrs R. Harris
Tumlow Satan	D	2.3.68	Tumlow Impeccable	Tumlow Odette	A. Collins	Mr and Mrs R. Harris
Taveys Badge	B	14.4.70	Iceberg of Tavey	Nieta of Tavey	Mr and Mrs S. Somerfield	Mrs J. Curnow
Studbriar Chieftain	D	12.8.68	Iceberg of Tavey	Eikon Jests Amazon	Mrs M. King	Owner
Whistleberry Achilles	D	25.10.66	Clanguard Comanche	Clanguard Cha Cha	R. Wilson	H. Rooney
Yucca of Tavey	B	17.9.69	Iceberg of Tavey	Nieta of Tavey	Mrs E. Edwards	Mrs J. Curnow
Flexor Flugelman	D	24.3.70	Tumlow Green Highlander	Tumlow Radiance	D. Crick	Owner
Highroyds Avenger	D	29.7.71	Nayrilla Adonis	Queen Wilhelmina of Zonneleen	T. Lamb	Owner
Mitrasandra Gay Lady of Findjans	B	22.8.71	Tumlow Satan	Findjans Fair Allyne	Mr and Mrs M. Page	Mr and Mrs M. Taylor
Stroud of Reksum	D	4.5.68	Dante of Tramerfield	Candy of Tavey	Mrs W. Barker	R. Musker
Tryphaena Titled Lady	B	14.7.71	Yachtsman of Tavey	Penny Poppet	Mrs E.P. Harrington-Gill	C. Blackman
Tinkazan Serengetti	B	30.1.71	Tinkazan Triogen Texas Ranger	Tinkazan Serenissima	Mrs J. Scheja	Owner
Taveys Icypants	B	30.4.71	Iceberg of Tavey	Nieta of Tavey	Mrs J. Curnow	Owner
Taveys Gridiron	D	8.3.71	Yachtsman of Tavey	Rusa of Tavey	Mrs J. Curnow	Owner
Vyleighs Valerian	B	3.2.72	Bonniedale Dougal	Hunsett Moonstone	R. Skinner and later Mrs O. Neave	Mrs H. Vyse

Name of Champion	Sex	Born	Sire	Dam	Owner	Breeder
Yachtsman of Tavey	D	17.9.69	Iceberg of Tavey	Nieta of Tavey	Mrs J. Curnow	Owner
Heidi of Travemunde	B	16.6.71	Achim Zeitgeist	Jenifer of Travemunde	Mr and Mrs A. Sheldon	J. Cole
Treasurequest Cristal	B	2.11.70	Treasurequest Annastock Xavier	Ruskins Dark Duchess	Mr and Mrs R. Law	A. Brown
Tinkazan Shinimicas	B	11.1.73	Camerons Snoopy of Tinkazan	Triogen Timely Reminder	Mr and Mrs D. Hilliard	Mrs J. Scheja
Heathermount Grenadier	D	29.3.71	Casper of Heathermount	Heathermount Quicksilver of Sonhende	Mrs K. Kennaman	Mr and Mrs W. Parker
Taveys Encore	B	14.5.74	Taveys Satellite	Taveys Icypants	Mrs J. Curnow	Owner
Royaltains Miss Haversham	B	22.9.72	Triogen Tornado	Royaltains Snow Gem	G. Clark	Miss P. Quinn
Royaltains Highwayman of Borain	D	4.6.71	Royaltains Prince Regent	Royaltains Lunar Mirth	Mrs P. Gledhill	Miss P. Quinn
Borains Raging Calm	B	20.3.74	Borains Warning Shot	Borains Born Forth	Mrs P. Gledhill	Owner
Kenstaff Tornado of Achenburg	D	23.8.73	Triogen Tornado	Sundown Sheba	Mrs M. Woodward	Mrs I. Marshall
Kirnvars Athos	D	10.3.71	Wilm von Forell	Bankers Amethyst	H. Curtis	Owner
Demos Skipper	D	6.1.72	Tumlow Whiplash	Knotsalls Ezmaralda	M. Turner	Owner
Chevington Royal Black Magic	D	5.4.75	Hillmora the Extremist	Chevington Royal Chiffon	Mr and Mrs I. Ould	Mrs O. Neave

Olderhill Seattle	B	2.2.74	Phileens Duty Free of Tavey	Olderhill Dhobi	Mrs D. Patience	Mrs S. Wilson
Dizown the Hustler	D	23.12.75	Taveys Satellite	Olderhill Salvador	Mrs D. Patience	Owner
Dizown Georgie Girl	B	23.12.75	Taveys Satellite	Olderhill Salvador	Mr and Mrs J. James	Mrs D. Patience
Olderhill Sheboygan	D	2.2.74	Phileens Duty Free of Tavey	Olderhill Dhobi	Mrs S. Wilson	Owner
Findjans Poseidon	D	13.4.74	Phileens Duty Free of Tavey	Mitrasandra Gay Lady of Findjans	Mr and Mrs M. Page	Owners
Jatras Raven	B	20.3.75	Findjans Poseidon	Jatras Blue Star	R. Gazley	Owner
Royaltains Unexpected Guest	B	27.11.74	Royaltains Reluctant Hero	Mystic Gay Heroine	Miss P. Quinn	C. Brown
Copper Bronze Anoushka	B	26.6.74	Phileens Duty Free of Tavey	Sophie Copper Bronze	Mrs S. Logan-Mitchell	Owner
Hillmora the Corsair	D	8.8.71	Wilm von Forell	Hillmora Triogen Torcella	Mr and Mrs I. Baird	B. Johnson
Merrist Reluctant Knight	D	19.1.74	Royaltains Reluctant Hero	Taveys Intrepid	R. Scott	Mrs G. Scott
Studbriar Dark N'Sassy of Zarwin	B	19.10.74	Studbriar Chieftan	Jatras Commanche Princess	M. Jones	Mrs M. King
Ariki Arataki	B	4.6.74	Studbriar Chieftain	Treasurequest Cristal	Mrs M. King	Mr and Mrs R. Law
Kaiserberg Helen	B	14.11.73	Kingsmeadow Blairderry Moss	Rembergs Bitter Sweet	D. More	Mrs A. Buist

Name of Champion	Sex	Born	Sire	Dam	Owner	Breeder
Arkturus Valans Choice	D	23.7.72	Linhoff the Pagan	Findjans Princess Pleasaunce	Mrs V. Harle	J. Nolan
Lucinian Nera	D	18.6.71	Clanguard Comanche	Heidi of Garmondsway	R. Peters	P. Brooks
Abbeyville Shooting Star	B	24.4.73	Stroud of Reksum	Triogen Too True	R. Peters	W. Barker
Ainsdale Sea Marauder	D	31.1.71	Heidiland Trouble Spot	Annastock Waternymph	Mrs J. Ainsley	Owner
Jasmeres Royal Melody	B	5.4.72	Taveys Gentleman of Jasmere	Borains Born Free of Jasmere	Mrs P. Judge	Mrs J. Crowe
Achenburg Juliette	B	31.7.72	Triogen Tornado	Achenburg Delilah	Mr and Mrs I. Wardopper	Mrs M. Woodward
Upfolds Admiral Blackfoot	D	13.7.74	Yachtsman of Tavey	Lisa's Black and Tan Fantasy	Miss E. Bradley	Dr Elliott
Hillmora the Explorer	D	8.12.73	Linhoff the Maestro	Hillmora the Capri	A. B. More	B. Johnson
Saxonhaus Black Bellman	D	9.5.71	Achim Zeigeist	Nayrilla Amethyst	Mrs M. K. Stamps	Mrs Hughes
Studbriar the Red	D	14.6.74	Phileens Duty Free of Tavey	Taveys Renaissance	Mrs M. King	Mrs J. Curnow and Mrs M. King
Kaybar Rheingold	B	13.1.75	Greif von Hagenstern from Barriminle	Karlakays Karmina	Mrs A. Sturdy	Mr and Mrs K. Cole
Varla My Silk and Satin	B	1.3.73	Auldrigg Pinza	Zweite Madchen	Mr and Mrs S. Mackay	Mr and Mrs R. Valerio
Ashdobes Brown Berry	B	1.11.75	Camerons Snoopy of Tinkazan	Ashdobes Venus	Mrs S. Mitchell	Owner
Sandean Aquarius	D	24.2.74	Roanoke Goldfinger	Black Belinda	Mrs R. Hedges	Mrs T. Brunton

Serky Sula Serape	D	8.4.72	Max of Index	Ortega Omen	A. Legget	Mrs Holden
Ikos Valerians Valor	D	15.10.74	Triogen Tornado	Vyleighs Valerian	Mr and Mrs I. James	R. Skinner
Taveys Ladyship of Shaheen	B	10.9.75	Taveys Gridiron	Camereich Daytrip of Tavey	Mrs E. Steggle	Mrs J. Curnow
Chater Man of the Moment	D	16.8.72	Triogen Tornado	Baroness of Tavey	J. MacKenzie	Mrs V. Killips
Davalogs Crusader	D	16.5.73	Tumlow Satan	Edwina Vivacious	Mr and Mrs A. Mullholland	F. Simmons
Javictreva Brief Defiance of Chater	D	6.4.75	Chater Icy Storm	Chater Moon Queen	Mrs V. Killips	Mrs N. Simmons
Borains Miss Royal	B	28.3.76	Flexor Flugelman	Borains Born Forth	Mrs P. Gledhill	Owner
Major Marauder	D	18.12.76	Ainsdale Sea Marauder	Crudos Amoroso	Mr and Mrs T. Jones	Mrs B. Horan
Alkay Alizanza	D	30.9.75	Stroud of Reksum	Roanoke Lucky Strike	W. Duggleby	A. Corbett
Dizown Bedazzled of Chaanrose	B	23.12.75	Taveys Satellite	Olderhill Salvador	Miss R. Lane	Mrs D. Patience
Phileens Ringmaster	D	13.8.74	Taveys Satellite	Kay Hills Outrigger	Mrs E. Edwards	Owner
Zalphas Harmony	B	10.10.75	Triogen Tornado	Jasmeres Royal Melody	Mrs A. Richardson	Mrs P. Judge
Studbriar the Godfather	D	3.10.76	Studbriar Chieftain	Jatras Commanche Princess of Studbriar	A. Geraghty	Mrs M. King
Pompie Alcyone	B	17.3.77	Findjans Poseidon	Pompie Sea Aphrodite	Mrs H. Partridge	Owner
Auldrigg Witchcraft	B	6.9.71	Auldrigg Pinza	Auldrigg Pickety Witch	Mrs F. Auld	Owner

Name of Champion	Sex	Born	Sire	Dam	Owner	Breeder
Zalphas Spirit	B	22.12.77	Findjans Poseidon	Jasmeres Royal Melody	R. Moore	Mrs P. Judge
Findjans Freya	B	8.3.77	Findjans Poseidon	Tanerdyce Michaelia	Mr and Mrs M. Page	Owners
Perihelias Madame Rochas	B	10.5.77	Taveys Gridiron	Jadans Aravon the Huntress of Perihelia	Mrs E. J. and Miss A. I. Lonsdale	Owners
Roanoke Marigold of Boreamond	B	12.2.77	Sandean Aquarius	Tinkazan Tabora	Mrs P. J. Tyler	J. Richardson
Sea Mistress of Ainsdale	B	18.12.76	Ainsdale Sea Marauder	Crudos Amoroso	Mrs J. Ainsley	Mrs B. Horan
Von Klebongs Solar Encore at Achenburg	D	17.7.78	Galaxys Solar Salute	Von Klebongs Dark Havoc	Mrs M. Woodward	Mrs J. Perry
Roanoke Swell-Fella	D	30.10.77	Upfolds Admiral Blackfoot	Roanoke Bonnie	T. M. Ager-Neave	J. Richardson
Highroyds Corry Belle	B	9.1.78	Highroyds Avenger	Studbriar Fortune Gal of Highroyd	Mr and Mrs N. Naylor	T. Lamb
I Can Boogie at Dizown	B	27.1.78	Dizown the Hustler	Olderhill Sioux	Mrs D. Patience	Mrs S. Wilson
Borains Night Watchman	D	2.7.78	Borains Warning Shot	Borains Forever Amber	Mrs P. Gledhill	Owner
Zalphas Midland Miss	B	22.12.77	Findjans Poseidon	Jasmeres Royal Melody	Mrs P. M. Judge	Owner
Chaanrose the Solitaire	B	3.2.79	Phileens Duty Free of Tavey	Dizown Bedazzled of Chaanrose	Miss R. Lane	Owner

298

Jasmeres Regal Star	B	13.12.78	Phileens Katmai	Jasmeres Regal Lady	C. J. Bagley	Mrs J. Crowe
Torjet Colonial Boy	D	21.5.80	Von Klebongs Solar Encore at Achenburg	Torjet Touch of Class	Mr and Mrs I. Wardropper and Mrs M. Woodward	Mr and Mrs I. Wardropper
Maganas Dark Damask	B	21.11.79	Javictreva Brief Defiance of Chater	Zalphas Lady Anna of Magana	Mr and Mrs J. B. Shaw	J. B. Shaw
Merrinores Modern Times	B	10.2.78	Flexor Flugelman	Merrinores Well-To-Do	Mr and Mrs M. J. Grier	Owners
Chornytan Fable	D	26.2.79	Chornytan Midnite Mark	Kittyhawk of Chornytan	D. E. Gandley	Mrs T. J. Toole
Dizown Razzamatazz	D	11.4.79	Ferrings Mike Victor	Olderhill Seattle	Mrs D. Patience	Owner
Taveys Ovation of Tancrey	B	10.8.76	Phileens Duty Free of Tavey	Taveys Winsome	Mrs J. Briscall	Mrs J. Curnow
Jasmeres Royal Festive	B	7.2.77	Highroyds Avenger	Jasmeres Regal Lady	Mrs J. Crowe	Owner
Orbiston Jaeger of Nethan	D	9.6.77	Nylana Gustav	Sonja Vontazia	P. S. McLean	J. Duffy
Highroyds Man of the Year	D	5.4.80	Jacade Mercedes of Mantoba	Studbriar Fortune Gal of Highroyd	Mr and Mrs J. D. Bamforth	T. Lamb
Studquest Black Velvet of Studbriar	B	23.6.79	Studbriar the Red	Studbriar Fortune Seeker	A. Coughlan	Mrs Amphlett
Borains Wild Alliance of Linzella	B	13.9.78	Flexor Flugelman	Borains Raging Calm	Mrs L. Satchell	Mrs P. Gledhill
Fillidons Carlton Cuckoo from Chornytan	B	16.6.79	Chornytan Midnite Mark	Yelitze of Achenburg	Mr and Mrs J. Sowden	G. Phillips

Name of Champion	Sex	Born	Sire	Dam	Owner	Breeder
Chevington Royal Virtue of Mantoba	B	30.12.79	Chevington Royal Black Magic	Vyleighs Valerian	Mrs P. M. Woodcock	Mrs O. Neave
Royal Bertie of Chevington	D	4.2.79	Chevington Royal Rianna	Ikos Criterion Maid	Mrs O. Neave	R. W. Skinner
Georgia Brown from Dizown	B	9.4.79	Dizown the Hustler	Gregarths Sonata	Mrs V. B. Corke	Mrs K. Kruger
Othertons Statesman	D	17.11.80	Merrist Reluctant Knight	Airborne of Otherton	Mr and Mrs P. B. Rock	Owners
Chevington Royal Virginia	B	30.12.79	Chevington Royal Black Magic	Vyleighs Valerian	R. G. David	Mrs O. Neave
Flexor Adonis	D	13.11.79	Flexor Neonlight	Merad Annabella	Mrs and Mrs G. Young	D. Crick
Ritlo Denzil	D	31.10.77	Gorgmari's Goliath	Ritlo Coren	P. C. Holloway	Dr M. L. Harris
Maxtay Meritorious	B	13.5.80	Javictreva Brief Defiance of Chater	Kingswinford Free Spirit	P. Taylor and K. Clarke	Mr and Mrs M. Dolman
Sateki Gin	B	6.3.80	Brutosh Roylat Maradidi	Zara Ind Diamond Thistle	D. Winterbourn	Owner
Halsbands Helmsman	D	12.9.80	Dizown Razzamatazz	Halsbands Manhatten	Mr and Mrs R. James	Owners
Chevington Royal Belle	B	9.8.80	Roanoke Swell-Fella	Chevington Royal Bianca	Mrs O. Neave	Owner
Vincedobe Eclipse	B	29.12.80	Major Marauder	Vincedobe Aurora	D. Anderson and Mrs Frost	Mr and Mrs Vincent
Vonmac Keegan	D	7.7.79	Drumpelier Bismarck	Vonmac Bonnie	Mr and Mrs F. J. Braid	Mrs McDonald

Name	Sex	Date	Sire	Dam	Breeder	Owner
Elrobans Good as Gold	B	24.9.81	Upfolds Admiral Blackfoot	Royaltains Dancing Flame	Mr and Mrs and Miss E. Bradley	Owners
Trevannick Master Mariner	D	13.7.80	Upfolds Admiral Blackfoot	Royaltain College Girl	Mr and Mrs C. B. Pascoe	Owners
Pompie Dutch Leiveling	B	29.4.81	Salvador vom Franckenhorst	Pompie Alcyone	Mrs H. Partridge	Owner
Findjans Chaos	D	5.6.82	Findjans Poseidon	Pompie Dione of Findjans	Mr and Mrs M. G. Page	Owners
Jenicks Debonaire	D	25.3.82	Jacade Mercedes of Mantoba	Highroyds Corry Belle	R. Masterton	Mr and Mrs N. Naylor
Findjans Bo Derick of Nyewood	B	23.1.82	Findjans Poseidon	Pompie Dione of Findjans	Mrs J. Rutter	Mr and Mrs M. G. Page
Chornytan Dinahawk	B	10.2.81	Chornytan Midnite Mark	Kittyhawk of Chornytan	Mrs T. J. Toole	Owner
Perihelias Resolution	D	19.12.81	Findjans Poseidon	Perihelias Madame Rochas	Mr and Mrs B. Bartle	Mrs and Miss Lonsdale
Chornytan Travelin' Light	D	23.6.82	Javictreva Brief Defiance of Chater	Chornytan Feather	Mr and Mrs A. Sargent	Mrs T. J. Toole
Dolbadarn Oriana	B	7.9.81	Merad Dark Tempest	Bremenville Miss Sonya	Mr and Mrs J. Higgins	Owners
Laurills High Flyer	B	30.9.80	Major Marauder	Royaltains High Hopes	Mrs L. Y. Green	Owner
Pampisford Pepper	B	7.3.82	Red Rebel of Chequers	Olga Black Pepper	Miss C. J. Green	Owner
Metexa Miss Brodie	B	7.5.80	Quanto vom Haus Schimmel	Metexa Midnight Surprise	Mr and Mrs J. McManus	Owners

Name of Champion	Sex	Born	Sire	Dam	Owner	Breeder
Pompie Sea Jade of Chancepixies	B	10.1.83	Flexor Adonis	Pompie Alcyone	D. Anderson and Mrs J. Frost	Mrs H. Partridge
Tashatrend Son of Adonis	D	12.3.82	Flexor Adonis	Natasha of Handa	Mrs K. King	J. R. Saville
Rheinbar Blakeney	D	3.5.79	Alkay Alizanza	Kaybar Rheingold	Mr and Mrs C. Hemmins	Mrs A. Sturdy
Bronsilk Copper Alanthus	D	26.10.82	Danceaway Sixth Former	Copper Black Pearl	Owners	Owners
Jiltrain Inter-City	D	21.8.81	Davalogs Crusader	Flexor Tamarisk	Mr and Mrs R. Thorpe	G. Rodgers
Essenbar Ebony Eyes	B	18.4.82	Varline Icon	Barrimilne Cover Girl	Mrs L. Clayton	Owner
Swanwite Flame Successor	D	8.2.81	Swanwite Flame Storm	Orbiston Thunderbolt	A. Legget	J. Hoolaghan
Mantoba High Voltage	D	17.12.82	Jacade Mercedes of Mantoba	Chevington Royal Virtue	Mrs P. M. Woodcock	Owner
Margins Flexibility	B	17.11.83	Flexor Adonis	Leos Sweet Sleepy Time Girl	Mr and Mrs Prowse	Mr and Mrs N. Barrett
Findjans Gelert	D	16.7.81	Findjans Poseidon	Pompie Dione of Findjans	Mr and Mrs R. H. Page	Mr and Mrs M. G. Page
Halsbands Redwing	B	7.11.82	Rosecroft By The Way to Bilsam	Halsbands Manhatten	R. James and J. Lewis	Owners
Dolbadarn Ace High	D	18.10.82	Davalogs Crusader	Bremenville Miss Sonya	Mr and Mrs K. Olney	Mr and Mrs J. Higgins

Sallates Ferris	D	27.4.85	Perihelias Resolution	Sigismunds Ice Cool Kate	Mrs Y. Bevans	Mrs G. E. Hunt
Metexa Movie Master	D	15.12.83	Graaf Carlos v.d. Edele Stam	Metexa McGuinness Fury	Mr and Mrs J. McManus	Owners
Corvic Cinnabar	B	14.11.82	Findjans Ikeya Seki	Georgia Brown from Dizown	Mrs V. B. Corke	Owner
Rittmeister Black Spartan	D	21.4.83	Ritlo Denzil	Ritlo Highland Mary	Mr and Mrs E. D. Phillips	Mr and Mrs K. McCormick
Crossridge the Jazzman	D	23.6.83	Dizown All That Jazz	Anna of Crossridge	Mr and Mrs M. R. Stewart	J. Crossley and Miss M. Detheridge
Jenicks Cruise Missile	D	1.9.84	Perihelias Resolution	Jenicks Missile Belle	S. Kay	Mr and Mrs N. Naylor
Chater the Ferryman	D	6.8.83	Achenburg Andrew	Lotus Eater of Chater	Mrs V. J. Philip	Owner
Dolbadarn Hawker Fury	D	12.5.83	Chornytan Midnite Mark	Bremenville Miss Sonya	Mr and Mrs M. J. Higgins	Owners
Clivalley She My Girl	B	14.2.82	Roanoke Everest	Jiltrains Head Girl	Mr and Mrs J. Hubball	C. McDonald
Dolbadarn Nite Star	B	11.4.84	Chornytan Travelin' Light	Dolbadarn Lile of Avelion	Mr and Mrs K. J. Olney	Mr and Mrs M. J. Higgins
Dizown I Can Boogie Too with Holtzburg	B	8.9.84	Findjans Chaos	I Can Boogie at Dizown	Mr and Mrs T. J. Holt	Mrs D. Patience
Jowendy Into Jazz	B	25.5.84	Dizown All That Jazz	Cracklin Rosie of Jowendy	Mrs W. J. Burge	Owner
Dolbadarn Dirty Girty	B	11.4.84	Chornytan Travelin' Light	Dolbadarn Lile of Avelion	Mr and Mrs A. R. Sargent	Mr and Mrs M. J. Higgins

Name of Champion	Sex	Born	Sire	Dam	Owner	Breeder
Nyewoods Bo Street Runner at Tanbowtra	D	10.12.84	Findjans Chaos	Findjans Bo Derick of Nyewood	Mrs W. Jackson	Mr and Mrs D. Rutter
Twinglo Le Juice of Bledig	B	21.11.84	Perihelias Resolution	Findjans Le Crunch	Mr and Mrs R. K. Braver and Mrs R. Beckerton	Mrs M. D. D'Cruze
Sundown Dancer of Pampisford	B	12.3.85	Red Rebel of Chequers	Pompie Heaven Sent	Mrs Y. Eggett	Mr and Mrs R. P. Houston
Dorusta Lutzow	D	10.2.80	Drumpelier Bismarck	Vonmac Brianna	D. Griffiths	D. Sumner
Chevington Royal Kashmere	B	28.5.83	Roanoke Swell-Fella	Kebunteh Magic Lass	Mr and Mrs A. Harper	Mrs O. Neave
Elrobans Scheherazade	B	3.3.84	Borains Night Watchman	Elrobans Royal Gold	Mr and Mrs R. Bradley	Owners
Crossridge the Carbon Copy at Lynfryds	D	22.3.84	Findjans Chaos	Dizown Copy Cat	Mr and Mrs F. P. Wilkes	J. Crossley and Miss M. Detheridge
Vonjolis Woman of the World	B	19.3.85	Highroyds Man of the Year	Black Princess	P. Stephenson and Mrs Hodgkins	Owners
Essenbar the Challenger	D	9.8.86	Quinto van de Kunnemaborgh at Vyleighs	Essenbar Athena	Mrs L. Clayton	Owner
Findjans Melee	B	18.4.85	Findjans Chaos	Findjans Alita	Mr and Mrs M. G. Page	Owners
Willows Stormy Satellite	B	22.1.85	Caerwent Midnight Storm	Cavanda Star	Mr and Mrs G. C. Doody	Owners

304

Name	Sex	Date	Sire	Dam	Breeder	Owner
Sallate Islay	B	29.5.86	Perihelias Resolution	Sallates Special Kay	B. C. Lewis	Mrs G. E. Hunt
Halsbands Wicked Wizard	D	31.10.83	Wizz Bang of Vickisfree	Halsbands Manhatten	J. H. Bruton	R. James and Miss J. Lewis
Shirdawns April Rain	B	24.4.85	Halsbands Helmsman	Alphadobes Merry Contessa	Mrs S. F. Cooper	Owner
Rumarks Kellys Eye	B	23.5.85	Tashatrend Son of Adonis	Scarlet Ribbon	M. E. Shipley and Miss R. Morrison	P. E. Osborne
Heimdalls Ero	D	19.3.84	Vonmac Nero	Barrimilne Dancing Queen	D. Stafford	Owner
Jostein Deja Vu	B	30.8.86	Dolbadarn Ace High	Josheb Boogie	S. D. Lowe	Owner
Dimrost Freedom Fighter	D	25.10.84	Pompie Dangerman at Dimrost	Khasamari Sieglinde at Dimrost	Mr and Mrs J. Nelson	Mr and Mrs R. Braid
Mantoba Whiplash	D	16.12.84	Jacade Mercedes of Mantoba	Chevington Royal Virtue of Mantoba	Mrs P. M. Woodcock	Owner
Halsbands Bugenhagen	D	31.10.83	Wizz Bang of Vickisfree	Halsbands Manhatten	R. James and Miss J. Lewis	Owners
Perihelias Lili Marlene	B	19.12.81	Findjans Poseidon	Perihelias Madame Rochas	Mrs E. J. and Miss A. I. Lonsdale	Owners
Pampisford Rebel Rouser	D	10.7.85	Red Rebel of Chequers	Olga Black Pepper	Mr and Mrs S. Fern	Miss C. J. Green
Sallates Frauline	B	27.4.85	Perihelias Resolution	Sigismunds Ice Cool Kate	Mrs G. E. Hunt	Owner
Intercity Shady Lady	B	19.2.85	Perihelias Redoubtable	Jiltrain Delabina	Mr and Mrs R. Thorpe	Owners

Name of Champion	Sex	Born	Sire	Dam	Owner	Breeder
Song and Dance Man	D	6.1.85	Crossridge The Jazzman	Bompers Black Pearl	Mrs S. Johnson	Mr and Mrs M. R. Stewart
Chancepixies Friend or Foe	B	10.6.85	Findjans Giovanni of Mascoll	Vincedobe Eternity of Chancepixies	M. Harvey	D. Anderson and Mrs J. Frost
Nyewoods Excalibur	D	12.12.85	Findjans Chaos	Findjans Bo Derick of Nyewood	Mrs J. Rutter	Owner
Dizown Hello Darling from Estridge	B	5.12.86	Marienburg Firedanza v. Tavey	Dizown Daisy Brown	Mrs L. Purser	Mrs D. Patience
Jowendys Kool Choice	D	3.8.86	Tamberg Ace High	Naughty But Nice at Jowendy	Mrs S. Mycroft	Mrs W. Burge

OBEDIENCE CERTIFICATE WINNERS

OBEDIENCE CHAMPIONS (Winners of Three Obedience Certificates)

Name of Champion	Sex	Born	Sire	Dam	Breeder	Owner and Handler	Year of Win
Ch. Jupiter of Tavey	D	22.3.52	Bruno of Tavey	Prinses Anja v't Scheepjeskerk	Mrs J. Curnow	Mrs J. Curnow and R. M. Montgomery (handler)	1954 & 1955
Lady Gessler of Bryan	B	29.8.82	McShane of Terian	Baroness of Mickalice	M. Coulson	P. Gavin	1988 & 1989
Winners of Two Obedience Certificates							
Lionel of Rancliffe	D	13.8.63	Ch. Jove of Cartergate	Juliette of Rancliffe	Mrs O. Morris	D. Tretheway	1968
Winners of One Obedience Certificate							
Yuba Adonis	D	18.5.60	Ch. & Ob. Ch. Jupiter of Tavey	Rotherhurst Celestial	Mrs L. Hadley	T. Hadley	1964
Heiner Rustic	D	26.2.62	Smoothfield Chico	Birchanger Dawn	A. Nash	I. Inskip	1968

WORKING TRIALS WINNERS AND QUALIFIERS

WORKING TRIALS CHAMPIONS

Name of Champion	Sex	Born	Sire	Dam	Breeder	Owner	Handler	Stake won & Date
Ulf v. Margarethenhof, P.D.ex., T.D.ex., U.D.ex., C.D.ex.	D	30.6.46	Hasso v.d. Neckarstrasse	Toska v. Margarethenhof	M. Thurling	C. C. Surrey	Sgt H. Darbyshire	P.D. 1949 P.D. 1950
Mountbrowne Karen, P.D. ex, T.D.ex., U.D.ex.	B	18.8.50	Astor v. Morgensonne	Donathe v. Begertal	C. C. Surrey	C. C. Surrey	PC R. Ling	T.D. 1954 P.D. 1955
Mountbrowne Julie, P.D.ex., T.D.ex., U.D.ex., C.D.ex.	B	7.1.50	W.T.Ch. Ulf v. Margarethenhof	Donathe v. Begertal	C. C. Surrey	C. C. Durham	Sgt T. Sessford	T.D. 1953 P.D. 1955
Joseph of Aycliffe, P.D.ex., T.D.ex., U.D.ex., C.D.ex.	D	18.4.52	Dober v. Oldenfelde	W.T.Ch. Mountbrowne Julie	C. C. Durham	C. C. Durham	Sgt W. McGorrigan	P.D. 1956 P.D. 1960
Chaanrose Night Queen, T.D.ex., W.D.ex., U.D.ex., C.D.ex.	B	2.9.78	Heathermount Flitzenjaeger	Olderhill Salvador	Miss R. Lane	J. Fleet	Owner	T.D. 1981 T.D. 1982
Linrios Domingo, P.D.ex., T.D.ex., W.D.ex., U.D.ex., C.D.ex.	B	21.12.79	Rioghals Bravura	Linrios Blanche	J. Arnott	J. Middleweek	Owner	T.D. 1982 T.D. 1983

WINNERS OF ONE WORKING TRIALS CERTIFICATE

Name	Sex	Born	Sire	Dam	Breeder	Owner	Handler	Stake won & Date
Mountbrowne Joe, P.D.ex., T.D.ex., U.D.ex., C.D.ex.	D	7.1.50	W.T.Ch. Ulf v. Margarethen-hof	Donathe v. Begertal	C. C. Surrey	Mrs Porterfield (for Dobermann Club)	Owner	P.D. 1953
Mountbrowne Jenny, T.D.ex., U.D.ex.	B	7.1.50	W.T.Ch. Ulf v. Margarethen-hof	Donathe v. Begertal	C. C. Surrey	C. C. Buckinghamshire	Sgt G. Jones	T.D. 1952
Anna of Aycliffe, P.D.ex., T.D.ex., U.D.ex., C.D.ex.	B	16.4.55	W.T.Ch. Ulf v. Margarethen-hof	Jenny of Ayclifden	C. C. Durham	C. C. Durham	PC Hutchinson	P.D. 1958
Arno of Aycliffe, P.D.ex., T.D.ex., U.D.ex., C.D.ex.	D	16.4.55	W.T.Ch. Ulf v. Margarethen-hof	Jenny of Ayclifden	C. C. Durham	C. C. Durham	Sgt H. Garth	P.D. 1959
Hawk of Trevellis, P.D.ex., T.D.ex., U.D.ex., C.D.ex.	D	10.6.62	Taveys Stormy Legion	Brumbies Black Bramble	Mrs D. Horton	H. Appleby	Owner	T.D. 1966

DOBERMANNS QUALIFYING AT CHAMPIONSHIP WORKING TRIALS

*Qualifying in Police Dog, Tracking Dog, Utility Dog & Companion Dog Stakes (P.D., T.D., U.D., C.D.)

Name	Sex	Born	Sire	Dam	Breeder	Owner	Handler
Vyking Drum Major	D	13.8.49	Vyking Don of Tavey	Vyking Wanda of Tavey	Mrs P. Korda	Mrs J. Faulks	Owner
Mountbrowne Olaf	D	14.1.52	W.T.Ch. Ulf v. Margarethenhof	Donathe v. Begertal	C. C. Surrey	C. C. Cheshire	Sgt Taylor
Mountbrowne Amber	B	28.5.55	Mountbrowne Odin	Ch. Reichert Judy	Mrs M. Porterfield	C. C. Northumberland	PC T. Yeouart, later Sgt J. Hyslop

*Qualifying in Police Dog, Utility Dog & Companion Dog Stakes (P.D., U.D., C.D.)

Name	Sex	Born	Sire	Dam	Breeder	Owner	Handler
Mountbrowne Odin	D	14.1.52	W.T.Ch. Ulf v. Margarethenhof	Donathe v. Begertal	C. C. Surrey	C. C. Surrey	PC W. Redwood
Joan of Ayfelde	B	18.4.52	Dober v. Oldenfelde	W.T.Ch. Mountbrowne Julie	C. C. Durham	C. C. Durham	PC Hedges
Jenny of Ayclifden	B	18.4.52	Dober v. Oldenfelde	W.T.Ch. Mountbrowne Julie	C. C. Durham	C. C. Durham	PC Welsh
Faust of Cartergate	D	28.3.56	Ch. Day of Cartergate	Lola of Cartergate	Miss E. M. Would	C. C. Lincolnshire	PC J. Bush
Maverick the Brave	D	12.12.58	Ch. Challenger of Sonhende	Kaitonias Rio	C. Seddon	C. Brockett	Owner
Yuba Adonis	D	18.5.60	Ch. & Ob. Ch. Jupiter of Tavey	Rotherhurst Celestial	Mrs L. Hadley	T. Hadley	Owner

*Qualifying in Tracking Dog, Utility Dog & Companion Dog Stakes (T.D., U.D., C.D.)

Name	Sex	Born	Sire	Dam	Breeder	Owner	Handler
Lorelei of Tavey	B	28.9.52	Tasso v.d. Eversburg of Tavey	Prinses Anja v't Scheepjeskerk	Mrs J. Curnow	Mrs J. Faulks	Owner
Mountbrowne Remoh	D	26.5.53	Bill v. Blauenblut	Mountbrowne Kandra	C. C. Surrey	C. C. Essex	PC P. Cousins
Mountbrowne Yukon	D	5.11.54	W.T.Ch. Ulf v. Margarethenhof	Ch. Reichert Judy	Mrs M. Porterfield	C. C. Bedfordshire, later C. C. Surrey	Sgt F. Pettit, later PC Proctor
Mountbrowne Astor	D	28.5.55	Mountbrowne Odin	Ch. Reichert Judy	Mrs M. Porterfield	C. C. Devon	PC Kendrick
Barnard of Caedan	D	6.12.59	Culloden of Skipwith	Doberean Pamela	C. A. Beere	I. Stewart	Owner
Gurnard Gloomy Sunday	D	1.11.63	Ch. Acclamation of Tavey	Gurnard Hedda	Mrs D. Billingham and A. Barnard	Mrs D. Billingham and A. Barnard	A. Barnard

*Qualifications available up to end of 1968.

*Qualifying in Tracking Dog, Working Dog, Utility Dog & Companion Dog Stakes (T.D., W.D., U.D., C.D.)

Name	Sex	Born	Sire	Dam	Breeder	Owner	Handler
Taveys Stormy Jael	B	25.10.63	Ch. Taveys Stormy Achievement	Taveys Stormy Zeminda	Mrs J. Curnow	Mrs J. Curnow and Mrs J. Faulks	Mrs J. Faulks
Dandy of Dovecote	D	6.2.63	Eddystone Lancelot	Smarty of Upend	M. Freeman	D. L. Milner	Owner
Dollar Premium	D	28.6.64	Ch. Tumlow Impeccable	Lacrosse Winning Ride	Mrs E. Peckham	Mrs R. Hooper	Owner
Japonicas Ochre	D	26.8.67	Ch. Oberan of Tavey	Sal Pride of Edward	Mrs Holt	Mr and Mrs H. E. Appleby	Mrs A. Appleby
Chorntyan Passenger	D	13.1.72	Tinsley's the Stormcloud	Chorntyan Delight	Mrs T. J. Toole	L S Christopher	Owner
Charis Aquarius	D	12.9.69	Trojan Achievement	Gretel Goddess of Gorsley	Mrs A. Higgs	E. Handscomb	Owner
Koriston Pewter Strike of Doberean	B	22.7.72	Royaltains Nicky Tams	Doberean Eclat of Tavey	Mrs A. E. Anderson	Mrs J. Faulks	Owner
Ch. Ashdobes Brown Berry	B	1.11.75	Camerons Snoopy of Tinkazan	Ashdobes Venus	Mrs S. Mitchell	Mrs S. Mitchell	Owner
Roanoke Serenade	B	2.12.75	Aust. Ch. Bonnie-dale Dougal	Black Baroness of Pintlehill	Mr and Mrs J. Richardson	Mr and Mrs A. Kingswell	A. Kingswell
Spartan Warrior at Jovin-Blak	D	26.7.79	Jovin-Blak Knite	Roanoke Martini	Mr and Mrs N. J. Mitchell	J. V. Alderson	Owner
Chilly's Gentle Giant	D	28.4.79	Ch. Dizown the Hustler	Star of Smallfield	N. Belson	C. J. Chillingworth	Owner

312

Name		Date	Sire	Dam	Breeder	Owner
Somerbys Bandoleer Bravado	D	5.5.81	Danargo Dynamic	Freda of Somerby	Mrs B. McGrath	T. Brace	Owner
Studbriar Royal Sentinel	D	30.7.81	Ch. Studbriar the Red	Studbriars Milady	Mrs M. King	P. J. Carroll	Owner
My Gem of Sunnygift	B	4.6.82	Apoldas Impelo	Harpersbury Resist Me Not	Mrs B. McGrath	Mrs J. Magness	Owner
Brocketsfield Mister Max	D	Jan. '83	Further particulars unknown		Miss M. Delaney	Owner
Flynns Flashy Fanny	B	6.10.85	Studbriar Royal Sentinel	Reds Black Beauty	Mrs S. Prior	P. J. Carroll	Owner

*From 1969 to December 1989

*Qualifying in Working Dog, Utility Dog & Companion Dog Stakes (W.D., U.D., C.D.)

Name	Sex	Born	Sire	Dam	Breeder	Owner	Handler
Wyndenhelms Escort	D	4.4.67	Ch. Acclamation of Tavey	Ch. Wyndenhelm AWOL	G. Thompson	G. Thompson	Owner
Contessa of Achenburg	B	1.12.67	Xuberance of Tavey	Katina of Trevellis	Mrs M. Woodward	P. Leigh	Owner
Tumlow Solitaire	B	16.12.67	Apolda Blunderbuss	Tumlow the Witch	Mr and Mrs Harris	Mrs S. Mitchell	Owner
Skipper of Ashdobe	D	27.11.69	Heiner Rustic	Tumlow Solitaire	Mrs S. Mitchell	Mrs S. Mitchell	Owner
Duchess Vanessa	B	22.10.70	Vanessa's Little Dictator of Tavey	Frankskirby's Fireparade	Mr and Mrs B. Garrat	Mr M. Thouless	Owner
Jimartys Macbeth of Vidal	D	30.7.71	Roanoke Double Diamond	Jimartys Lancia Flavia	Mr and Mrs J. E. Burrell	C. Hooper	Owner
Danargo Dynamic	D	9.4.73	Ch. Triogen Tornado	Achenburg Fair Fortune	Mrs A. F. Griffiths	A. L. Griffiths	Owner
Ashdobes Vaguely Great	B	23.7.79	Ch. Findjans Poseidon	Ch. Ashdobes Brown Berry	Mrs S. Mitchell	Mrs S. Mitchell	Owner
Lorac Christophe	D	30.9.79	Jimartys Sandman	Weefores Beautiful Girl	Mrs C. Turnbull	Mr and Mrs J. Luke	J. Luke
Kessler Another Realm	D	7.6.81	Ch. Von Klebongs Solar Encore at Achenburg	Merrist Aphrodite	Mrs C. Jackson	D. Henry	Owner
Taranda Flamboyant Lady	B	21.10.80	Ch. Merrist Reluctant Knight	Soekis Shapely Lady	Mr and Mrs R. Dowden	Mrs C. M. Fleet	J. Fleet

Name	Sex	Born	Sire	Dam	Breeder	Owner	Handler
Purdey at Jovin-Blak	B	18.3.84	Chevington Royal Nimrod	Wyncab Lucky Girl	Mrs I. C. Davies	J. V. Alderson	Owner
Saucy Fraulein	B	18.7.85	Graaf Carlos v.d. Edele Stam	Whispering Waunder	A. More	Mrs J. Dempster	Owner
Daleys Deb	B	25.3.83	Linrios Canticle from Barrimilne	Fenns Delight	Mrs B. J. Fennemore	Mrs D. Cronin	T. Brace
The Khan of Sunnygift	D	29.8.85	Bavarian of Barrimilne	Starglatt Sheer Delight	Mr & Mrs D. Magness	Mrs J. Magness	Owner

*From 1969 to December 1989

*Qualifying in Utility Dog Stakes (U.D.ex) (from 1949 to December 1989)

Name	Sex	Born	Sire	Dam	Breeder	Owner	Handler
Donathe v. Begertal	B	28.3.48	Zar v. Stahlhelm	Asta v. Teufenstal	K. Ehlebracht	C. C. Surrey	Sgt A. Osment
Mountbrowne Justice	D	7.1.50	W.T.Ch. Ulf v. Margarethenhof	Donathe v. Begertal	C. C. Surrey	C. C. Kent	Sgt S. Lawrie
Mountbrowne Juno	B	7.1.50	W.T.Ch. Ulf v. Margarethenhof	Donathe v. Begertal	C. C. Surrey	C. C. Lancashire	Sgt H. Herdman
Mountbrowne Kim	D	18.8.50	Astor v. Morgensonne	Donathe v. Begertal	C. C. Surrey	C. C. West Riding	–
Brumbies Black Baroness	B	1.9.52	Carle of Combepeter	Betti of Cartergate	Mrs P. Davis	D. Kingsberry	Owner

Name	Sex	Born	Sire	Dam	Breeder	Owner	Handler
Alouette of Aycliffe	B	16.4.55	W.T.Ch. Ulf v. Margarethenhof	Jenny of Ayclifden	C. C. Durham	C. C. Durham	PC Aikenhead
Asta of Aycliffe	B	16.4.55	W.T.Ch. Ulf v. Margarethenhof	Jenny of Ayclifden	C. C. Durham	C. C. Durham	PC Brett
Diana of Aycliffe	B	11.8.57	Culloden of Skipwith	Joan of Ayfelde	C. C. Durham	C. C. Durham	–
Doberean Patience	B	30.3.59	Ch. Taveys Stormy Abundance	Lorelei of Tavey	Mrs J. Faulks	Mrs J. Faulks	Owner
Flame of Aycliffe	B	27.4.59	Culloden of Skipwith	Joan of Ayfelde	C. C. Durham	C. C. Bedfordshire	PC Fulcher
Fangio of Aycliffe	D	27.4.59	Culloden of Skipwith	Joan of Ayfelde	C. C. Durham	C. C. Dorset, later G. Clark	PC Williams, later R. Skelhorne
Bracken of Cartergate	B	6.8.59	Ch. Claus of Cartergate	Ch. Helena of Cartergate	Miss E. M. Would	J. Bush	Owner
Ch. Wyndenhelms AWOL	B	25.7.60	Ch. Caliph of Trevellis	Ch. Bowesmoor Mona	G. Thompson	G. Thompson	Owner
Goliath of Dissington	D	26.12.60	Bowesmoor Sancho	Bambi of Dissington	Mrs E. M. Blair	C. C. Bedfordshire	PC N. Gorham
Lancon Skipper	D	31.7.51	Astor v. Morgensonne	Mountbrowne Juno	C. C. Lancashire	C. C. Lancashire	–
Mountbrowne Pluto	D	4.7.52	W.T.Ch. Ulf v. Margarethenhof	Mountbrowne Kandra	C. C. Surrey	C. C. East Riding	PC Peacock
Bowesmoor Gina	B	20.7.56	Treu v.d. Steinfurthohe	Helga v. Kleinwaldheim	Mrs M. Porterfield	C. C. Essex	PC T. Bierne

Name	Sex	Date	Sire	Dam	Breeder	Owner	Handler
Bowesmoor Herma	B	23.4.61	Old Boy	Vervain Rhythm	Mrs M. Porterfield and H. Darbyshire	C. C. Devon	PC Farrow
Bowesmoor Otis	B	15.12.61	Smoothfield Chico	Doocloone Dear Delinquent	Mrs D. H. Bamford	J. O. Whytock	Owner
Pagan Privateer	D	2.5.62	Ch. Acclamation of Tavey	Bracken of Cartergate	J. Bush	J. Bush	Owner
Mountbrowne Peter	D	28.4.65	Fury of Dissington	Ina of Trevellis	M. V. Downes	C. C. Surrey	PC M. Juniper
Dena of Illustria	B	18.4.62	Illustria Tumlow Storm Ahead	Eurydice of Trevellis	Mrs W. Garrod	M. J. Garrod	Owner
Harast Tomlyn	D	28.8.73	Japonicas Ochre	Hareaway Hebe	Mr and Mrs H. Appleby	Mr and Mrs H. Appleby	Mrs A. Appleby
Helroy Hotspur	D	13.2.71	Chater Kings Reward	Helroy Lady Courage of Graybarry	Mrs J. Glossop	L. Parker	Owner
Byron Burnt Sienna	B	21.4.75	Baron of Balbeggie	Swift of Balbeggie	Mrs J. Stocks	P. J. Carroll	Owner
Ch. Chevington Royal Black Magic	D	5.4.75	Hillmora the Extremist	Chevington Royal Chiffon	Mrs O. Neave	Mr and Mrs I. Ould	I. Ould
Jupiters Solo Orbit	D	20.10.76	Ch. Highroyds Avenger	Woodland Pride	G. Wilson	Mrs A. S. Wilson	G. Wilson
Charcoal Lady	B	27.3.77	Tinsleys March from Sousa	Bronze Venus	O. N. Poulton	K. Rhodes	Owner
Navua Billy Broonzy	D	3.2.79	Jimartys Sandman	Chavez Forget Me Not	Mrs S. M. Tanner	J. Daft	Owner

Name	Sex	Born	Sire	Dam	Breeder	Owner	Handler
Koriston Polonaise of Doberean	B	3.4.78	Royaltains Nicky Tams	Koriston Superstarlet	Mrs A. E. Anderson	Mrs J. Faulks	Owner
Ikos Imperial Priestess	B	9.11.80	Ch. Royal Bertie of Chevington	Tamars Lady of the Lake	R. W. Skinner	Mrs D. Easter	Owner
Ashdobes Vaguely Noble	D	23.7.79	Ch. Findjans Poseidon	Ch. Ashdobes Brown Berry	Mrs S. Mitchell	M. J. Crickett	Owner
Rizpahs Burning Ambition	B	22.5.80	Jupiters Solo Orbit	Copper Bronze Bridget	Mr and Mrs G. Wilson	A. Roach	Owner
Rioghal Cervantes	D	4.1.84	Edcath Registus	Linrio Enterprise	M. Grierson	John Middleweek, later, Mrs. C. Lethaby	Mrs C. Lethaby
Raggedhall Star	B	22.5.82	Chillys Gentle Giant	Raggedhall Raven	Mrs J. Pope	P. Merling	Owner
Opals Speculator	D	30.5.85	Ch. Chater the Ferryman	Charlottes Lucky Opal	Mrs J. Hardwick	Mrs J. Hardwick	Owner
Zenoan Reluctant Warrior	D	21.4.80	Wladek von Szczein	Elisa of Kenstaff	S. E. Thomas	R. Carter	Owner
Shardains Lady Gem	B	7.8.86	Ch. Dorusta Lutzow	Othertons Donah	J. Skitt	D. Morris	Owner
Vickisfree Starpitcher	D	7.7.84	Reltans Black Madness	Vickisfree Rebecca	Mrs J. Bird	A. Waite	Owner
Othertons Trialist	B	4.9.83	Ch. Highroyds Man of the Year	Airborne of Otherton	Mr & Mrs P. B. Rock	J. Daft	Owner
Bojenhoff Mistress Delilah	B	2.5.83	Barrimilne Benno	Bojenhoff Gypsy Greta	Mr & Mrs R. Beesley	Mrs V. Isherwood	Owner

*Qualifying U.D. (qualification discontinued after 1968)

Name	Sex	Born	Sire	Dam	Breeder	Owner	Handler
Astor v. Morgensonne	D	29.3.48	Sigmar	Asta v. Schulzenhof	E. Raginski	C. C. Surrey	–
Prinses Anja v't Scheepjeskerk	B	3.7.48	Graaf Dagobert v. Neerlands Stam	Alindia v't Scheepjeskerk	Mrs K. Demout	Mrs J. Curnow	Mrs A. Montgomery
Mountbrowne Bruce	D	15.6.55	Alex v. Rodenaer	Mountbrowne Kandra	C. C. Surrey	C. C. Northumberland	Pc Glendinning
Gin von Forell	D	23.5.60	Ger. Ch. Dirk v. Goldberg	Diana vom Oelberg	E. Wilking	Mrs M. Bastable	Owner

DOBERMANN CLUB WORKING TESTS DIPLOMA WINNERS (to October 1989)

Name	Sex	Born	Sire	Dam	Breeder	Owner & Handler	Test Passed
Lorelei of Tavey	B	28.9.52	Tasso v.d. Eversburg of Tavey	Prinses Anja v't Scheepjeskerk	Mrs J. Curnow	Mrs J. Faulks	I II
Carlo Eversburg of Romsley	D	24.4.58	Alex v. Rodenaer	Pride of Stonecross	J. C. Baugh	Mrs B. Murphy	I
Triogen Tallulah	B	20.6.58	Ch. Taveys Stormy Achievement	Triogen Bandeau of Tavey	A. B. Hogg	V. J. Lowe	I II
Classic of Trevellis	B	5.6.58	Ch. Taveys Stormy Abundance	Ch. Satin of Tavey	Mrs D. Horton	B. Horton	I
Doberean Patience	B	30.3.59	Ch. Tavey's Stormy Abundance	Lorelei of Tavey	Mrs J. Faulks	Mrs J. Faulks	I II
Brumbies Bandit	D	8.3.55	Birling Rebel	Brumbies Black Baroness	D. Kingsberry	D. Kingsberry	I
Mangrypin Sombrero	D	21.11.58	Treu v.d. Steinfurthohe	Mahadeo Early Edition	I. Bradbury	G. Myers	I
Illustria Elissa of Trevellis	B	9.11.59	Aguila of the Tamerlane	Classic of Trevellis	Mrs D. Horton	M. J. Garrod	I
Ch. Wyndenhelms AWOL	B	25.7.60	Ch. Caliph of Trevellis	Ch. Bowesmoor Mona	G. Thompson	G. Thompson	I II IV

Name	Sex	Date	Sire	Dam	Breeder	Owner	
Maverick the Brave	D	12.12.58	Ch. Challenger of Sonhende	Kaitonia's Rio	C. Seddon	C. Brockett	I III III
Hawk of Trevellis	D	10.6.62	Taveys Stormy Legion	Brumbies Black Bramble	Mrs D. Horton	B. Horton, later H. E. Appleby	I III III IV
Dena of Illustria	B	18.4.62	Illustria Tumlow Storm Ahead	Eurydice of Trevellis	Mrs W. Garrod	M. J. Garrod	I
Gurnard Gloomy Sunday	D	1.11.63	Ch. Acclamation of Tavey	Gurnard Hedda	Mrs D. Billingham and A. Barnard	Mrs D. Billingham and A. Barnard (handler)	I II III IV
Dandy of Dovecote	D	6.2.63	Eddystone Lancelot	Smarty of Upend	M. Freeman	D. L. Milner	I III III
Wyndenhelms Cormorant	B	8.6.64	Ch. Acclamation of Tavey	Ch. Wyndenhelms AWOL	G. Thompson	R. Hodge	I
Quizmaster of Siddley	D	19.1.63	Ch. Taveys Stormy Wonder	November Mist of Siddley	V. J. Lowe	V. J. Lowe	I
Havildar of Trevellis	D	10.6.62	Taveys Stormy Legion	Brumbies Black Bramble	Mrs D. Horton	H. E. Appleby	I III III
Dollar Premium	D	28.6.64	Ch. Tumlow Impeccable	Lacrosse Winning Ride	Mrs E. Peckham	Mrs R. Hooper	I III IV
Fredo of Rhodesdobe	B	12.2.64	Ch. Annastock Lance	Rhodesdobe Ousewhip Alethea	K. Rhodes	K. Rhodes	I II
Rhodesdobe Ousewhip Alethea	B	29.7.62	Mangrypin Sombrero	Smoothfield Diamond	G. Myers	K. Rhodes	I
Zonneleen Tarnmor Admiration	D	29.9.64	Ch. Taveys Stormy Wonder	Rombermor Mein Chats	Mr and Mrs B. Roper	J. Wynne	I

Name	Sex	Born	Sire	Dam	Breeder	Owner & Handler	Test Passed
Barrimilne Freshman	D	14.7.65	Gin von Forell	Brumbies Black Hornbeam	L. E. Wainwright	G. Kelly	I
Taveys Stormy Jael	B	25.10.63	Ch. Taveys Stormy Achievement	Taveys Stormy Zeminda	Mrs J. Curnow	Mrs J. Curnow and Mrs J. Faulks (handler)	I II
Mountbrowne Peter	D	28.4.65	Fury of Dissington	Inga of Trevellis	M. V. Downes	C. C. Surrey (handler: Pc M. Juniper)	I II
Pompie the Bosun	D	12.7.64	Pompie Seaman	Hiltonrookery Flora Jane	A. J. Partridge	M. G. Page	I
Militiaman of Levenay	D	–	Ruptrech of Manford	Roma of Levenay	Mr and Mrs W. W. Berry	R. Cakebread	I
Hareaway Hamilton	B	5.7.66	Vanessas Little Dictator of Tavey	Taveys Stormy Beclette	Miss B. Elliott	C. Hooper	I II
Easterns Own	D	14.5.66	Vanessa's Little Dictator of Tavey	Devastation Top Girl	C. White	J. E. Burrell	I
Wyndenhelms Escort	D	4.4.67	Ch. Acclamation of Tavey	Ch. Wyndenhelms AWOL	G. Thompson	G. Thompson	I II
Helroy Carrickgreen Climax	D	6.12.63	Carrickgreen Cordon Bleu	Carrickgreen Cluny	D. P. Clark	Mrs J. Glossop	I
Annastock Sirius	D	18.5.66	Ch. Taveys Stormy Nugget	Annastock Kate of Sawgate	Mrs J. Parkes	B. Pole	I
Gemsback of Deelcee	D	14.4.67	Ruptrech of Manford	Gazelle of Deelcee	D. E. Chandler	R. T. Gazley	I

Name	Sex	Date	Sire	Dam	Breeder	Owner	Awards
Chater Kings Reward	D	6.12.66	Ch. Crontham King	Heidiland High Society	Mrs V. Killips	P. Eales	I
Helroy Lady Courage of Graybarry	B	1.4.66	Brumbies Barleycorn	Inga of Trevellis	E. W. Fletcher	Mrs J. Glossop	I
Panzer of Kronsforde	D	17.2.64	Ch. Taveys Stormy Master	Gerda of Kronsforde	H. Brookfield	H. Brookfield	I
Japonicas Ochre	D	26.8.67	Ch. Oberan of Tavey	Sal Pride of Edward	Mrs Holt	H. E. Appleby	I II
Xerxes of Furzebeam	D	12.6.68	Edencourts Banker	Wyndenhelms Cormorant	R. Hodge	R. Hodge	I
Barrimilne Sheer Pride	B	27.2.68	Wilm von Forell	Barrimilne the Temptress	Mrs M. Bastable	Mrs C. Gudgeon	I
Gurnard Simon	D	20.9.67	Vanessa's Little Dictator of Tavey	Ch. Gurnard Gemma	Mrs D. Billingham and A. Barnard	Mrs D. Billingham and A. Barnard (handler)	I
Pride of Cheshunt	B	15.7.68	Jammu Salmbukk	Katie's Biscuit Barrel	J. Pullan	L. Parker	I
Gin von Forell	D	23.5.60	Ger. Ch. Dirk v. Goldberg	Diana vom Oelberg	E. Wilking	Mrs M. Bastable	I
Tumlow Solitaire	B	16.12.67	Apolda Blunderbuss	Tumlow the Witch	Mr and Mrs R. Harris	Mrs S. Mitchell	I II IV
Twilight Traveller	D	9.2.69	Dollar Premium	Heidi of Molsheim	Miss S. Elson	Miss S. Elson	I
Triogen Talent Spotter	D	26.9.68	Ch. Triogen Tornado	Triogen Tropical Splendour	A. B. Hogg	A. L. Griffiths	I
Charis Aquarius	D	12.9.69	Trojan Achievement	Gretel Goddess of Gorsley	Mrs A. Higgs	E. Handscomb	I II III IV

Name	Sex	Born	Sire	Dam	Breeder	Owner & Handler	Test Passed
Kudu of Furzebeam	B	3.2.65	Filibuster of Sonhende	Conquest of Dumbrill	Mrs T. Puddephat	R. H. Jackson	I
Sym Comforter			No further details available			S. Moss	I
Skipper of Ashdobe	D	27.11.69	Heiner Rustic	Tumlow Solitaire	Mrs S. Mitchell	Mrs S. Mitchell	I II IV
Blitzkreiger of Eaton	D	23.5.68	Wilm von Forell	Jansue of Wyndham	D. Powell	R. Nosowitz	I
Placide of Tavey	B	5.6.68	Ch. Iceberg of Tavey	Rusa of Tavey	Mrs J. Curnow	Mrs J. Rutter	I
Oakfairs Debutante	B	9.10.68	Wilm von Forell	Oakfairs Carmen v. Riedlhof	Mr and Mrs G. Turner	G. Turner	I
Hareaway Hebe	B	5.7.66	Vanessa's Little Dictator of Tavey	Taveys Stormy Beclette	Miss B. Elliott	H. E. Appleby	I
Jimartys Lancia Flavia	B	9.2.69	Dollar Premium	Heidi of Molsheim	Miss S. Elson	Mrs M. Burrell	I
Taveys Alliance of Vidal	D	21.4.70	Kavkaunas Orbital Storm	Suffraget of Tavey	Mrs J. Curnow	J. E. Burrell	I
Trumpkin Black Rose	B	2.7.70	Ch. Triogen Traffic Cop	Marnie from Ifieldwood	D. J. Evans	D. J. Evans	I II
Kickshaw of Furzebeam	B	20.3.66	Zouave of Furzebeam	Conquest of Dumbrill	Mrs T. Puddephatt	Mrs S. Gray	I
Achenburg Fair Fortune	B	3.11.70	Exclusive of Annastock	Baia of Achenburg	Mrs M. Woodward	Mrs A. F. Griffiths and T. Brace (handler)	I IA
Harast Astrid	B	31.7.71	Japonicas Ochre	Hareaway Hebe	Mr and Mrs H. E. Appleby	Mrs L. Knapp	I

Name	Sex	Date	Sire	Dam	Owner	Breeder	Class
Helroy Hotspur	D	13.2.71	Chater Kings Reward	Helroy Lady Courage of Graybarry	Mrs J. Glossop	L. Parker	I II III IV
Chornytan Passenger	D	13.1.72	Tinsley the Stormcloud	Chornytan Delight	Mrs T. J. Toole	L. S. Christopher	I II
Oakfairs Eulenspiegel	D	6.12.60	Timo v.d. Brunoburg	Oakfairs Carmen v. Riedlhof	Mr and Mrs G. Turner	G. Turner	I
Helroy Hot Cockles	B	13.2.71	Chater Kings Reward	Helroy Lady Courage of Graybarry	Mrs J. Glossop	P. Eales	I
Harast Joe	D	31.7.71	Japonicas Ochre	Hareaway Hebe	Mr and Mrs Appleby	Mrs A. Warby	I
Pompie Sunset Shell	B	22.6.67	Easterns Own	Pompie Sea Urchin	Mrs H. Partridge	M. G. Page	I
Karlakays Kruger	D	5.5.72	Wilm von Forell	Ch. Kingroy Karla Kay	M. Witham and P. O'Connor	E. Handscomb	I
Greenling Black Nugget	D	19.4.70	Lowenbrau Artisan of Courage	Tylerann Princess Starglow	Mrs Linger	T. Fletcher	I
Helroy Hot Toddy	D	13.2.71	Chater Kings Reward	Helroy Lady Courage of Graybarry	Mrs J. Glossop	J. Bushell	I
Helroy High Jump	D	2.6.68	Wilm von Forell	Helroy Lady Courage of Graybarry	Mrs J. Glossop	R. Nosowitz	I
Darford Maxwell	D	22.7.69	Alex of Brandenberg	Lively Lady	Dr A. Campbell	T. Radford	I
Duchess Vanessa	B	22.10.70	Vanessa's Little Dictator of Tavey	Frankskirbys Fireparade	Mr and Mrs B. Garrat	M. Thouless	I IA II III

Name	Sex	Born	Sire	Dam	Breeder	Owner & Handler	Test Passed
Danargo Dynamic	D	9.4.73	Ch. Triogen Tornado	Achenburg Fair Fortune	Mrs A. F. Griffiths	A. L. Griffiths	I IA II III IV
Illustria's Porthos	D	1.7.73	Xerxes of Furzebeam	Illustria's Eve	M. J. Garrod	M. J. Garrod	I
Rajah	D	16.2.72	Rajah	Emma	Not known	Commissioner of the Metropolitan Police (owner) PC R. Squire (handler)	I II III
Great Tarquin	D	12.9.69	Trojan Achievement	Gretel Goddess of Gorsley	Mrs A. Higgs	Mrs P. Vaudrey	I II
Koriston Pewter Strike of Doberean	B	22.7.72	Royaltains Nicky Tams	Doberean Eclat of Tavey	Mrs A. E. Anderson	Mrs J. Faulks	IA I II
Ch. Ashdobes Brown Berry	B	1.11.75	Camerons Snoopy of Tinkazan	Ashdobes Venus	Mrs S. Mitchell	Mrs S. Mitchell	I III IV
Ch. Hillmora the Explorer	D	8.12.73	Linhoff the Maestro	Hillmora the Capri	B. Johnson	A. B. More	I IA II
Gurnard Golla	D	8.7.74	Ch. Tumlow Satan	Demos Soraya	A. Barnard	A. Barnard	I
Pompie Black Canasta	D	13.3.75	Ch. Arkturus Valans Choice	Pompie Sea Fleurette	A. J. Partridge	P. J. Carroll	I
Blacks Silhouette	B	1.5.73	Wilm von Forell	Finmear Black Pearl	D. L. Eaton	D. L. Eaton	I
Pompie Theseus	D	9.3.75	Ch. Arkturus Valans Choice	Pompie Sea Aquamarine	A. J. Partridge	B. K. Spiers	I
Quinsana Beau Geste of Ambari	D	26.8.74	Royaltains Oliver Twist	Royal Symbol of Chevington	Mrs C. Smith	Dr J. D. Pratten	I

Name	Sex	Date	Sire	Dam	Breeder	Owner	
Woodlords Dominator	D	2.9.74	Taveys Satellite	Rathkeel Penny Black	Mrs C. J. Cowan	D. L. Eaton	I
Stonebank Happy Harry	D	10.10.74	Ch. Triogen Tornado	Hopemanne Happy Hilary	P. Williams	G. A. Bingham	I IA II
Kaiserberg Bathtub Gin	B	21.12.74	Ch. Stroud of Reksum	Rembergs Bitter Sweet	Mrs S. Buist	D. M. Coulter	I
Byron Burnt Sienna	B	21.4.75	Baron of Balbeggie	Swift of Balbeggie	J. Stocks	P. J. Carroll	I IA II
Ch. Chevington Royal Black Magic	D	5.4.75	Hillmora the Extremist	Chevington Royal Chiffon	Mrs O. V. Neave	I. Ould	I IA II
Jovin-Blak Knite	D	24.11.73	Ch. Iceberg of Tavey	Eastern Feluccas	J. V. Alderson	J. V. Alderson	I IA
Jimartys Black Diamond Bay	D	13.8.76	Taveys Alliance of Vidal	Jimartys Sand Dancer	Mr and Mrs J. E. J. Burrell	J. E. J. Burrell	I IA II
Tonio's Bombardier	D	6.6.76	Ch. Arkturus Valans Choice	Roving Moonspinner	R. Peacock	M. Thouless	I IA II III
Findjans Ikeya-Seki	D	26.4.75	Phileens Duty Free of Tavey	Ch. Mitrasandra Gay Lady of Findjans	Mr and Mrs M. G. Page	H. Whiter	I IA
Schreider of Mercia	D	No further particulars				P. Lakin	I
Garath St. David	D	Dec.1974	'Rescue' dog, so breeding unknown			J. Middleweek	I IA II
Black Ice	D	21.5.76	Phileens Duty Free of Tavey	Helaman Beatrice	Mrs A. Y. Higgs	Mrs I. Green	I IA II
Jovin Blak Jeny	B	24.11.73	Ch. Iceberg of Tavey	Eastern Feluccas	J. V. Alderson	A. Ward	I

Name	Sex	Born	Sire	Dam	Breeder	Owner & Handler	Test Passed
Vyleighs Mustang	D	28.6.76	Canterilla Cutlass	Vyleighs Strider	Mrs H. M. Vyse	Mrs H. M. Vyse	I
Parabar Black Chiffon	B	7.4.77	Ch. Chevington Royal Black Magic	Taveys Lamé	Mrs B. Grant-Parkes	Mrs M. Ould	I IA
Charcoal Lady	B	26.3.77	Tinsleys March from Sousa	Bronze Venus	Mrs N. O. Poulton	K. Rhodes	I IA
Sandjak of Jimartys	D	13.5.77	Taveys Satellite	Jimartys Flexabella	Mr and Mrs J. E. J. Burrell	Mr and Mrs J. E. J. Burrell	I
Luke the Drifter	D	31.8.76	Chaka the Warrior	Demo the Adventuress	Mrs S. Fitchett	S. Dawes	I
Jimartys Sandimans	D	22.6.76	Jimartys Sandman	Jimartys Cressida	Mr and Mrs J. E. Burrell	Mrs P. Ainsworth	I
Chater French Connection	D	24.4.76	Ch. Javictreva Brief Defiance of Chater	Chater High Society	Mrs V. J. Killips	K. D. Clarke	I
Thelos Orea Gobelaz	B	19.9.77	Sea King	Pompie Sea Fenella	Mr and Mrs B. R. Bennett	D. Dennis	I
Frankskirby Jubilee Flame	D	5.6.77	Phileens American Express	Frankskirby Red Christel	Mr and Mrs B. M. J. Spaughton	Mrs C. Tucker	I IA
Roanoke Serenade	B	2.12.75	Aust. Ch. Bonniedale Dougal	Black Baroness of Pintlehill	Mr and Mrs J. Richardson	A. Kingswell	I
Jubilee Queen of Jimartys	B	13.5.77	Taveys Satellite	Jimartys Flexabella	Mr and Mrs J. E. E. Handsford Burrell		I IA II

328

Name	Sex	Date	Sire	Dam	Breeder	Owner	Class
Koriston Polonaise of Doberean	B	3.4.78	Royaltains Nicky Tams	Koriston Superstarlet	Mrs A. E. Anderson	Mrs J. Faulks	I IA
W.T.Ch. Chaanrose Night Queen	B	2.9.78	Heathermount Flitzenjaeger	Olderhill Salvador	Miss R. Lane	J. Fleet	I IA
Apoldas Lady Fair	B	18.9.77	Ch. Hillmora the Explorer	Apoldas Hot Chocolate	Mrs D. Baker	A. B. More	I
Springthorpes Solar Star	D	–	Drindod Sir Galahad	Jade of Dinas	Mrs J. Francis	M. A. Plant	I
Jimartys Jezebel	B	21.6.78	Sandjak of Jimartys	Jimartys Burning Hope	Mr and Mrs J. E. Burrell	Mrs O. Passant	I
Ch. Dizown Bedazzled of Chaanrose	B	23.12.75	Tavey's Satellite	Olderhill Salvador	Mrs D. Patience	Miss R. Lane	I
Midnight Intruder	D	4.11.78	Drindod Sir Galahad	Jumping Jill	D. J. Lewis	Mrs A. Bell	I
Jimartys Close Encounter	D	22.6.78	Sandjak of Jimartys	Jimartys Burning Hope	Mr and Mrs J. E. Burrell	K. Hughes	I
Merryns Dick Turpin	D	11.7.78	Ch. Royaltains Highwayman of Borain	Merad Admiration	Mrs J. Gibbs	R. Higgins	I
Navua Billy Broonzy	D	3.2.79	Jimartys Sandman	Chavez Forget Me Not	Mrs S. M. Tanner	J. Daft	I IA
Jimartys Sand Flame	B	27.3.79	Jimartys Black Diamond Bay	Jimartys Sand Mystery	Mr and Mrs J. E. Burrell	Mrs I. Green	I IA
Parabar Black Queen	B	7.4.77	Ch. Chevington Royal Black Magic	Taveys Lamé	Mrs B. Grant-Parkes	Mrs L. Griffiths	I

Name	Sex	Born	Sire	Dam	Breeder	Owner & Handler	Test Passed
Chillys Gentle Giant	D	28.4.79	Ch. Dizown the Hustler	Star of Smallfield	N. Belson	C. J. Chillingworth	I IA II III IV
Otherton Soubrette	B	2.4.78	Stonebank Warlord	Duchess of Otherton P. B. Rock		Mrs O. Hole	I
Baronstern Silver Arrow	D	14.10.77	Ch. Hillmora the Explorer	Quandris Baroness	Mrs M. Frankish	Mrs P. Ainsworth	I
Ashdobes Vaguely Great	B	23.7.79	Ch. Findjans Poseidon	Ch. Ashdobes Brown Berry	Mrs S. Mitchell	Mrs S. Mitchell	I IA II IV
W.T.Ch. Linrios Domingo	B	21.12.79	Rioghal Bravura	Linrio Blanche	J. Arnott	J. Middleweek	I IA II III
Spartan Warrior at Jovin-Blak	D	26.7.79	Jovin-Blak Knite	Roanoke Martini	Mr and Mrs N. J. Mitchell	Mr and Mrs N. J. J. V. Alderson	I IA II III IV
Jimartys Proud Salopian	D	1.5.79	Ch. Olderhill Sheboygan	Sand Jil from Jimartys	Mr and Mrs J. E. J. Burrell	Mr and Mrs J. E. J. Burrell	I
Jimartys Wagabit	D	27.3.79	Jimartys Black Diamond Bay	Jimartys Sand Mystery	Mr and Mrs J. E. S. Dawes Burrell	Mr and Mrs J. E. S. Dawes	I
Raggedhall Raven	B	21.6.79	Pompie Black Canasta	Daymays Foxtrot	Mrs J. Pope	Mrs J. Pope	I
Ashdobes Vaguely Noble	D	23.7.79	Ch. Findjans Poseidon	Ch. Ashdobes Brown Berry	Mrs S. Mitchell	M. J. Crickett	I IA II IV
Airborne Warrior	D	25.12.79	Auldrigg Son of a Witch	Heidi Tinkerbelle	Mrs E. J. Collinson	Mrs D. Easter	I IA
Ch. Dorusta Lutzow	D	10.2.80	Drumpelier Bismarck	Vonmac Brianna	D. Sumner	D. Griffiths	I IA

Name	Sex	Date	Sire	Dam			Class
Zenoan Reluctant Warrior	D	21.4.80	Wladek von Szczein	Elisa of Kenstaff	S. E. Thomas	R. Carter	I IA II III
Krystal Clear Vijentor	B	12.1.77	Phileens Duty Free of Tavey	Katherine of Kenstaff	A. D. McCarthy	Mrs J. M. Jakeman	I
Rizpahs Burning Ambition	B	22.5.80	Jupiters Solo Orbit	Copper Bronze Bridget	Mr and Mrs G. Wilson	A. Roach	I IA
Sparrowhall the Sorceror	D	30.5.78	Chornytan Mr Mighell of Sparrowhall	Olderhill Oriole	Mrs V. Hockmeyer	S. C. Hancox	I
Royaltains Lonely Pride	B	7.2.80	Space Quest of Royaltain	Ch. Royaltains Unexpected Guest	Miss P. Quinn	Mrs W. J. Jackson	I IA
Whispering Waunder	B	17.3.80	Ch. Hillmora the Explorer	Nivella High Stepper	Mrs J. E. Philpot	A. B. More	I
Studbriar Royal Sentinel	D	30.7.81	Ch. Studbriar the Red	Studbriars Milady	Mrs M. King	P. J. Carroll	I IA II III IV
Somerbys Bandaleer Bravado	D	5.5.81	Darnago Dynamic	Freda of Somerby	Mrs B. McGrath	T. Brace	I IA II III IV
Pegasus Thor of Demond	D	7.4.80	Damors the Warlord	Drumfire Athena	Mrs L. Bissett	W. Mondey	I IA II
Jacris Rouge Royale	B	13.11.79	Jimartys Sandman	Jubilee Queen of Jimartys	E. G. Hansford	E. G. Hansford	I IA
Olderhill Kirsty	B	13.1.81	Ch. Borains Night Watchman	Olderhill Olga	Mrs S. Wilson	Mrs S. Cooper	I
Ikos Imperial Priestess	B	9.11.80	Ch. Royal Bertie of Chevington	Tamars Lady of the Lake	R. W. Skinner	Mrs D. Easter	I IA

Name	Sex	Born	Sire	Dam	Breeder	Owner & Handler	Test Passed
Hans of Jimartys	D	23.2.81	Salvador von Frankenhorst	Jimartys Gem	Mrs J. Hollis	J. Burrell	I IA
Jimartys Adventuress	B	26.6.78	Jimartys Sandjak	Burning Hope of Jimartys	J. Burrell	Mrs D. Smith	I IA II IV
Danargo Intimate Miss	B	2.10.80	Danargo Dynamic	Jamboree Picturebook	Mrs C. Rycroft and A. L. Griffiths	Mrs M. Griffiths	I
Symbol of Lear	B	1.2.79	Rheydt Hawk	Inger of Raleigh	Mr and Mrs B. Carter	F. Judson	I
Starlight Sheer Delight	B	13.3.81	Ch. Hillmora the Explorer	Gregarths Bonbon Bay	Mr and Mrs Graham	Mrs J. Magness	I
Deltynas Helen	B	11.10.81		Details not known		Mr R. and Mrs S. Burgess (handler)	I
Ashdobes Great Crusader	D	2.2.82	Ch. Davalogs Crusader	Ashdobes Vaguely Great	Mrs S. Mitchell	Mrs S. Mitchell	I IA II IV
My Gem of Sunnygift	B	4.6.82	Apoldas Impelo	Harpersbury Resist Me Not	Mrs P. McGrath	Mrs J. Magness	I IA II IV
Shaheen Golden Days	D	1.1.82	Studbriars The Sentinel	Chimera Black Rose of Shaheen	Mrs R. Steggle	R. Prior	I IA
Wernlies Barola	D	10.8.82	Ch. Chevington Royal Black Magic	Rheinbar Belinda	J. Ainsworth	J. Scandrett	I
Charlottes Lucky Opal	B	12.5.81	Ryuker Rothaar of Regensburg	Footloose and Fancy Free	G. Hackett	Mrs J. Hardwick	I IA IV

Name	Sex	Date	Sire	Dam	Owner	Breeder	Codes
Filans Night Raider	D	27.11.81	Dargais Border Minstrel	Jimartys Wood Sprite	N. R. Hunter	P. Rogers	I
Jimartys Lucifer	D	19.3.82	Jimartys Proud Salopian	Flash Anna from Jimartys	Mr and Mrs J. E. Burrell	Mrs D. Smith	I IA II
Shonas Path of Peace at Dhobie	B	28.2.80	Taveys Diploma	Shonas Black Velvet	Mrs Ross	Mrs S. Jaffa	I
Suemels Phantom Queen	B	28.7.79	Phileens Duty Free of Tavey	Studbriars Jubilee Princess	Mrs V. King	Mrs S. Bailey	I
Daleys Deb	B	25.3.83	Linrio Canticle from Barrimilne	Fenns Delight	Mrs Fennemore	Mrs D. Cronin	I IA II IV
Evam Titania	B	5.8.83	Apoldas Impelo	Starglatt Sheer Delight	Mrs J. Magness	Mrs M. Judson	I IA
Rioghal Cervantes	D	4.1.84	Edcath Aegistus	Linrio Enterprise	M. Grierson	J. Middleweek	I
Petrax Prospero	D	14.2.83	Ironman Overlord	Princess Pretty Penny at Petrax	Mrs G. Read	J. Challis	I IA II
Karlsfield Fighting Hope	D	8.12.83	Ironman Overlord	Jentels Lady of Karlsfield	Mrs J. Daney	Mrs T. Marie	I
Wallheath Mothers Day Girl	B	29.3.81	Ch. Chevington Royal Black Magic	Showgirl of Chornytan	P. Cluett	P. Adams	I IA II
Black Satin King	D	28.6.80	Ch. Major Marauder	Crudos Carmina	M. Staples	D. Mann	I
Kaiser of Red House	D	28.8.79	Ch. Dizown the Hustler	Roanoke Aralia	A. O'Keeffe	Mrs C. Vines	I
Purdey at Jovin-Blak	B	18.3.84	Chevington Royal Nimrod	Wyncar Lucky Girl	Mrs I. C. Davies	J. Alderson	I IA II

Name	Sex	Born	Sire	Dam	Breeder	Owner & Handler	Test Passed
Simela Dai Girl	B	2.5.83	Ch. Royal Bertie of Chevington	Wallheath Mothers Day Girl	P. Adams	P. Adams	I IA II
Bojenhoff Mistress Delilah	B	2.5.83	Barrimilne Benno	Bojenhoff Gypsy Greta	Mr and Mrs R. Beesley	Mrs V. Isherwood	I IA
Vivluc Rosie Rit	B	26.9.79	Knight of Romercastle	Vivluc of Takeley	Mrs V. Lucas	Mrs P. Dawson	I
Raggedhall Star	B	10.5.82	Chillys Gentle Giant	Raggedhall Raven	Mrs J. Pope	P. Morling	I
Thunderstar Black Wonder	D	26.3.81	Barrimilne Black Adder	Debbie Nokeshot of Thunderstar	Mrs E. Chandler	Mrs V. Isherwood	I
Pompie Hot Toddy	D	10.10.79	Ch. Findjans Poseidon	Pompie Fleur Lys	Mrs H. Partridge	G. Dawson	I IA
Jimartys Sandy T'Other	D	28.11.83	Dorusta Lutzow	Sand Jil of Jimartys	Mr and Mrs J. E. Burrell	Mrs L. Griffiths	I
Bequerelle Top Mettle	D	31.8.83	Trooper of Jowendy at Zordia	Bequerelle Schonne	Mrs G. Barwick	Mrs J. Watkins	I IA II
Barrimilne Beachcomber	D	2.12.81	Linrio Don Juan from Barrimilne	Barrimilne Tally	Mrs M. Bastable	A. Rogers	I
Sultans Black Swift	D	2.10.82	Ch. Hillmora the Explorer	Ikos Black Symphony	P. O'Conner	R. Ball	I IA II
Petrax Perilous	D	15.10.84	Ch. Bronsilk Copper Alanthus	Princess Pretty Penny at Petrax	Mrs G. Read	Mrs G. Purrott	I
Opals Speculator	D	30.5.85	Chater the Ferryman	Charlottes Lucky Opal	Mrs J. Hardwick	Mrs J. Hardwick	I IA

Name	Sex	Date	Sire	Dam	Breeder	Owner	
Red Black Beauty	B	8.10.83	Chillys Gentle Giant	Tamars Lady Hamilton	Mrs M. Chillingworth	Mrs S. Prior	I
Pantgwyn Duchess	B	5.8.85	Canis Major	Lady Suzzanah	Mrs S. A. Mills	Mrs B. Upton-Taylor	I IA
Saucy Fraulein	B	18.7.85	Graaf Carlos v.d. Edele Stam	Whispering Waunder	A. More	Mrs J. Dempster	I IA II
Flynns Flashy Fanny	B	6.10.85	Studbriars Royal Sentinel	Reds Black Beauty	Mrs S. Prior	P. J. Carroll	I IA
Lady Lobelia	B	11.5.85	Chevington Royal Shane	Landymoor Jolie Jacasta	R. M. Goddard	Mrs J. Parker	I
The Khan of Sunnygift	D	28.9.85	Bavarian of Barrimilne	Starglatt Sheer Delight	Mr and Mrs D. Magness	Mrs J. Magness	I IA
Running Free	D	16.5.83	Ch. Borains Night Watchman	Valentine Dream	N. M. Hicks	B. Worboys	I IA
Midnight Phantom of Arun	D	9.1.84	Locksacre Image of Harvey	Morning Cloud of Scorrier	Mrs J. Pannell	Mrs L. Lowe	I
Vickisfree Starpitcher	D	7.7.84	Reltans Black Madness	Vickisfree Rebecca	Mrs J. Bird	A. Waite	I
Sayyadina Chani	B		Further particulars unknown			Mrs J. Graves	I
Chevington Royal High Rebel	D	25.11.84	Ch. Roanoke Swell-Fella	Chevington Royal Sheer Elegance	Mrs O. Neave	J. Graves	I IA
Shardains Lady Gem	B	7.8.86	Ch. Dorusta Lutzow	Othertons Donah	J. Skitt	D. Morris	I
Anders Crocs	D	23.3.85	Prince of Woodside	Syreenas Holliberi	M. Connett	A. Ware	I IA

Name	Sex	Born	Sire	Dam	Breeder	Owner & Handler	Test Passed
Ritlo Full of Magic	D	14.2.84	Ritlo Highland Monarch	Ritlo Full of Grace	Dr M. L. Harris	I. Ould	I IA
Chornytan the Chosen Hawk	D	29.9.86	Ch. Dolbadarn Hawker Fury	Ch. Chornytan Dinahawk	Mrs T. J. Toole	Mrs J. Graves	I
Maclachlan Gemstone Demon	D	8.12.84	Ch. Othertons Statesman	Wallheath Lady of the Moment	Mr and Mrs Barrett	A. Scott	I
Diamond Commissar of Jacris	D	26.7.85	Pompie the Flying Dutchman	Jimartys Satin	Mr and Mrs Parsons	E. Hansford	I
Magnums Too of Bilsam	D	12.1.87	Bilsam Sudden Impact	Goughs Gemma	M. Charalambous	Miss C. Vines	I
Kenives Progress	D	23.12.84	Rathkeel Rakes Progress	Enchanting Rogue	Mrs Francis	Miss K. Lamb	I
Barrimilne Brown Baron	D	2.5.86	Quinto v.d. Kunne-maborgh at Vyleighs	Barrimilne Naughty Lady	Mrs M. Bastable	Mrs J. Dempster	I
Dalys Copper Cornerway	D	31.8.86	Azur La Mare	Sacha Distell	A. P. Sutton	Mrs L. Werry	I
Merryns Nightwalker	D	25.9.86	Merryns Magnum	Merryns Zenobia	Mrs J. Gibbs	Mrs L. Partleton	I
Princess Mechico	B	1.6.86	Linhoff Braint of Lankirk	Valrons Shalimar	P. Brady	C. Cowley	I
Jimartys Dot	B	20.12.87	Jimartys Dashing Knight	Laika v.d. Rameler Marke	Mr and Mrs J. Burrell	J. Burrell	I

DOBERMANNS IN POLICE SERVICE

Name	Sex	Born	Sire	Dam	Breeder	Owner	Handler
Ulf v. Margarethenhof	D	30.6.46	Hasso v.d. Neckarstrasse	Toska v. Margarethenhof	M. Thurling	C. C. Surrey	Sgt H. Darbyshire
Astor v. Morgensonne	D	29.3.48	Sigmar	Asta v. Schulzenhof	E. Raginski	C. C. Surrey	–
Donathe v. Begertal	B	28.3.48	Zar v. Stahlhelm	Asta v. Teufenstal	K. Ehlebracht	C. C. Surrey	Sgt A. Osment
Mountbrowne Joe	D					Mrs M. Porterfield for the Dobermann Club	Mrs M. Porterfield
Justice	D	7.1.50	W.T.Ch. Ulf v. Margarethenhof	Donathe v. Begertal	C. C. Surrey	C. C. Kent	Sgt S. Lawrie
Juno	B					C. C. Lancashire	Sgt H. Herdman
Jenny	B					C. C. Buckinghamshire	Sgt G. Jones
Julie	B					C. C. Durham	Sgt T. Sessford
Mountbrowne Karen	B	18.8.50	Astor v. Morgensonne	Donathe v. Begertal	C. C. Surrey	C. C. Surrey	PC Ling
Kandra	B					C. C. Surrey	–
Kola	B					C. C. West Riding	–
King	D					C. C. Suffolk	–
Kim	D					C. C. West Riding	–

Name	Sex	Born	Sire	Dam	Breeder	Owner	Handler
Mountbrowne Odin	D	14.1.52	W.T.Ch. Ulf v. Margarethenhof	Donathe v. Begertal	C. C. Surrey	C. C. Surrey	PC W. Redwood
Olaf	D					C. C. Cheshire	Sgt Taylor
Onyx	D					C. C. East Sussex	PC Horsecroft
Otis	B					C. C. Cheshire	–
Mountbrowne Pablo	D	4.7.52	W.T.Ch. Ulf v. Margarethenhof	Mountbrowne Kandra	C. C. Surrey	C. C. Cheshire	–
Pluto	D					C. C. East Riding	PC Peacock
Pedro	D					–	–
Pinto	D					C. C. Dorset	–
Paula	B					–	–
Mountbrowne Remoh	D	26.5.53	Bill v. Blauenblut	Mountbrowne Kandra	C. C. Surrey	C. C. Essex	PC P. Cousins
Reina	B					C. C. Kent, later C. C. Surrey	–
Mountbrowne Tasco	D	24.3.54	W.T.Ch. Ulf v. Margarethenhof	Mountbrowne Kandra	C. C. Surrey	C. C. Hertford-shire	PC E. Pugh
Tasso	D					C. C. Lancashire	PC Alston
Taxel	D					C. C. Shropshire	PC Roberts
Mountbrowne Yukon	D	5.11.54	W.T.Ch. Ulf v. Margarethenhof	Ch. Reichert Judy	Mrs M. Porterfield	C. C. Bedford-shire, later C. C. Surrey	Sgt F. Pettit, later PC Proctor
Yager	D						
Mountbrowne Amber	B	28.5.55	Mountbrowne Odin	Ch. Reichert Judy	Mrs M. Porterfield	C. C. Northumberland	PC T. Yeouart, later Sgt J. Hyslop
Astor	D					C. C. Devon	PC Kendrick
Arras	D					–	–
Alger	D						

Name	Sex	Date	Sire	Dam			
Mountbrowne Barry	D	15.6.55	Alex v. Rodenaer	Mountbrowne Kandra	C. C. Surrey	C. C. Kent	–
Bruce	D					C. C. Northumberland	PC Glendinning
Mountbrowne Dinco	D	20.11.55	W.T.Ch. Ulf v. Margarethenhof	Mountbrowne Reina	C. C. Surrey	C. C. Surrey	PC W. Redwood
Mountbrowne Shifta	D	Further particulars unknown			C. C. Surrey		–
Mountbrowne Peter	D	28.4.65	Fury of Dissington	Ina of Trevellis	M. V. Downes	C. C. Surrey	PC M. Juniper
Copper of Buckinghamshire	D					C. C. Buckinghamshire	–
Lancon Skipper	D	31.7.51	Astor v. Morgensonne	Mountbrowne Juno	C. C. Lancashire	C. C. Lancashire	–
Lancon Pilot	D				C. C. Lancashire	C. C. Lancashire	PC Rolands
Joan of Ayfelde	B	18.4.52	Dober v. Oldenfelde	W.T.Ch Mountbrowne Julie	C. C. Durham	C. C. Durham	PC P. Hedges
Jenny of Ayclifden	B						PC Welsh
Joseph of Aycliffe	D						PC W. McGorrigan
Arno of Aycliffe	D	16.4.55	W.T.Ch. Ulf v. Margarethenhof	Jenny of Ayclifden	C. C. Durham	C. C. Durham	PC H. Garth
Argus	D						PC S. Regan
Anna	B						PC Hutchinson
Asta	B						PC Brett
Alouette	B						PC Aikenhead
Adella	B						PC Scott
Amanda	B						–
Anita	B						PC Wheatley

Name	Sex	Born	Sire	Dam	Breeder	Owner	Handler
Diana of Aycliffe	B	11.8.57	Culloden of Skipwith	Joan of Ayfelde	C. C. Durham	C. C. Durham	–
Flame of Aycliffe	B	27.4.59	Culloden of Skipwith	Jenny of Ayclifden	C. C. Durham	C. C. Bedfordshire	PC Fulcher
Fangio	D					C. C. Dorset, later W. G. Clark	PC Williams, later R. Skelhorne
Argus of Northumbria	D	29.5.59	Bowesmoor Kuno	Mountbrowne Amber	C. C. Northumberland	C. C. Northumberland	PC Crisp
John v. Waldhorst	D	22.6.60	Lasso v. Zyraksgarten	Quinda v.d. Ansbornquelle	–	C. C. Durham	PC S. Regan
Greif	D	7.4.55	Bruno of Tavey	Baba Black Sheep	Mrs D. M. Ince	C. C. Hertfordshire	PC H. Appleby
Faust of Cartergate	D	28.3.56	Ch. Day of Cartergate	Lola of Cartergate	Miss E. M. Would	C. C. Lincolnshire	PC J. Bush
Goliath of Dissington	D	26.12.60	Bowesmoor Sancho	Bambi of Dissington	Mrs E. M. Blair	C. C. Bedfordshire	PC N. Gorham
Fagin	D	?.8.65	Zouave of Furzebeam	Highbrooks Andromeda	M. Witham	C. C. Hertfordshire	PC E. Pugh
Bowesmoor Dana	B	26.5.53	Bill v. Blauenblut	Mountbrowne Kandra	C. C. Surrey	C. C. Dorset	PC P. Thrasher, later Sgts Highmore & Green
Bowesmoor Gina	B	20.7.56	Treu v.d. Steinfurthohe	Helga v. Kleinwaldheim	Mrs M. Porterfield	C. C. Essex, later C. C. Hertfordshire	PC T. Bierne

Bowesmoor Herma Hain Hero	B D D	23.4.61 Old Boy	Vervain Rhythm	Mrs M. Porterfield and H. Darbyshire	C. C. Devon C. C. Devon Commissioner of the Metropolitan Police	PC Farrow PC Lane PC Geeves
Metpol Fritz	D	Prob. 1953 Birling Roimond	Frieda von Casa Mia of Upend	L. Hamilton-Renwick	Commissioner of the Metropolitan Police	PC Dines
Rajah	D	16.2.72 Rajah	Emma	Not known	Commissioner of PC R. Squire the Metropolitan Police	PC R. Squire
Collectors Choice	D	2.10.73 Silver Dollar of Tyrhin	Llyswen of Marley	L. Neale	C. C. South Wales	PC P. Wilson
Chornytan Ace High	D	24.4.77 Chornytan Midnite Mark	Skylark of Chornytan	Mrs T. J. Toole	C. C. Lincolnshire	PC M. Edwards
Chornytan Shadow	D	6.1.84 Quinsana Mickey Finn of Sparrowhall	Chornytan Laughing Girl	Mrs T. J. Toole	C. C. Cambridgeshire	PC J. Parker

BIBLIOGRAPHY

Brearley, Joan McDonald. *The Book of the Doberman Pinscher*, T.F.H. Publications, 1976

Frankenberger, Ernst. *My Dobermann* (translated by Marga Shaw), Akademische Druck-u, Verlagsanstalt, Graz, Austria, 1985

Gruenig, Philipp. *The Doberman Pinscher*, Orange Judd, New York, 1951

Ladd, Mark. *Dobermann Champions of the UK*, distributed under the auspices of the Midland Dobermann Club, 1985

Noted Breed Authorities. *The Complete Doberman Pinscher*, Howell Book House, New York, 1967

Wilhelm, André. *The Dobermann*, Kaye and Ward Ltd (translated from *Le Dobermann*, Crépin-Leblond et Cie, Paris, 1961)

Chadwick, Wilf. *Dog Training, Your Pet to Champion*, Burnedge Press, 1986

Smythe, R.H., M.R.C.V.S. *The Conformation of the Dog*, Popular Dogs, 1957

Volhard and Fisher. *Training Your Dog*, Howell Book House, New York, 1983

Walker, Dr Alan D., BSc., PhD. *Fit for a Dog*, Davis-Poynter, 1980

White, Kay. Articles in *Kennel Gazette*, May 1985 to January 1988, The Kennel Club, London

Nicholas, Anna Katherine. *The World of Doberman Pinschers*, T.F.H. Publications, 1986

KENNEL NAMES AND AFFIXES
EUROPE

Bavaria
Begertal
Bismarcksaule
Blankenburg
Blauenblut
Brandenburg
Brunia
Brunoberg

Dobberhof
Domstadt

Edele Stam
Ehrgarten
Eichenhain
Emsperle
Engelsburg
Eversburg

Fayette Corner
Felsingpass
Ferrolheim
Finohoehe
Forell
Franckenhorst
Frankenland
Furstenfeld

Germania
Glueckswinkel
Goldberg
Grammont

Hagenstern
Hagenstolz
Heerhof
Heinrichsburg

Herthasee
Hohenwurtzburg
Hollingen

Ilm-Athen

Jaegerhof

Kastanienhof
Kellergrund
Kleinwaldheim
Koningstad
Kunnemaborgh

Mandurahof
Margarethenhof
Morgensonne

Neckarstrasse
Neerlands Stam
Norden Stam

Oelberg

Rameler Marke
Rauhfelsen
Rehwalde
Rheinperle
Rivals
Roemerhof
Roeneckenstein
Romberg
Ruppertsburg

Sandberg
Scheepjeskerk

Schwedenhecke
Siegestor
Sigalsburg
Simbach
Simmenau
Sonnenhoehe
Stahlhelm
Starkenburg

Steinfurthohe
Sudhoek

Wachtparade
Waldhorst
Weimar-Eisenach
Wellborn
Westfallenhalle

USA and Canada

Ahrtal

Brown

Camereich

Damasyn
Doberman
Dow

Ebonaire
Elbe
Elfred

Gra-Lemor

Haus Schimmel
Haydenhill
Highbriar

Kay Hills
Kilburn

Liquorish

Marienburg
Marienland
Marks Tey
Moorpark
München

Pontchartrain

Rancho Dobe
Rosecroft
Ru-Mar

Stebs

Tannenwald
Tedell
Toledobe
Tri-Lees

Westphalia
Westwind
White Gate

Great Britain

Achenburg
Annastock
Ashdobe
Auldrigg
Aycliffe

Baronstern
Barrimilne

Barztova
Bilsam
Birling
Bledig
Bondend
Borain
Boreamond
Bowesmoor

Brief
Brumbies

Caedan
Carnagh
Carrickgreen
Cartergate
Chaanrose
Chancepixies
Charis
Chater
Chevington
Chornytan
Chrilise
Clanguard
Corvic
Crossridge

Damocles
Danargo
Darford
Dartrian
Deelcee
Delmordene
Dirksby
Dissington
Dizown
Doberean
Dolbadarn
Dolina
Dumbrill

Edcath
Edencourt
Elroban
Essenbar

Fairbrigg
Findjans
Flexor
Frankskirby
Furzebeam

Gekelven
Gurnard

Halsband
Harast
Heathermount

Heidiland
Heimdall
Helroy
Hensel
Highroyd
Hillmora
Holtzburg

Ikos
Illustria

Jasmere
Jatra
Javictreva
Jenick
Jimarty
Jovin Blak
Jowendy

Kaiserberg
Karlakay
Kaybar
Kilmuir
Kinraith
Knecht
Koriston
Krieger

Lancon
Linhoff
Linzella
Lynfryds

Mabaro
Magana
Mangrypin
Mantoba
Merrist
Merryn
Metexa
Metpol
Milperra
Moorbridge
Mountbrowne

Nayrilla
Northumbria
Nyewood

Oakfair
Olderhill
Orbiston

Pampisford
Perihelia
Petrax
Phileen
Pompie
Popladene

Quinsana

Rathkeel
Rheinbar
Rhodesdobe
Rioghal
Roanoke
Romsley
Royaltain
Ruskie

Sallate
Sanjyd
Sataeki
Saxonhaus
Siddley
Sigismund
Sonhende
Sophreta
Sorkie
Stonebank

Studbriar
Swanwite

Tanbowtra
Tavey
Tickwillow
Tinkazar
Tinkazan
Tramerfield
Trevellis
Triogen
Tumlow
Twinglo

Upend

Valmara
Varla
Vickisfree
Vidal
Vivluc
Vonmac
Vonmills
Vyking
Vyleigh

Whistleberry
Wyndenhelm

Zeitgeist
Zonneleen

DOBERMANNS MENTIONED IN THE TEXT

347

Index